Graphics
for
Architecture

Kevin Forseth

with David Vaughan

VAN NOSTRAND REINHOLD COMPANY
— New York

VNR

Copyright © 1980
by Van Nostrand Reinhold Company Inc.

Library of Congress Catalog Card Number 79-12915

ISBN 0-442-26390-2

Printed in the United States of America.

Van Nostrand Reinhold Company Inc.
115 Fifth Avenue
New York, N.Y. 10003

Van Nostrand Reinhold Company Limited
Molly Millars Lane
Wokingham, Berkshire RG11 2PY, England

Van Nostrand Reinhold
480 La Trobe Street
Melbourne, Victoria 3000, Australia

Macmillan of Canada
Division of Canada Publishing Corporation
164 Commander Boulevard
Agincourt, Ontario M15 3C7, Canada

16 15 14 13 12 11 10 9 8

Library of Congress Cataloging in Publication Data

Forseth, Kevin, 1949—
    Graphics for architecture.

    Includes index.
    1. Architectural drawing—Technique. 2. Architectural rendering—Technique. 3. Architecture—Composition, proportion, etc.—Technique. 4. Perspective—Technique. I. Title.
NA2708.F67   720'.28   79-12915
ISBN 0-442-26390-2

Contents

Acknowledgments

I want to thank two very talented students for their special efforts toward completing this book:

Don Blair, who suggested the poster analogy for page layouts and whose sensitive hand and eye produced many of the designs and drawings; and David Vaughan, whose wide range of skills and tremendous capacity for work enabled him to help with the written material, design work, and many of the toned drawings.

Many other students helped in various capacities. I am grateful to Scott Wiemer for the hundreds of hours he spent drafting; to Todd Wetherilt for assisting with the drafting and design work; and to Dale Brown, Ann Ringlein, and Bob Mabrey for their contributions.

Professors Tom Laging, Wayne Attoe and Rod Lamberson deserve credit for their critical evaluation of early drafts and for contributing building designs.

The encouragement of my mentor, Professor Tim McGinty, who showed me how to think and draw and who somehow taught me to enjoy hard work, will always be appreciated.

This book was supported with Area of Excellence Faculty Development Funds provided through the College of Architecture at the University of Nebraska. I must state my debt to W. Cecil Steward, the Dean of the College of Architecture, and to Homer Puderbaugh, the Chairman of the Department of Architecture, for their generous and enthusiastic support of the project.

Finally, I want to express my gratitude to Forrest Wilson, whom I have never met in person, for making the book possible.

for Katie

Introduction

The material for this book was assembled primarily for beginning students of architecture and interior design. Its main purpose is to illuminate typical methods for mechanically constructing design drawings.

Written to serve as a text for a one-semester course in graphic constructions and as a handy reference manual for use in the design studio, its contents are organized and presented to combine textbook learning sequences with the ready reference qualities of a handbook.

As a text illustrated procedures and examples are carefully presented to help beginning students with the often difficult task of learning to construct their drawings. Concept drawings are included to help clarify basic ideas.

As a handbook the format was designed to emphasize drawings and illustrations rather than written explanations, which were kept short and concise. Every effort was made to assemble the book so that the quality and clarity of its illustrations and the care with which it is laid out would make it a good reference for the office or design studio.

In order to devote more pages to the difficult and essential task of explaining the principles and procedures behind architectural graphic constructions, this book does not include a chapter on equipment. For reference purposes, however, a typical range of drafting supplies is illustrated here (1-11).

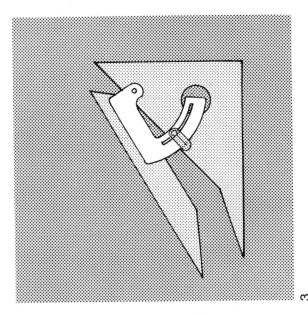

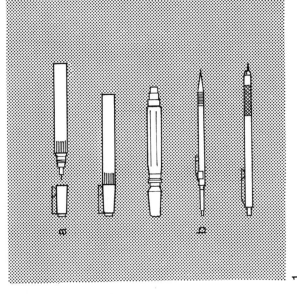

1

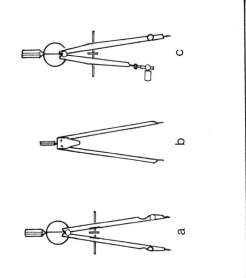

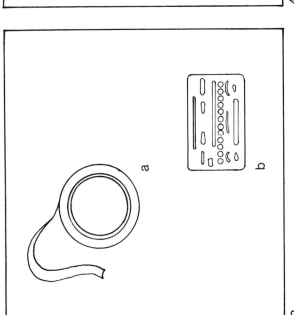

3

4

2

1
a   Technical pens
b   Mechanical pencils
2
a   Tape
b   Eraser shield
3   Variable triangle
4
a   Compass
b   Calipers
c   Compass with adaptor for technical pens

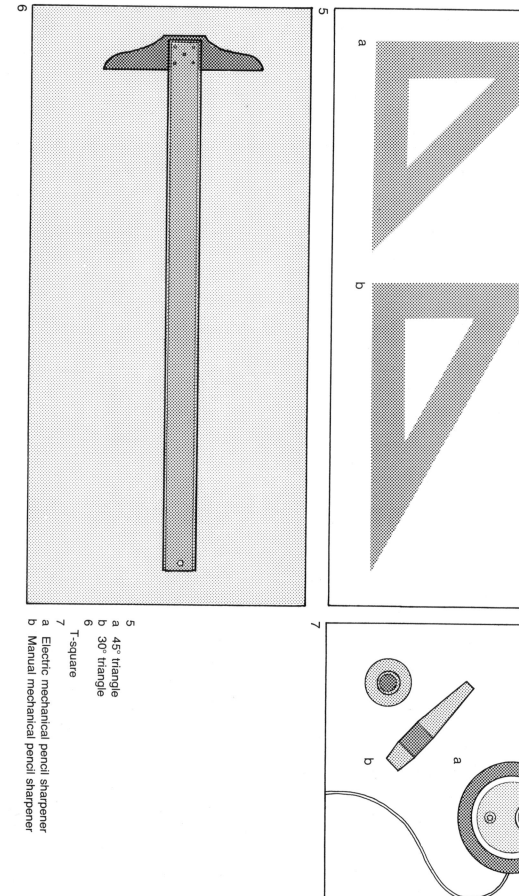

5 a 45° triangle
  b 30° triangle
6   T-square
7 a Electric mechanical pencil sharpener
  b Manual mechanical pencil sharpener

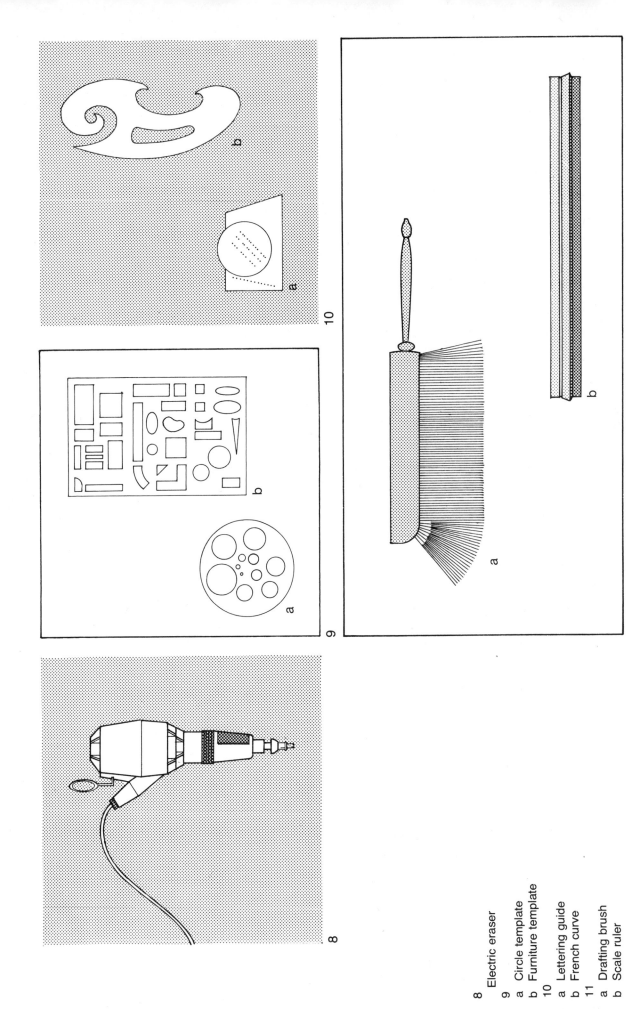

9

8   Electric eraser

9   a Circle template
      b Furniture template

10 a Lettering guide
      b French curve

11 a Drafting brush
      b Scale ruler

Pictorial Effect

Projection System

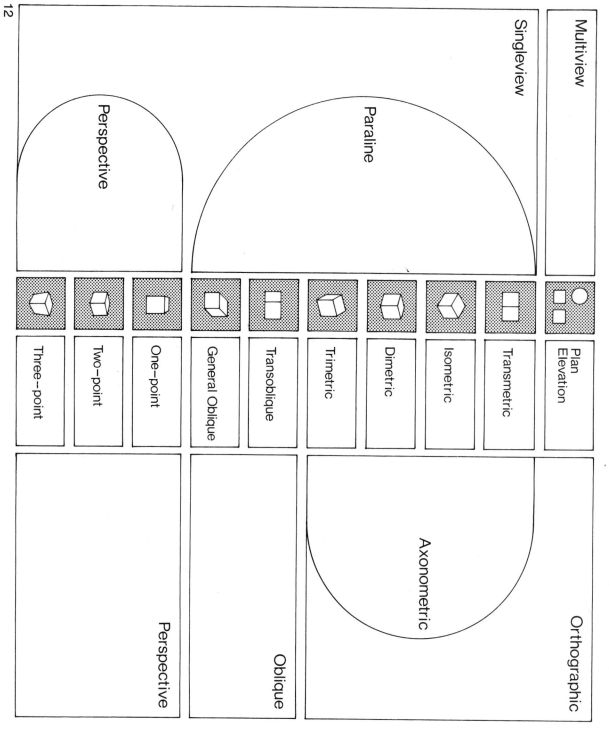

Pictorial Effect		Projection System
Multiview	Plan / Elevation	Orthographic
Singleview	Transmetric	
	Isometric	
Paraline	Dimetric	Axonometric
	Trimetric	
	Transoblique	Oblique
	General Oblique	
	One-point	
Perspective	Two-point	Perspective
	Three-point	

12

Design Drawings

The ten small rectangles in the chart to the left (12) illustrate the primary design drawings. The chart's left and right sides show two approaches to organizing and learning about the types of design drawings.

The left half groups design drawings by their pictorial effect. The pictorial-effect approach is based on a learning process that encourages the application of a set of rules and examples to a particular drawing problem in order to cosmetically create the desired design drawing's image or effect.

The chart's right side organizes design drawings by projection-system technique. The learning process associated with this approach involves an understanding of the fundamental principles of drawing construction and the application of these principles to the creation of a specific drawing type.

Both learning approaches have advantages and disadvantages. In each chapter projection-system rules and examples are presented and discussed as a means of more thoroughly understanding and appreciating the portions of each chapter devoted to pictorial-effect drawings.

Seldom is a clear distinction made between the two approaches. Both do have as their center of concern the same design drawings and are thus intimately related. The distinguishing difference exists in the depth of understanding that one approach provides over the other. This distinction can be illustrated through analogy.

A man plants a garden by following the instructions printed on the back of the seed package. His botanist neighbor also plants a garden, applying his understanding of seed germination and plant growth to ensure that each seed is properly planted and cared for. Both gardens will be successful, but the neighbor's garden may grow faster, look better, and be more productive. In essence the same is true of the pictorial-effect and the projection-system approaches.

Pictorial-effect drawings are rendered by following a set of directions, whereas projection-system drawings grow out of an understanding of fundamental drawing theory and provide a more flexible and productive approach to design drawing.

This chapter briefly introduces the different design drawings and the factors that influence their appearance. Later chapters explain their method of construction and application more fully.

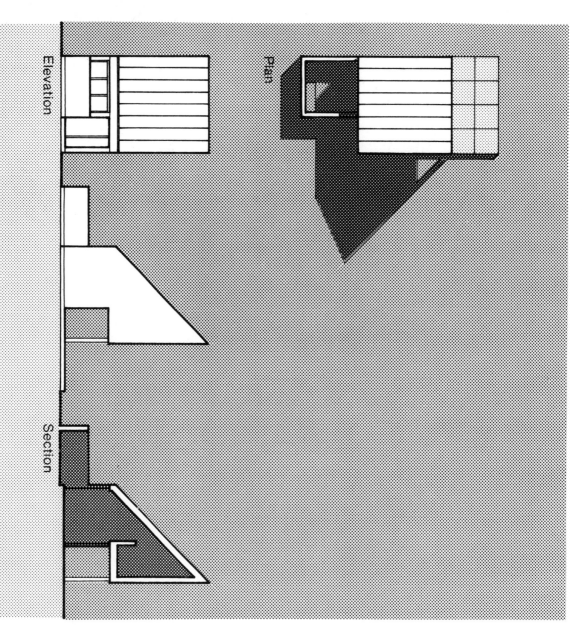

Plan

Elevation

Section

The learning process associated with the pictorial-effect grouping of design drawings has the characteristic approach of a paint-by-number set.

Following step-by-step directions, a finished drawing can be constructed by using one of the primary design drawings as a pattern.

For example, suppose that an exterior view of a building showing the general massing of the structure is to be drawn. An isometric design drawing might be chosen as the approach, and by following the basic rules for constructing an isometric a finished drawing can be quickly completed.

The approach stresses the practical applications of both multiview and singleview drawings without the need to understand the more abstract principles of design drawing.

Design drawings defined by their pictorial effect include multiview and singleview drawings.

Multiviews

Plans, elevations, and sections are the three types of multiview drawings (13). No single multiview drawing can communicate the true configuration of a three-dimensional object. Depending on the complexity and detail of the object, each independent drawing may need to provide supplemental information in additional drawings.

Singleviews

Singleview design drawings simultaneously communicate more than one side of an object in the same view.

Both paraline and perspective drawings are singleview drawings. The difference between paraline and perspective drawings is visually apparent. In a paraline drawing any two parallel lines remain infinitely parallel (15); in a perspective drawing parallel lines appear to converge at a common vanishing point (14).

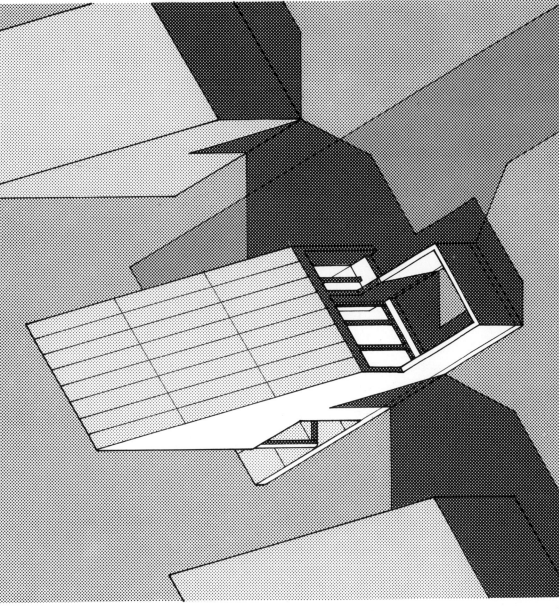

15

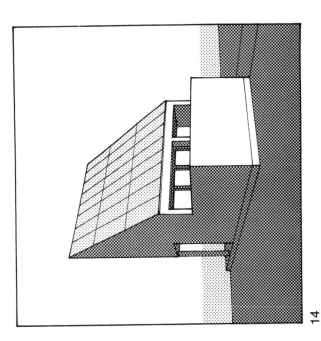

14

Description of a Typical Projection System

To explain how design drawings are organized in terms of differences in their projections, a kit of parts for assembling a model of a typical projection system is needed. The kit of parts includes:

1. a three-dimensional object
2. a picture plane for capturing the object's projected image
3. projector rays for projecting the object to the picture plane's surface
4. a viewer to observe the object's image on the picture plane

The pictorial drawing to the left (16) serves as our model. In the model a viewer is observing a building's two-dimensional image on the surface of a picture plane. The image on the picture plane was obtained by projecting points from the building's actual surface to the picture plane's surface. The projected points on the picture plane were then connected to form the building's image. This image varies as the relationship between the projector rays and the picture plane varies. For example, the model illustrates a form of orthographic projection because projector rays are oriented perpendicular to the picture plane.

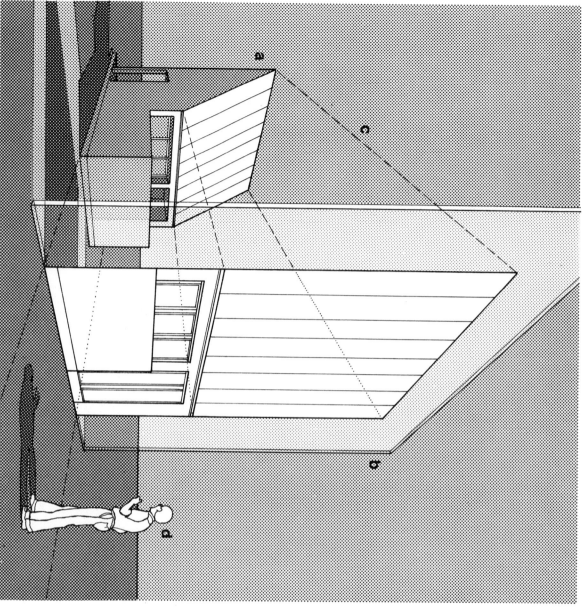

16

16
a Three-dimensional object
b Picture plane
c Projector rays
d Viewer

Types of Projections

Projector rays intersect the picture plane in one of three systematic ways (17). Each systematic intersection defines a family of design drawings based on projection.

Orthographic Projections

If all projectors meet the picture plane at right angles, the image on the picture plane is an orthographic projection. Plans, elevations, sections, and axonometrics belong to the family of orthographic projections.

Oblique Projections

Projections parallel to each other and at an oblique angle to the picture plane produce oblique projections on the picture plane. Transobliques and general obliques belong to the family of oblique projections.

Perspective Projections

Projectors forming various angles to the picture plane and converging to a common vanishing point produce perspective projections. One-point, two-point, and three-point perspectives belong to the family of perspective projections.

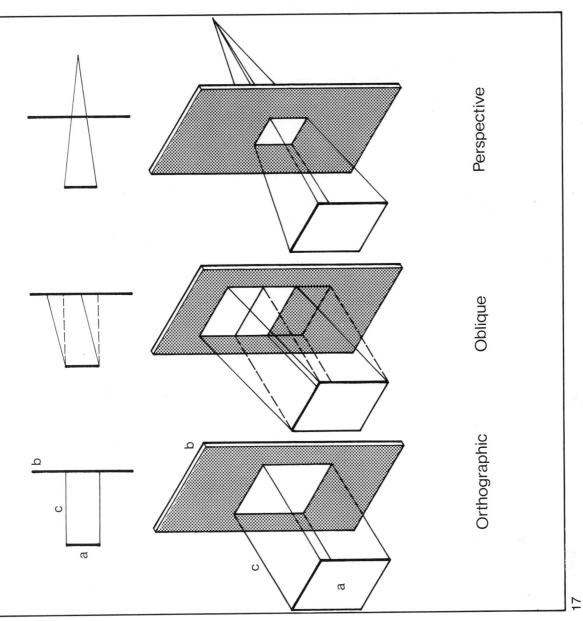

Orthographic   Oblique   Perspective

17

17
a Object
b Picture plane
c Projector rays

15

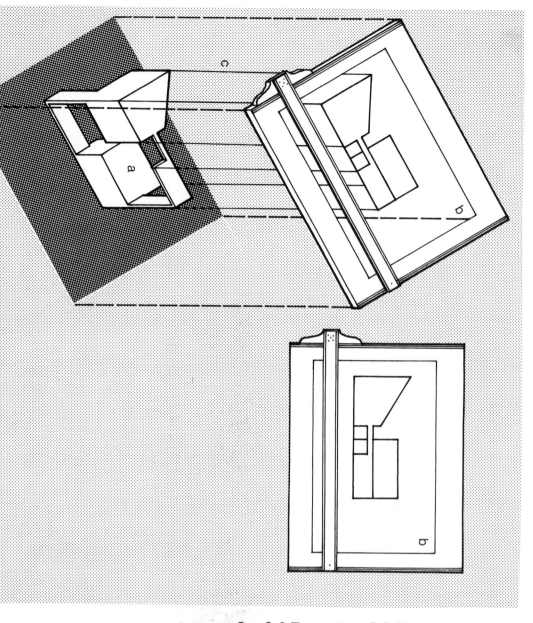

18

Regardless of the type or complexity of a completed design drawing, its sheet of paper technically serves as a picture plane, and the phantom of the depicted object or scene exists three-dimensionally somewhere in the picture plane's vicinity.

If all projectors meet the picture plane at right angles, the resulting image on the picture plane is an orthographic projection. Shown at left (18) is an example of an orthographic projection.

The family of orthographic projections includes multiviews and axonometrics. The difference between a multiview and an axonometric is based on the orientation of the actual object with respect to the picture plane.

Multiviews: Plans, Elevations, and Sections

If one principal face of an object is oriented parallel to the picture plane, its orthographic image is called a multiview. Plans, elevations, and sections are types of multiview drawings. The drawing to the left (18) illustrates a multiview elevation.

The chapter on multiviews describes this material in greater detail.

18
a Object
b Picture plane
c Projector rays

Axonometrics: Transmetrics, Isometrics, Dimetrics, and Trimetrics

If multiple sides of an object appear in the same orthographic image on the picture plane, the resulting view is called an axonometric. Transmetrics, isometrics, dimetrics, and trimetrics belong to the family of axonometric drawings.

Since three sides of the building appear in the same orthographic image, the drawing to the right (20) illustrates an axonometric.

The chapter on paralines describes axonometrics in greater detail.

19 Pictorial

20
a Object
b Picture plane
c Projector rays

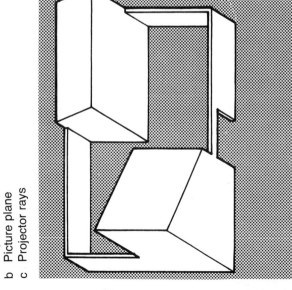

19

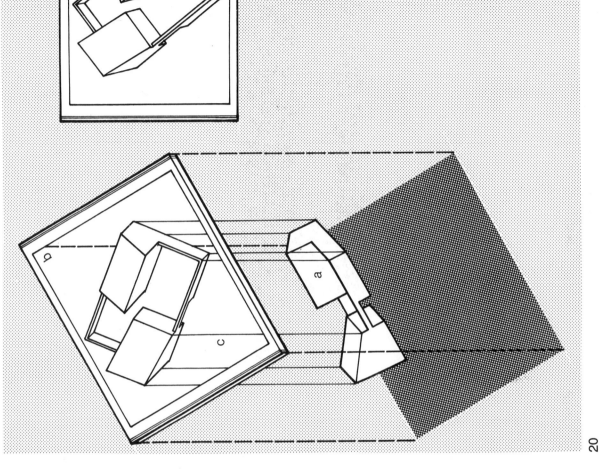

20

Oblique Projection

If all projectors are parallel to each other and at an oblique angle to the picture plane, the image on the picture plane is an oblique projection.

The family of oblique projections includes transobliques and general obliques. The difference between a transoblique and a general oblique is based on the orientation of the actual object: general obliques project three faces of a building into the picture plane, while transobliques project only two. Since three sides of the building appear in the same oblique image, the drawing to the left (21) illustrates a general oblique.

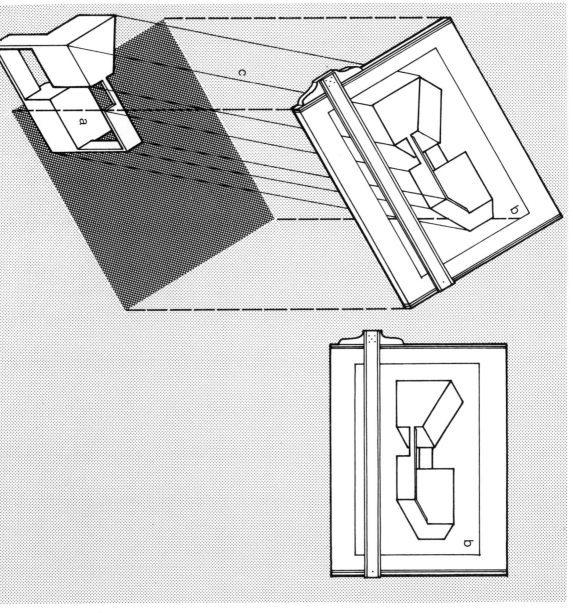

21
a Object
b Picture plane
c Projector rays

If all projectors converge to a common vanishing point, their intersection with the picture plane produces a perspective image of an object.

The family of perspective projections includes one-point, two-point, and three-point perspectives. Their differences are based on the orientation of the actual object with respect to the picture plane.

One-point Perspective

If one face of a rectilinear object is parallel to the picture plane, its perspective image is called a one-point.

Two-point Perspective

If one set of a rectilinear object's parallel edges is parallel to the picture plane and no faces of the actual object are parallel to the picture plane, the resulting image is a two-point perspective. The drawing to the right (22) illustrates a two-point perspective.

Three-point Perspective

If no faces or edges of a rectilinear object are parallel to the picture plane, the resulting image is a three-point perspective.

The chapter on perspectives describes these differences in greater detail.

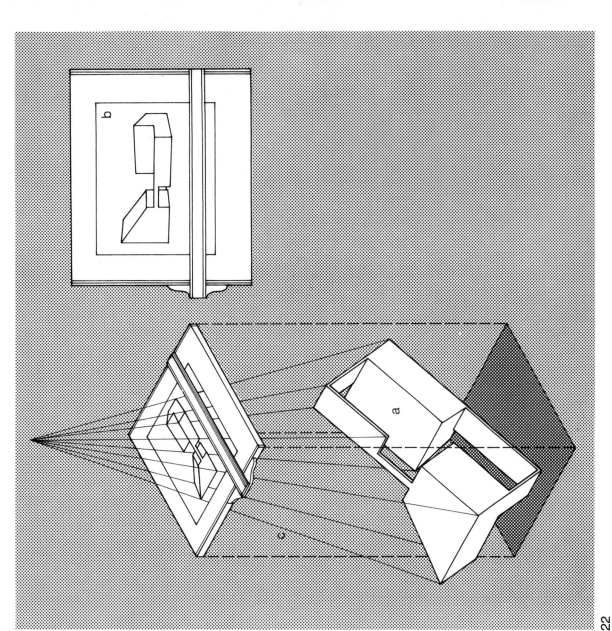

22

22
a Object
b Picture plane
c Projector rays

Multiviews

The three types of multiview drawings are plans, elevations, and sections. Individually the drawings cannot adequately communicate the configuration of a three-dimensional object. They require additional drawings to provide a complete understanding of the entire object.

Although multiview drawings lack the three-dimensional quality of paraline and perspective drawings, they have the advantage of being able to express the accurately scaled dimensions of objects, buildings, and environments.

Plans, elevations, and sections are also examples of orthographic-projection drawing. A major goal of all orthographic drawing is the determination of a true configuration: length of a line, shape of a plane, position of a point, location and angle of an intersection, and representation of irregular and complex shapes.

The first portion of this chapter defines a vocabulary, outlines basic rules, and provides a systematic approach to the basic theory of orthographic projection. This material, based on the principles of descriptive geometry, is particularly useful to the designer in such diverse applications as accurate model building, estimating quantity of materials, and repairing warped bicycle wheels.

The last portion of this chapter briefly discusses plans, elevations, and sections as basic design-presentation drawings. Rooted in orthographic drawing theory, architectural multiview drawings illustrate buildings and environments clearly and precisely.

An understanding of fundamental words and phrases is essential to comprehend the principles of orthographic projection. Commonly used and accepted terms form the gist of the basic vocabulary defined below.

Picture Plane (PP)

A picture plane is the two-dimensional planar surface that records the image of an object or building. There are three basic picture planes: horizontal, frontal, and profile (23).

The horizontal picture plane (H) is a level plane. It is always parallel to level ground and to the surface of placid mountain lakes.

The frontal picture plane (F) is a vertical plane that is perpendicular to the horizontal picture plane. Frontal elevations are viewed on the frontal plane.

The profile picture plane (P) is perpendicular to both the horizontal and the frontal plane. Right and left elevations are always viewed on the profile plane.

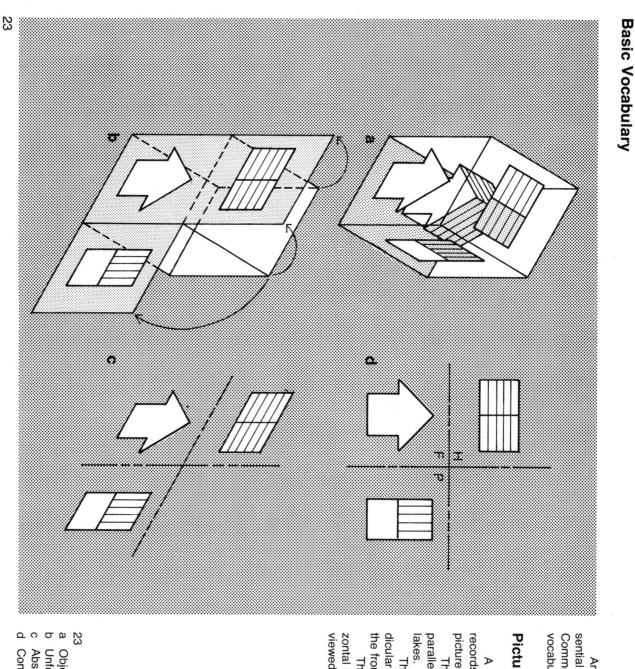

23

a Object surrounded by picture plane box
b Unfolded picture plane box
c Abstracted unfolded box
d Convention for expressing related picture planes

View

The image that an observer sees projected on a picture plane is called a view (24).

Plan view

A plan view (25) is the image of an object that appears on the horizontal picture plane. A bird flying directly above a building might regularly enjoy this view.

Elevation View

Elevation views (25) project directly from the plan view and appear on both the frontal and the profile plane.

Auxiliary view

Auxiliary views (25) project directly from the plan view but are not front, rear, left, or right elevations.

Inclined view

Inclined views (25) project from views other than the plan and appear on sloped picture planes.

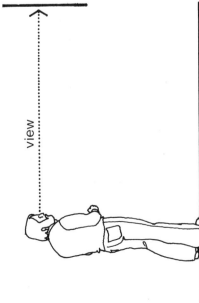

24

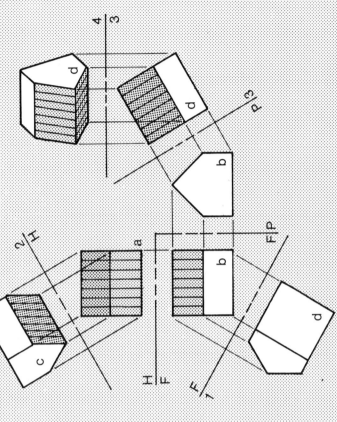

25

25
a Plan view
b Elevation view
c Auxiliary view
d Inclined view

23

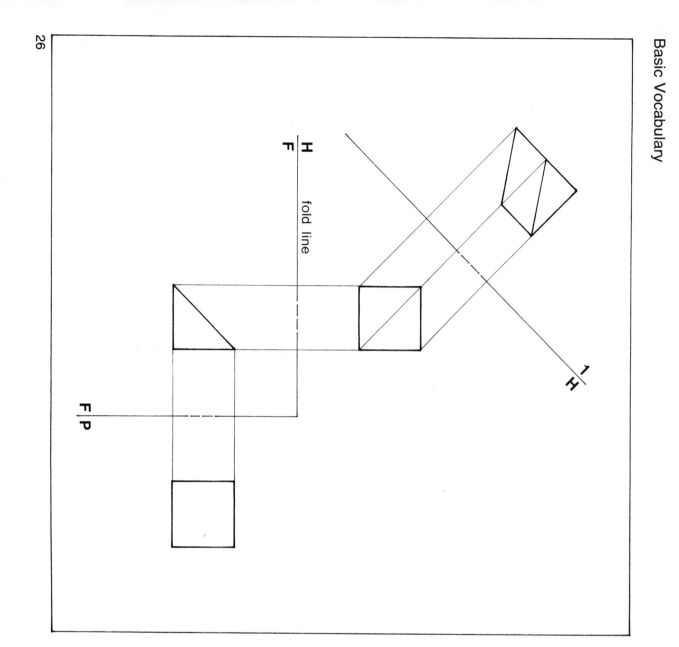

Fold Line

The fold line depicts the line of intersection between perpendicular picture planes (26).

Notation System

Picture planes are referenced at their fold lines with letters and numbers. The horizontal, frontal, and profile picture planes are always labeled with the letters H, F, and P, respectively. All other picture planes are referenced with numbers. By convention the letters and numbers are paired and placed on either side of the fold line (26).

One-view Drawings

A one-view drawing is an orthographic projection that describes an image of a three-dimensional object.

A one-view drawing can be constructed by beaming imaginary lines from every point on the object or building to the surface of a picture plane. These lines, called projector rays or projectors, always intersect the picture plane at right angles (27).

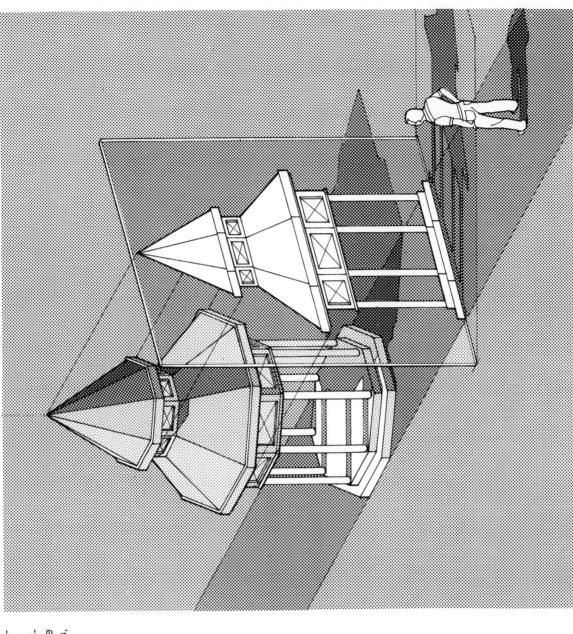

27

A two-view drawing is an orthographic projection that depicts two related images of an object or building (28). A two-view drawing is constructed in the same manner as a one-view drawing. Points on an object are connected by imaginary projector rays to its image on the picture plane. Remember that projector rays are always perpendicular to the surface of the picture planes.

The two images in a two-view drawing must lie in related picture planes and obey the related-picture-plane rule: related picture planes are perpendicular and share a common edge.

A two-view drawing, for example, might record the image of the front and side, the top and side, or the bottom and front but never the front and back views of an object. The front and back views do not occur in perpendicular picture planes and do not share a common edge. The drawing could not correctly be called a two-view drawing. To avoid the inconvenience of having to peer around the corner to see the second view in a two-view drawing, it is rotated 90° (29) to bring it into the same plane of view as the first drawing. A fold line is drawn along the common edge to indicate that the two views are actually in perpendicular picture planes.

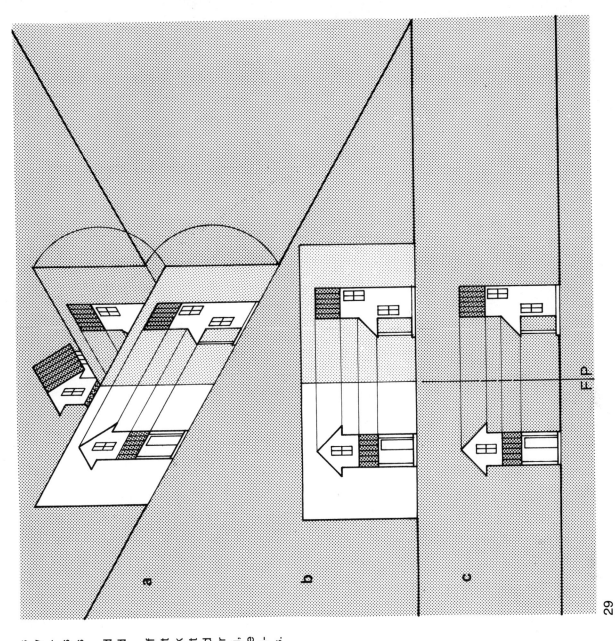

29

29 Revolved profile plane
a Both picture planes contained in the plane of this page
b Convention for expressing two related picture planes

Three-view Drawings

A three-view drawing depicts three related images of an object by conceptually surrounding it on three sides with picture planes.

The house in the illustration (30) is wrapped on three sides with mutually perpendicular picture planes. Each of the picture planes contains an orthographic image of the building. The images are connected to the building by imaginary projector rays that intersect the picture plane at right angles. By convention the picture planes are labeled H, F, P — horizontal, frontal, and profile picture planes, respectively.

The horizontal and profile picture planes can be unfolded until all three views appear in the same plane. By revolving the horizontal and profile picture planes about the frontal plane the three images that previously could be viewed only by moving around the house are now seen in a single flat plane.

The illustration (31) shows how the two sides are unfolded to view all three images in the same plane as the frontal plane.

31

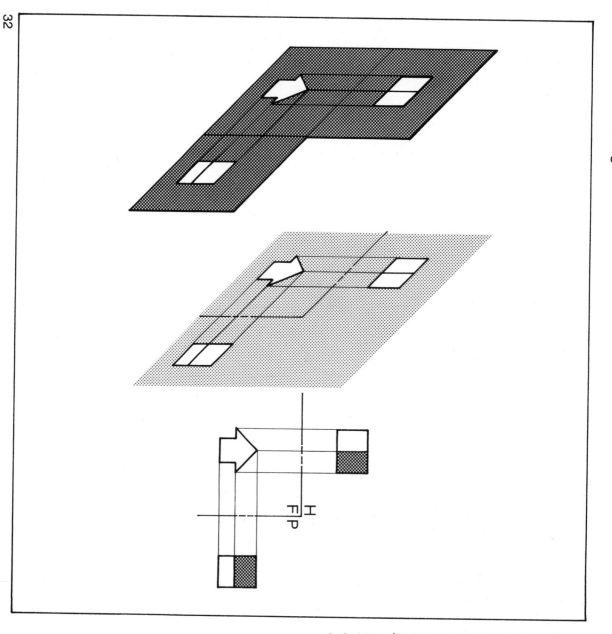

32

The standard manner for depicting three-view drawings is to revolve the three picture planes so that their images are all viewed in the same plane: a three-dimensional object abstractly represented in two dimensions. Each view is labeled, and the scaled front elevation, right elevation, and plan view appear in the same plane (32, 33).

The following observations can be made about three-view drawings.

1. Fold lines represent the line of intersection between two perpendicular picture planes.

2. Points on one picture plane can be located on an adjacent picture plane by using projector rays that are perpendicular to fold lines. Always project points of objects across fold lines with projector rays that are perpendicular to the fold lines.

3. The distance from a point on an object in the horizontal picture plane to its fold line with the frontal picture plane is equal to the distance from the same point in the profile picture plane to its fold line with the frontal plane. This observation is the basis for what will later be defined as the skip-a-plane rule.

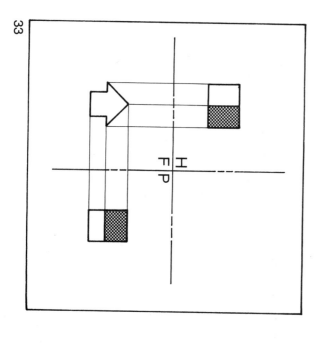

33

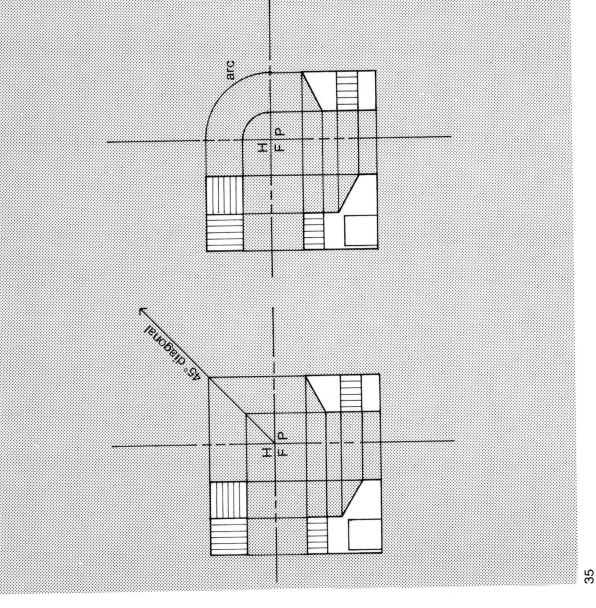

35

Transferring Related Distances

There are two simple methods for transferring the distances from the fold line to points on the horizontal plane to the profile plane.

1. Draw a diagonal at the intersection of the fold lines and transfer the distances as illustrated (35).

2. Use the intersection of the fold lines as the center for circular arcs that transfer the distance as illustrated (35).

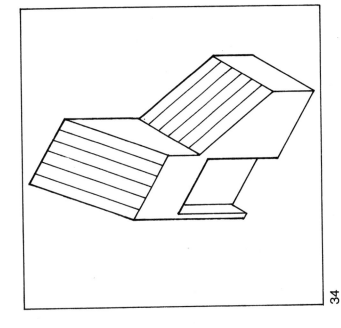

34

Six-view Drawings

A six-view drawing depicts six images of an object or building by conceptually enclosing it in a picture-plane box. In a six-view drawing three additional views are possible: left elevation, rear elevation, and bottom plan view.

The sequence of drawings (36, 37) illustrates the unwrapping of a six-sided picture-plane box. The last illustration (37) shows the notation for representing a picture-plane box unfolded in this manner.

The picture-plane box can be folded back into a cube by bending the planes along the fold lines 90° until a three-dimensional cube is formed. The cube can again be unfolded in a variety of ways.

36

The observations made about three-view drawings also apply to the six-view drawings.

1. Each fold line represents the line of intersection between two perpendicular picture planes.

2. Points on one picture plane can be located on an adjacent picture plane by using projector rays that are perpendicular to fold lines. Always project points of objects across fold lines with projector rays that are perpendicular to the fold lines.

3. The distance from a point on the building to a fold line in one picture plane is equal to the distance of that same point to its fold line in both the picture plane that is on the opposite side of the cube and the picture plane diagonally to the right or left. This observation will be more clearly explained later as the skip-a-plane rule.

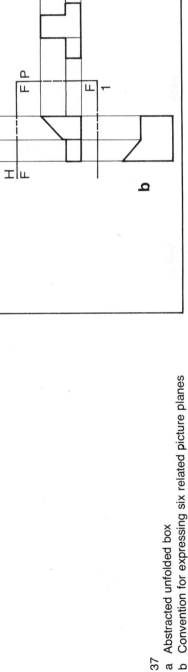

a

b

37 Abstracted unfolded box
a Abstracted unfolded box
b Convention for expressing six related picture planes

Auxiliary Views

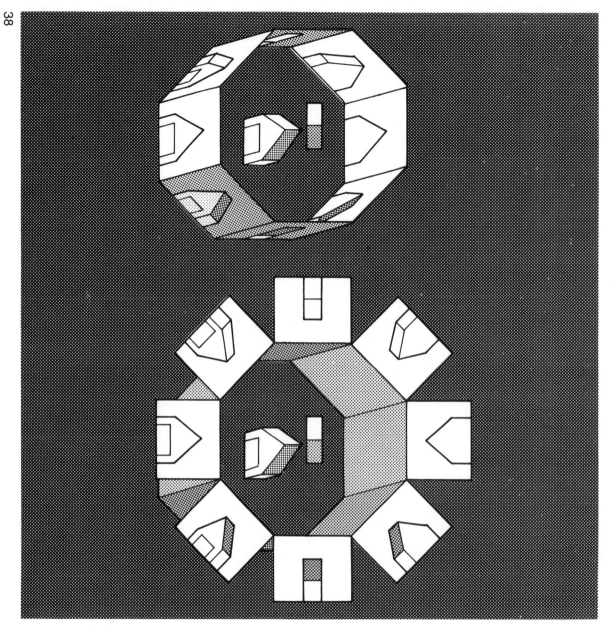

Auxiliary views are elevation drawings other than the front, rear, right, and left elevations projected directly from the plan view.

The sequence of drawings to the left (38) shows a narrow house surrounded by eight elevations. The convention for expressing this three-dimensional configuration is depicted to the right (39). Four of the elevations are the principal elevations: front, rear, right, and left. The other four elevations, which are not parallel to the walls of the house, are auxiliary-view elevations.

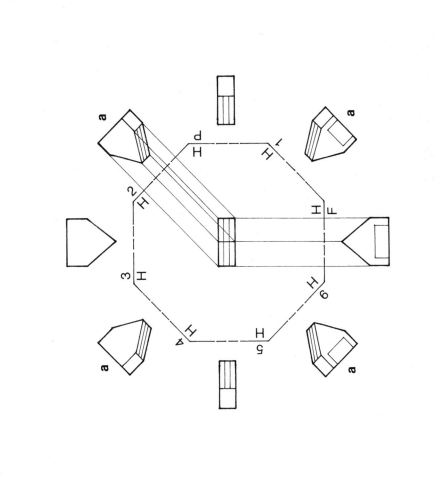

An infinite number of auxiliary views can be generated. For example, the house can be surrounded by sixteen vertical picture planes. Four of the sixteen projected images would be principal elevations and twelve would be auxiliary-view elevations. Any fold line introduced off the plan, except the four principal fold lines, will generate an auxiliary-elevation view.

39

39

a   Auxiliary view

40

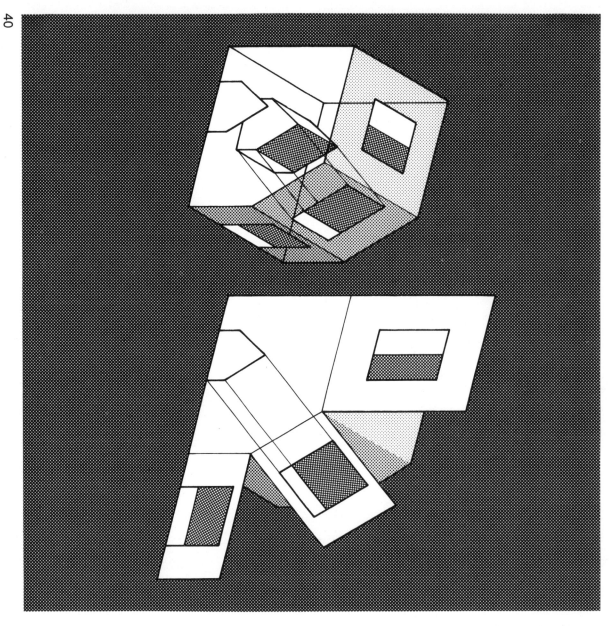

Inclined views enable a building to be viewed orthographi-cally from all angles. An inclined view is projected from an eleva-tion view or another inclined view and is always seen on a sloped picture plane (40, 41). It is never projected from a plan view.

The addition of auxiliary and inclined views to the vocabulary of orthographic projection provides the capacity to project any view of an object or building that is desired.

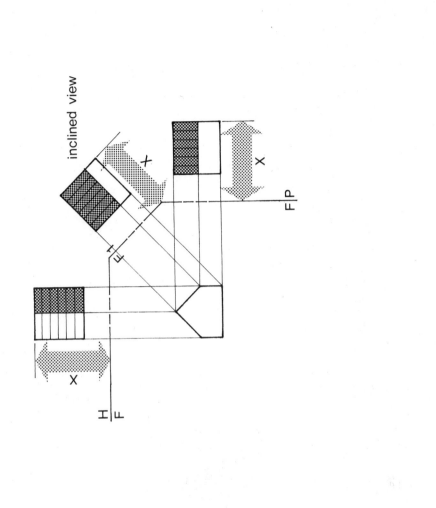

inclined view

F/P

H/F

X

X

X

The observations that were made about three- and six-view drawings also apply to auxiliary- and inclined-view drawings.

1. Each fold line represents the line of intersection between two perpendicular picture planes.

2. Points on one picture plane can be located on an adjacent picture plane by using projector rays that are perpendicular to fold lines. Always project points of objects across fold lines with projector rays that are perpendicular to the fold lines.

3. The distance from a point on a building to a fold line in one picture plane is equal to the distance from that same point to its fold line in every other picture plane. This observation will be more clearly explained later as the skip-a-plane rule.

Concrete and Abstract

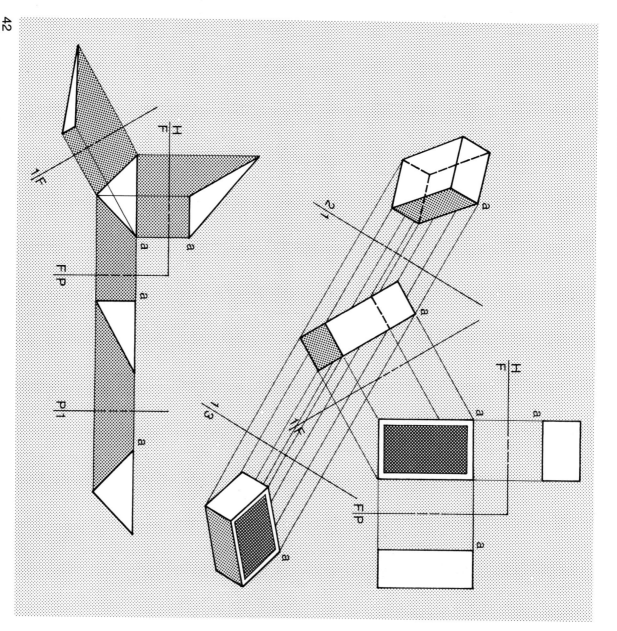

Points, lines, and planes are the basic geometric pieces used to abstractly represent any shape. Complex shapes can be broken down into these basic geometric components and depicted as orthographic drawings.

Drawings of familiar objects, such as speaker boxes (42), can be fairly easily understood when rotated, unfolded, and depicted in any of the standard orthographic views. Abstract geometric configurations such as points, lines, and planes are sometimes more difficult to visualize.

The observations made about two-, three-, six-, auxiliary-, and inclined-view drawings can be stated as rules and used to more clearly understand and analyze the relationships between orthographic drawings of abstract geometric configurations. Readily observed in orthographic drawings of familiar objects, these rules also apply to the more abstract geometric drawings.

A point on an object in one view projects at a right angle across the common fold line to its corresponding location on the object in an adjacent view.

Everything projects across fold lines at right angles: 2-H pencils, Rietveld chairs, middle-aged professors, buildings, geometric planes, and lines all follow this rule (43).

Always project points of objects into adjacent picture planes across fold lines with projector rays that are perpendicular to the fold line.

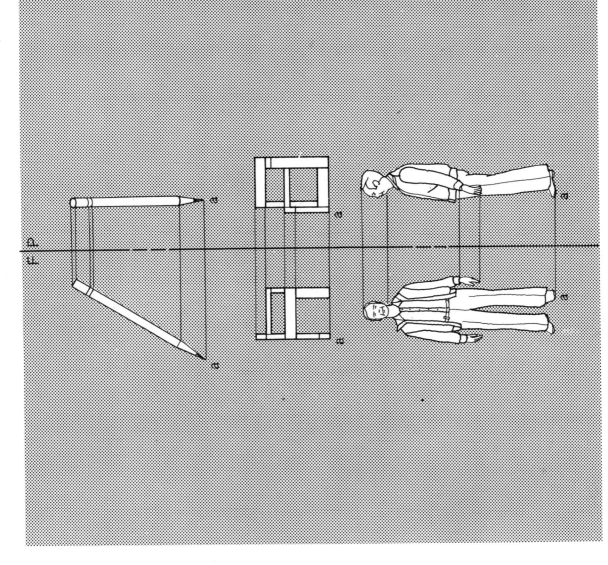

43

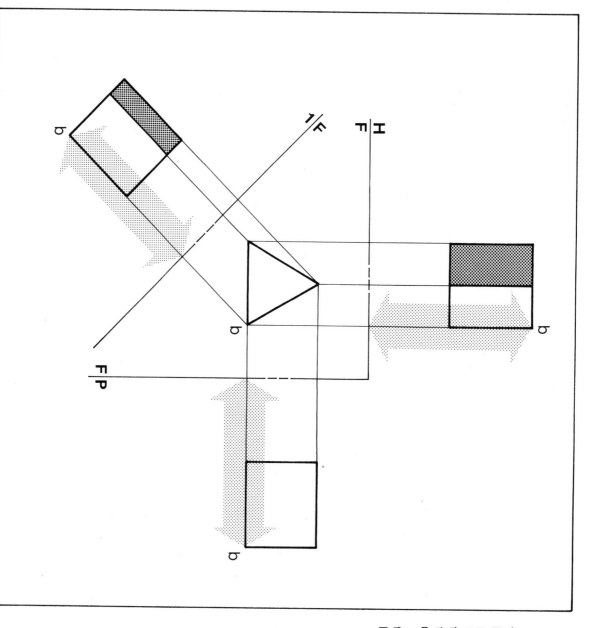

The distance from a point on an object to the fold line in one view is the same as its distance from the fold line in every other view.

The skip-a-plane rule can be visually explained in the illustration to the left (44). Mark off the distance from point B to fold line HF in the horizontal view. From the HF fold line leap-frog (skip a plane) over the frontal view to the F1 fold line. The distance from F1 to point B is equal to the original distance marked off from B to the HF fold line in the H view. The rule applies uniformly. Each of the distances marked off by the arrows are equal and are separated from one another by a skipped plane.

Two views separated by a skipped plane yield equal distances measured from the same point to their respective fold lines.

Fold-line Rule

A new fold line may be introduced anywhere in a drawing.

A new fold line can be drawn on either side of and at any distance from an existing view without affecting the resultant image.

The view projected across a new fold line is affected by the angle of the fold line. The resultant image changes as the angle of the fold line changes.

Fold lines can be drawn at any distance from an existing view without affecting the resultant images as long as the angles remain the same (45, 46).

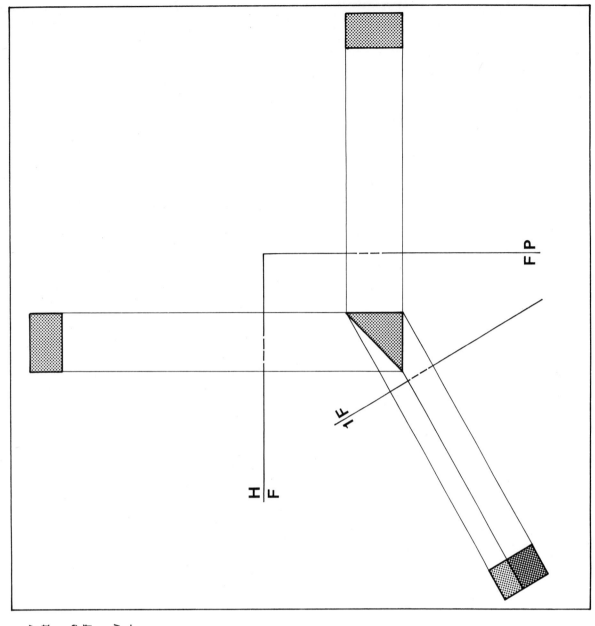

46

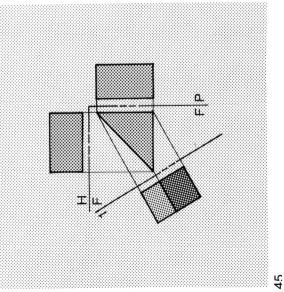

45

Four Basic Images

The purpose of this section is to explore methods of finding the elusive true dimensional measurements of building edges and surfaces that are not parallel to any given picture planes. All such measurements can be made with the concepts and procedures used to find the four basic images of lines and planes. The four basic images — or views, as they are sometimes called — include the true length and point images of a line and the true shape and edge images of a plane.

The true length image of the pencil appears on the picture plane that is oriented parallel to the pencil (47).

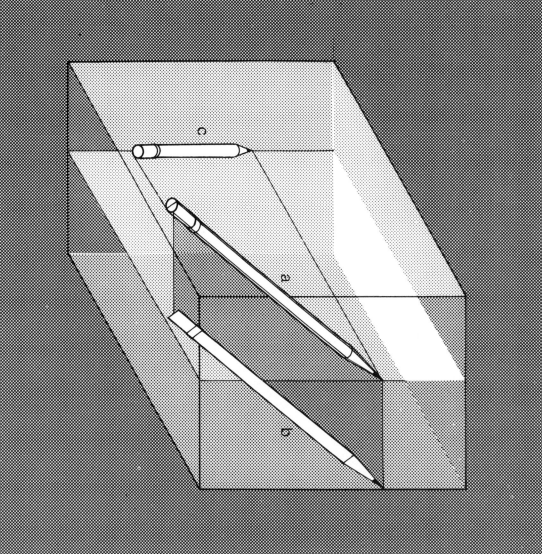

47
a Actual pencil
b True length image of pencil
c Foreshortened image of pencil

True Length Image of a Line

A line must be parallel to the picture plane in order for its true length to be seen. If a line is parallel to a fold line, it will appear in its true length image in the view across the fold line (48).

To find the true length image of a line:

1. If a line does not already appear in its true length in any given view, draw a fold line parallel to the line.

2. Project across the fold line to obtain the line's true length image.

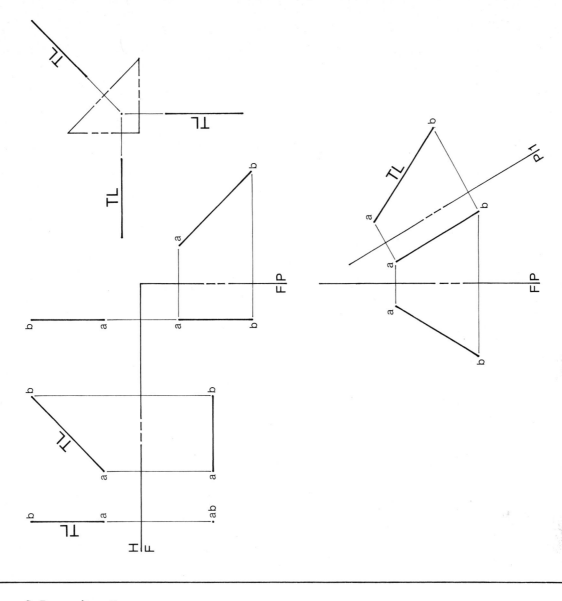

48

The point image of the pencil — its end view — appears on the picture plane that is oriented perpendicular to the pencil (49).

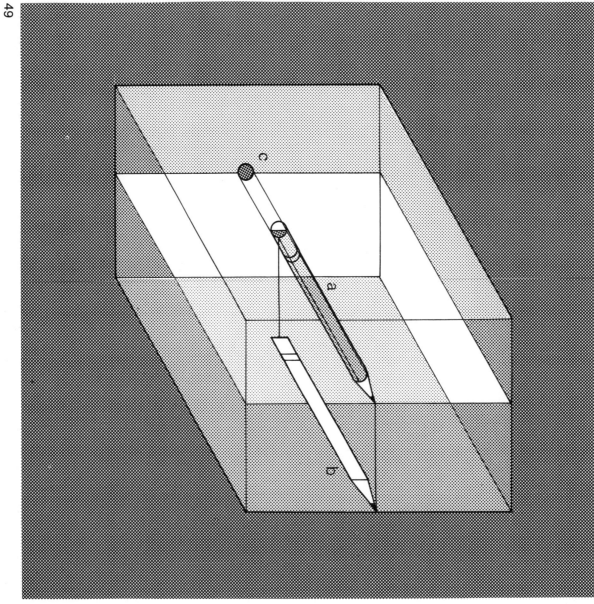

49

a Actual pencil
b True length image of pencil
c Foreshortened image of pencil

True Point Image of a Line

A line appears as a point in the pair of views whose picture planes are perpendicular to the line. If a fold line is constructed perpendicular to a true length line, the point image of the line will project across the fold line (50, 51).

To find the point image of a line:
1. Begin with a true length image of the line.
2. Construct a fold line perpendicular to the true length line.
3. Project across the fold line to obtain the point image of the line.

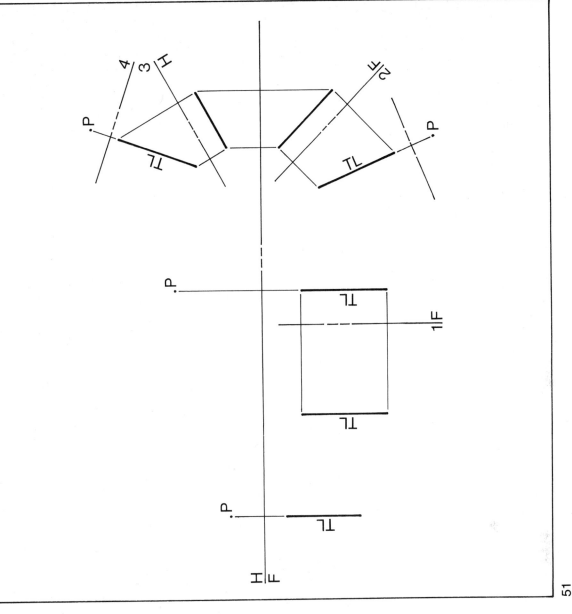

50 a Point image of chimney
    b True length image of chimney

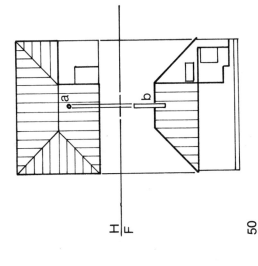

51

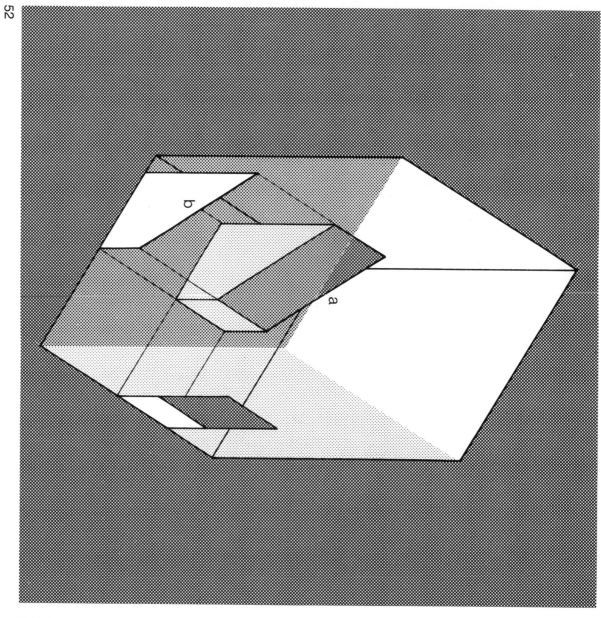

52

The building's pitched roof plane (52) appears as an edge on the picture plane that is oriented perpendicular to its surface.
The upper and lower horizontal edges of the shed roof appear as points in the view that shows the whole roof plane as an edge.

52
a Actual roof plane
b Edge image of roof plane

True Edge Image of a Plane

If a line on a plane appears as a point, the plane will appear as a line in the same view. If the point image of a line that is contained in a plane can be found, the plane will appear as an edge or line in the same view (53).

To find the edge image of a plane:

1. Find a true length line on the plane. If one is not there already, make one: pick a view. Draw a line on the plane from one side of the plane to the other. Make this line parallel to a fold line. Project this line into an adjacent view to obtain its true length.

2. Find the point view of the true length line and carry the points defining the plane into the same view. The resulting image will be an edge view of the plane.

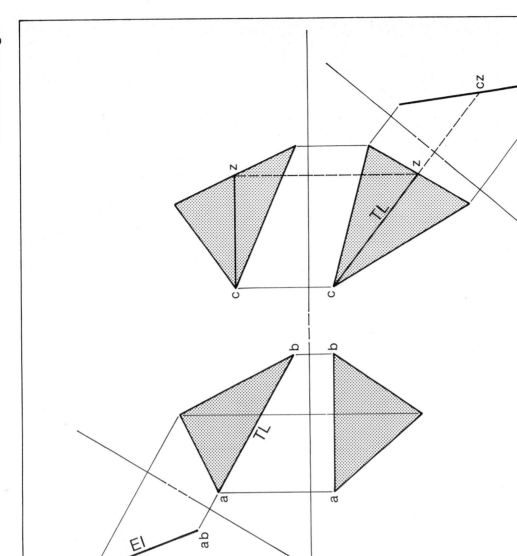

53

54

The true size and shape of the building's pitched roof (54) appear on a picture plane that is oriented parallel to the roof's surface.

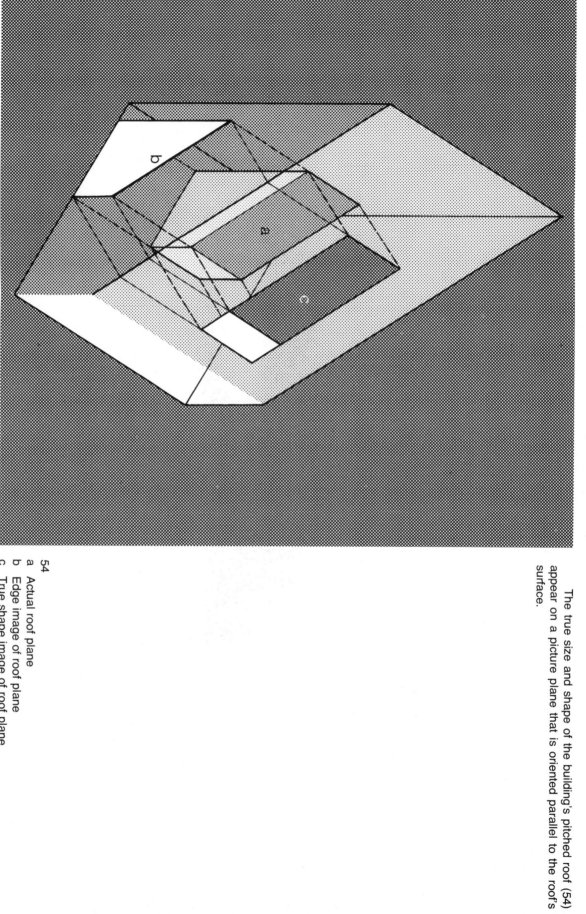

54
a   Actual roof plane
b   Edge image of roof plane
c   True shape image of roof plane

True Size Image of a Plane

A plane appears in its true size and shape on a picture plane that is parallel to the plane. By constructing a fold line parallel to the edge image of the plane its true size image can be found in the view across the fold line (55, 56).

To find the true size image of a plane:

1. Find an edge image of the plane.
2. Construct a fold line parallel to the edge image.
3. Project the plane across the fold line. The resulting image will be the true size image of the plane.

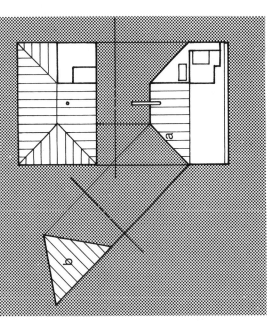

55
a Edge image of roof plane
b True shape image of roof plane

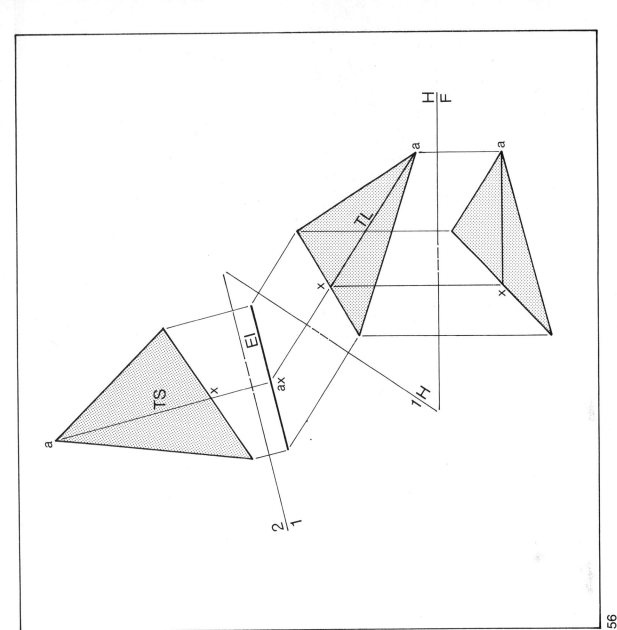

56

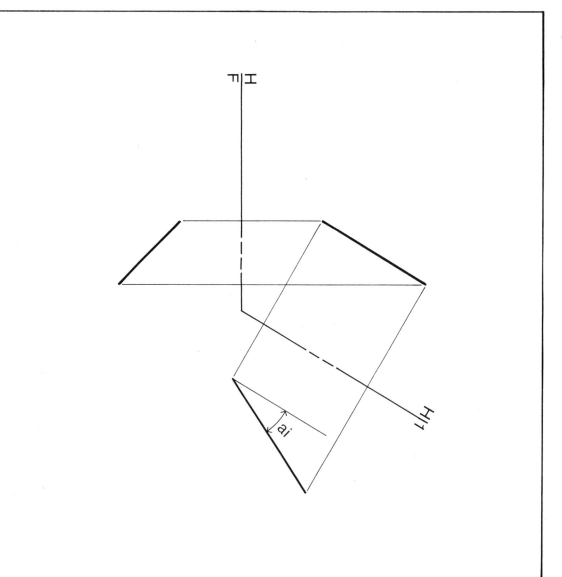

The procedures for finding the four basic images of lines and planes are employed to find the basic angles and intersections between lines and planes.

Inclination of a Line

An angle of inclination is the true or smallest angle formed between a line and a horizontal plane. The inclination of a line can be measured only in an elevation view that shows the true length image of the line (57).

To find the inclination of a line:

1. Construct a fold line parallel to the plan view of the given line.

2. Project the line across the fold line, obtaining its true length image.

3. Measure the angle formed between the line's true length image and a horizontal line. The horizontal line must be parallel to the fold line constructed from the plan view. This usually means that the horizontal line is not horizontal on the sheet of paper.

Several conventions are used to express the resulting angle (page 65).

Inclination of a Plane

An angle of inclination is the true or smallest angle between a line or plane and a horizontal. The inclination of a plane is measured in an elevation view that shows the plane as an edge (58).

To find the inclination of a plane:

1. If a true length line is not already given, construct one in the plan view of the plane.

2. Find the point image of this true length line and project the plane into the same view, obtaining the edge view of the plane.

3. Measure the angle between the plane's edge image and a horizontal line. This horizontal line should always be parallel to the fold line separating the constructed elevation and the given plan view.

4. Use an appropriate convention to express this angle (page 65).

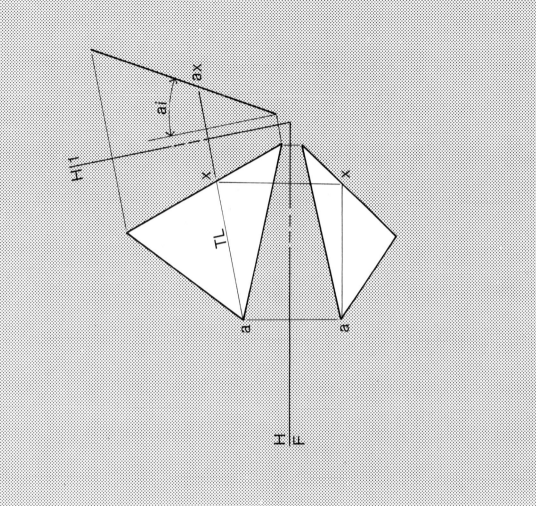

Intersection of a Line and a Plane

A line must intersect a plane that is not parallel to the line. One way to find this point of intersection is to construct an edge image of the plane, transferring the line to the same view (59).

Edge-image Method

To find the intersection of a line and plane using the edge-image method:

1. Construct a view showing the plane's edge image and transfer the line into the same view.

2. Project the point of intersection in the constructed view to the line in the adjacent view. The meeting of projector and line locates the position where the line pierces the plane in the adjacent view.

3. Project this piercing point from view to view and from line to line. Each intersection of projector and line marks the position where the line and the plane meet.

There is also a method of finding which part of a line is hidden behind a plane in any view (page 60).

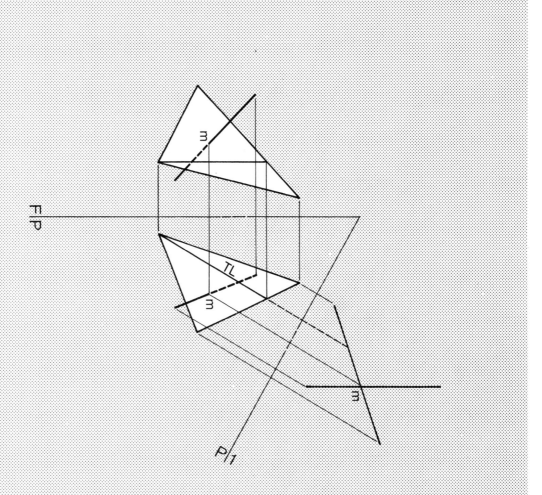

F P

TL

m

m

m

P 1

Cutting-plane Method

If the edge image of a plane — called the cutting plane — is positioned over a view of the line, then the point of intersection between the line and the plane can be located without constructing additional views. Since the added cutting plane is drawn in edge view, its line of intersection with the given plane is easily plotted in the adjacent view. The position where this line of intersection and the given line meet in the adjacent view marks the point of intersection between the line and the plane (60).

To find the intersection of a line and a plane using the cutting-plane method:

1. Position a cutting plane over a given view of the line. The cutting plane and the line appear as the same line in this view.

2. Project the line of intersection between the cutting plane and the given plane into the adjacent view.

3. The point where the given line and the line of intersection between the cutting plane and the given plane meet in the adjacent view marks the intersection of the given line and the plane.

4. Transfer this point of intersection from view to view.

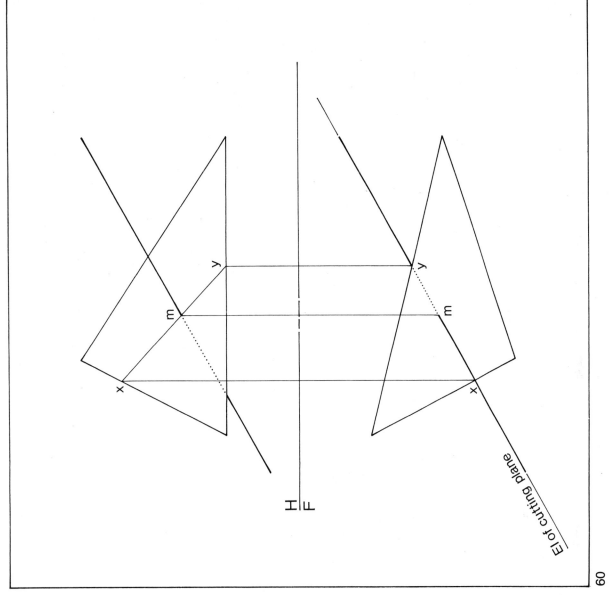

60

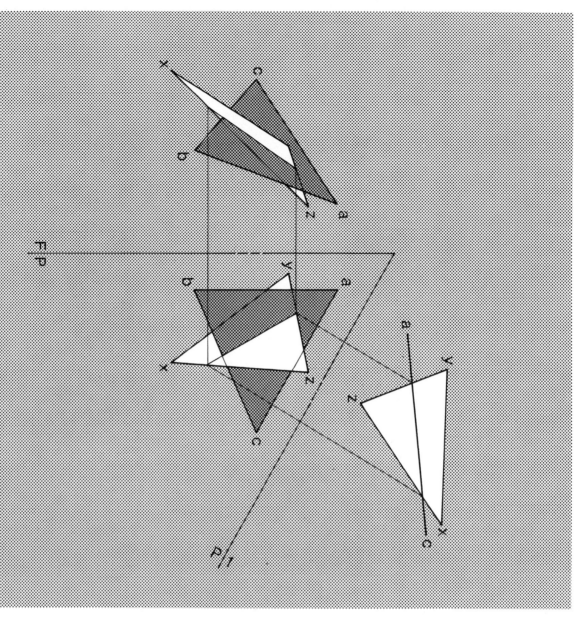

Intersecting Planes

Two nonparallel planes intersect along a straight line. This line of intersection can be found in a view that shows one of the planes as an edge (61).

Edge-image Method

To find the line of intersection between two planes using the edge-image method:

1. Construct the edge image of one plane and carry the other plane into the same view.

2. Transfer points of intersection from the edge-image view into adjacent views.

Cutting-plane Method

To find the line of intersection between two nonparallel planes, apply the cutting-plane method (page 53) twice: position edge images of cutting planes over two edges of a given plane. Find the intersection of each edge with the other plane and connect their points of intersection with a straight line (62).

To find the line of intersection between two planes using the cutting-plane method:

1. Position cutting planes over two edges of a given plane.

2. Use the cutting-plane method (page 53) to locate the point where each line receiving a cutting plane intersects the other plane.

3. Connect the pair of edge-line intersections with the other plane with a straight line. This straight line defines the line of intersection between the given planes.

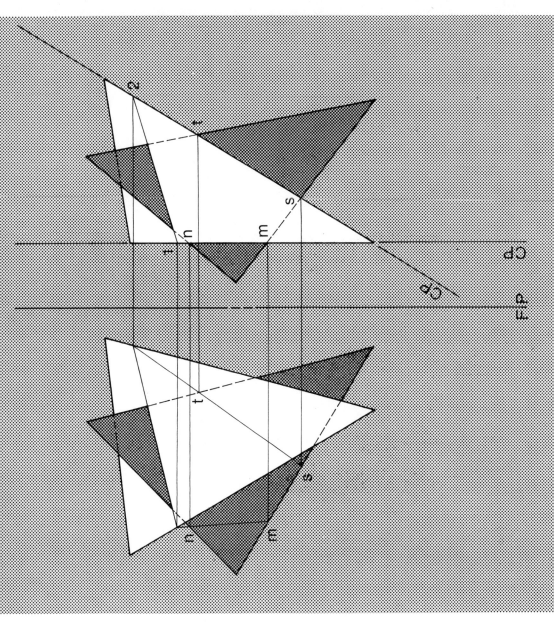

62

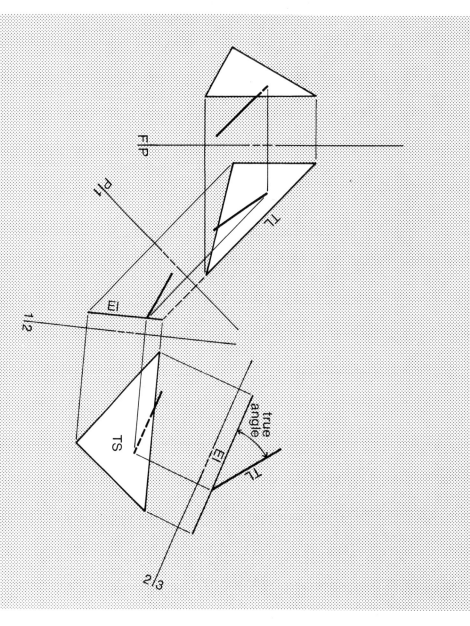

Angle between a Line and a Plane

The true angle between a line and a plane is found in views that show the plane as an edge and the line in its true length.

All views adjacent to the true size image of a plane show the plane in edge view. By projecting an edge view of the plane that also shows the line in true length the special view showing the plane as an edge and the line in its true length can be found (63).

To find the angle between a line and a plane:

1. Construct a true shape image of the plane. Carry the line into the same view.

2. Find the true length image of the line in a view adjacent to the true shape image of the plane.

3. Measure the true angle between the edge image of the plane and the true length image of the line. This angle is expressed in degrees.

Angle between two Planes

The true angle between two intersecting planes is called the dihedral angle. It is measured in a plane that is perpendicular to the line of intersection between the two planes. To measure the angle between two planes requires a view showing both planes as edges (64).

To find the dihedral angle between two intersecting planes:

1. Construct the line of intersection between the given planes.

2. Find the true length image of this line of intersection. Carry the given planes into this view.

3. Find the point image of the true length line. The given planes should both appear in edge image in this view.

4. Measure the dihedral angle between the given planes. This angle is expressed in degrees.

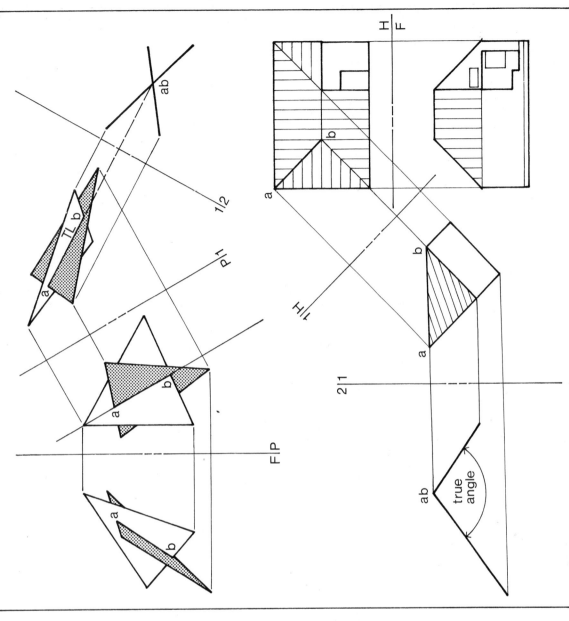

64

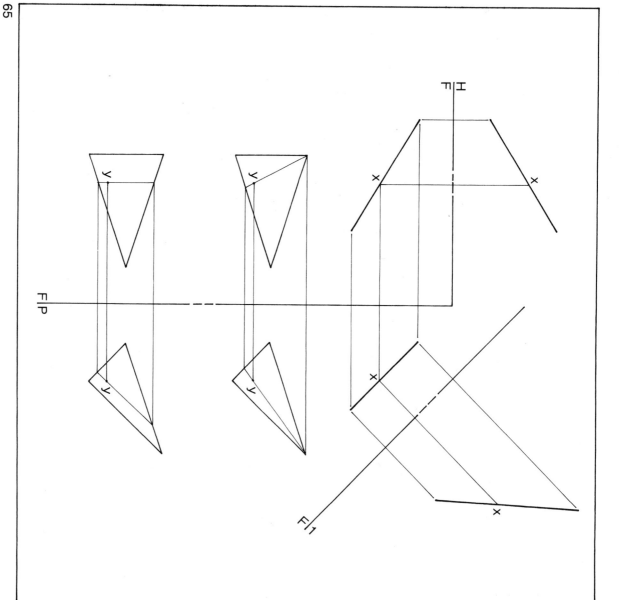

65

Locating a Point on a Line

To project a point on a line in one view to the same location along the line in an adjacent view, simply project the point across the fold line until it meets the line in the adjacent view (65).

Locating a Point within a Plane

Projecting a point on a plane from view to view usually requires more information than the drawing provides, because the point often floats unattached within the plane (65). To project a point on a plane from view to view, construct a line within the plane that contains the point. Use the intersections of the line with the edges of the plane to project the line from view to view. Project the point from line to line, locating the point within the different views of the plane.

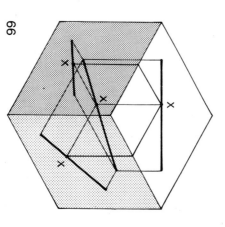

66

Warped Planes

Planes bounded by three straight edges are always flat. Planes bounded by four or more edges are not always flat. They may be warped.

If straight lines are drawn between corners on a many-sided flat plane, their points of intersection must line up along common projectors between views (67).

To test for the flatness of a plane:

1. Construct intersecting straight lines from all corners of the plane in a pair of adjacent views.

2. Transfer the points of intersection between the lines constructed on the plane from one view to the other.

3. If the points of intersection between the lines constructed on the planes line up along common projectors, the surface is flat.

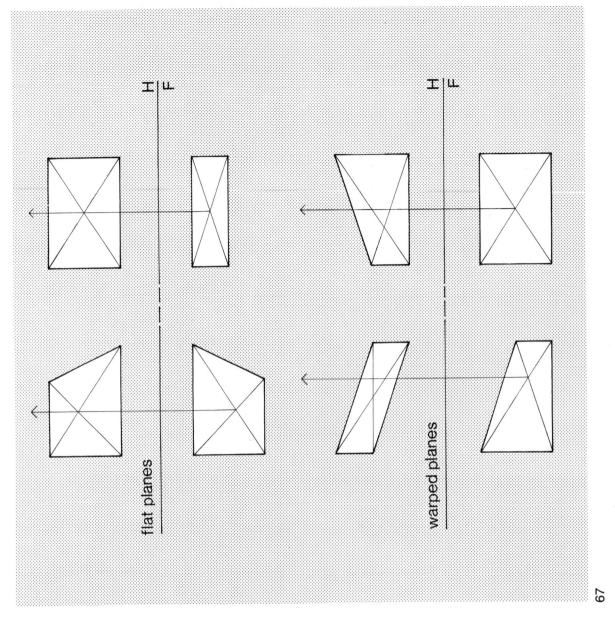

flat planes

warped planes

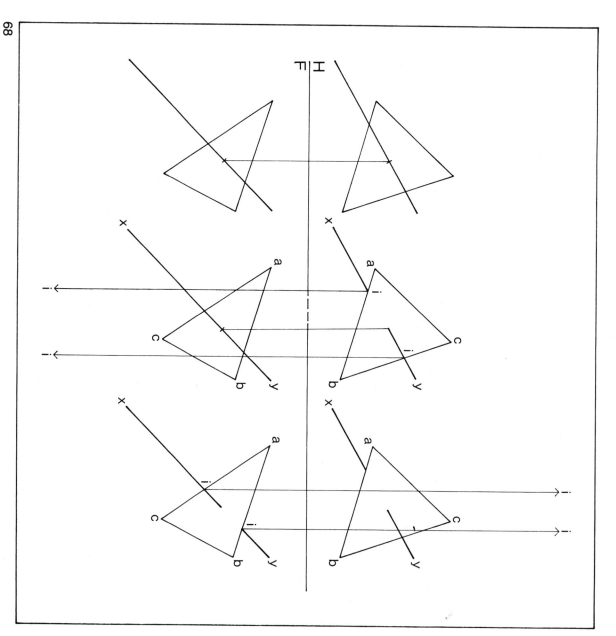

Abstract Hidden Lines

Abstract geometric forms, such as intersecting lines and planes in space, are often difficult to visualize in three dimensions, which makes it difficult to find their hidden lines. The following procedure is designed to locate hidden lines within these abstract configurations. Which of two object lines is closer to the picture plane in a particular view is determined by observing which is closer to the fold line in an adjacent view (68).

1. Project the apparent intersection of two object lines — for example, the apparent intersection between a given line and a given planar edge — into an adjacent view.

2. Track along this projection line until it meets one of the two object lines in the adjacent view. The object line that is closer to the fold line in the adjacent view — the first line met by the projector ray — is closer to the picture plane and therefore not hidden in the original view.

Hidden Lines

Hidden lines reveal edges that would not otherwise appear in a particular view of an object. As if x-rayed, edges located behind objects suddenly become visible.

To avoid confusing hidden lines with visible object lines, the former are represented by dashes (70).

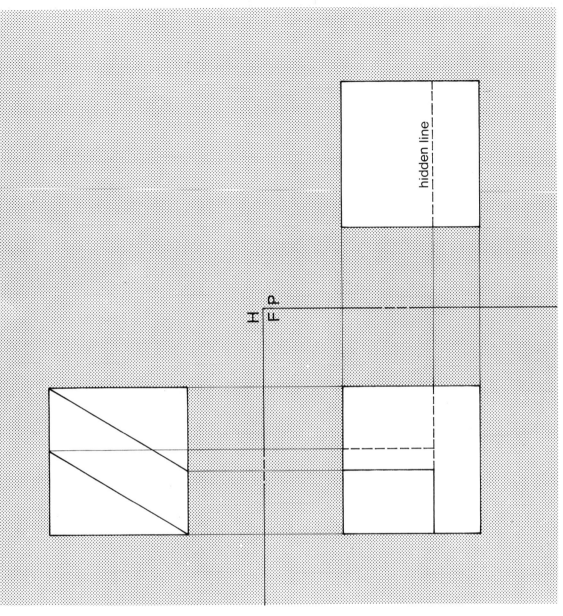

70

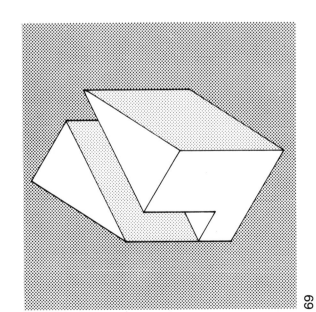

69

Circles and Irregular Shapes

There are no straight lines in curves, so circles and irregular shapes must be transferred point by point from view to view (71).

To transfer circles and irregular shapes from one view to another:

1. Divide the circle or irregular shape into points. The finer the divisions along the curve, the more accurate the resulting projection. These divisions can be made at regular or irregular intervals along the curve.

2. Transfer each point along the curve into an adjoining view.

3. Connect the projected points with a smooth, continuous curve. For drafted drawings use a french curve.

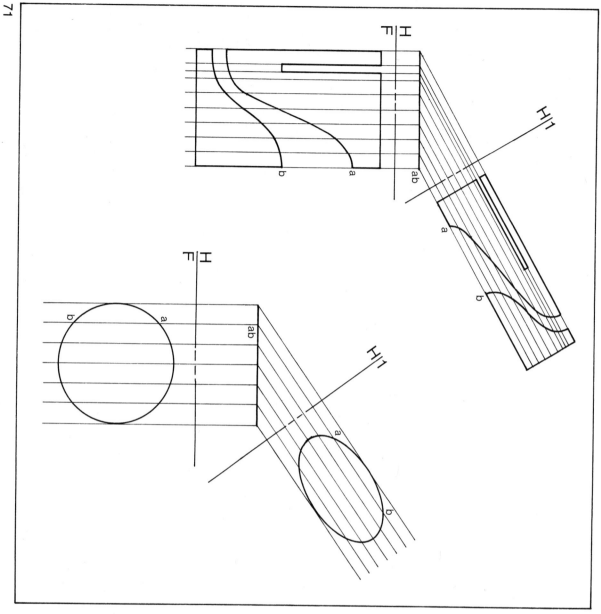

71

Complex Shapes

Complex graphic configurations present two problems: the problem of projecting a new view of an intricate shape and the problem of locating intersections within specific views of the shape.

To project new views, the best strategy is to project big shapes first and then to subdivide them.

To find points and lines of intersections, isolate and solve each intersection separately. Remember that volumes can be broken down into planes, which in turn can be reduced to lines and points. Be patient. It often takes longer to solve a complicated problem than to solve each of its component parts (72).

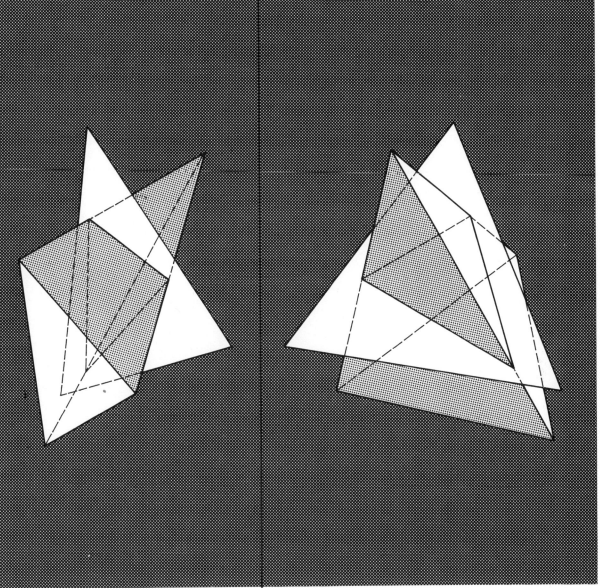

72

Plan Direction of Lines

Two conventions are commonly used to express the plan direction of nonvertical lines (73).

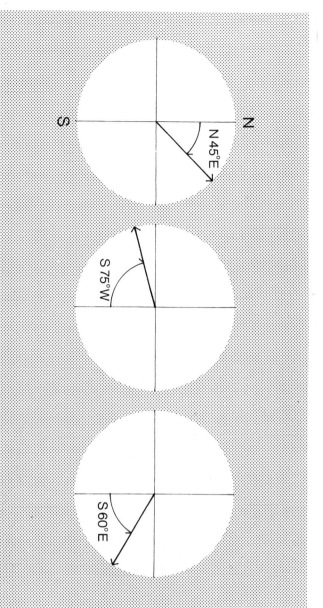

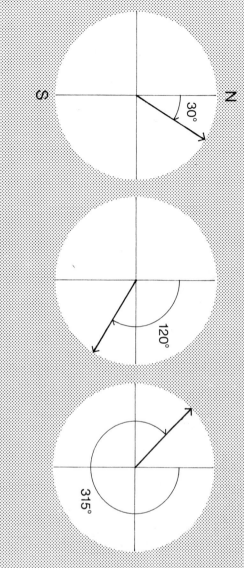

Bearing

The bearing direction of a nonvertical line is expressed in degrees. It is measured as the acute angle between a directional line and due north or south. This angle is always measured in the plan view.

Examples: N 45° E
S 75° W
S 60° E

Azimuth

Azimuth is measured clockwise from due north. It is expressed in degrees. Measure azimuth in the plan view only.

Examples: 30°
120°
315°

Inclination of a Line

By definition an angle of inclination represents the true vertical angle formed between a sloping line or plane and a horizontal. The following conventions are used to describe this angle of inclination (74):

Slope Angle

Slope angle is measured in degrees.
Example: 32°

Grade

Grade is measured as a percent.
Example: rise/run = 62/100 = 62%

Slope Ratio

Slope ratio is measured as a fraction with 12″, whichever is larger, for the rise or run.
Example: 7/12

Directional inclined lines are prefaced with a plus or minus sign to indicate whether they point up (+) or down (−). For example, an inclined line can have a slope angle of −32°.

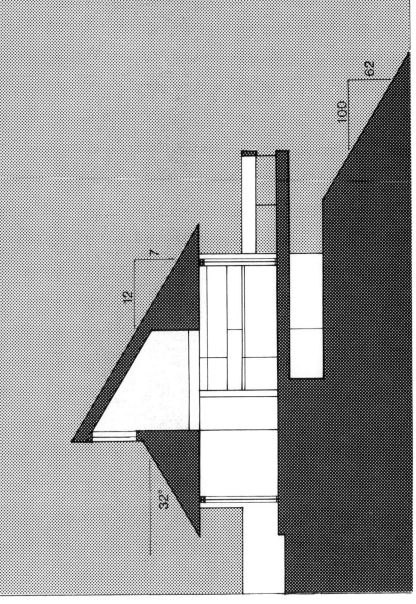

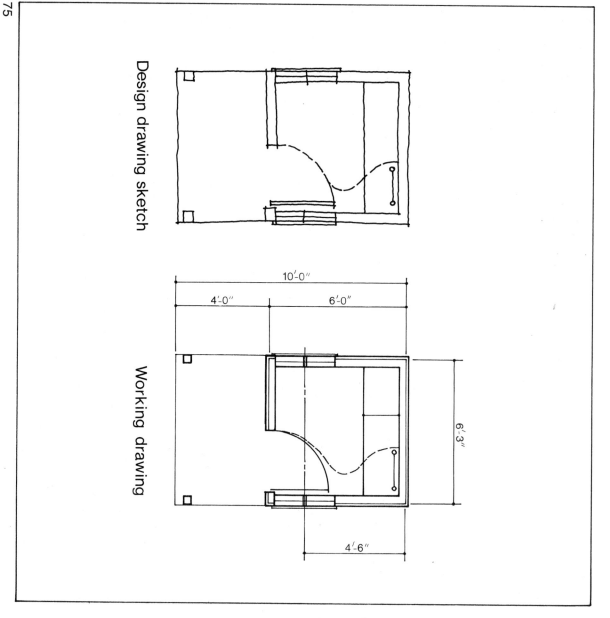

Design drawing sketch

Working drawing

Architectural multiview drawings are used throughout all three stages of the design process as:

1. Design drawing sketches (75)
2. Design presentation drawings
3. Working drawings and construction documents (75)

Multiview drawings have already been described as an orderly projection system that is useful as a problem-solving tool at the third stage of design development and refinement. This portion of the chapter discusses pictorial-effect multiview drawings as basic design-presentation drawings.

Simple plan, elevation, and section drawings are commonly used to visually describe buildings to clients and others who might have difficulty in understanding more technical architectural drawings.

Based on the principles of orthographic projection, they are dimensionally scaled and, when drawn showing the placement of furniture and door and window details, provide a sense of proportion and scale.

As the most commonly used and understood of architectural drawings, plans, elevations, and sections communicate buildings and environments clearly and precisely.

The drawings on this page illustrate two different approaches for orthographically depicting a building.

Below (76) a building is drawn using projected views separated by fold lines. The same building, drawn as an architectural design-presentation sequence with emphasis on pictorial effect, is illustrated to the right (77).

This approach, without fold lines, is preferred for presentation drawings. Fold lines are meaningless to people unacquainted with orthographic drawing theory.

Presentation drawings with properly oriented plans above any elevation communicate the interrelationships between drawings without reference to fold lines.

Some of the typical drawings used in design presentations are illustrated and discussed on the following pages.

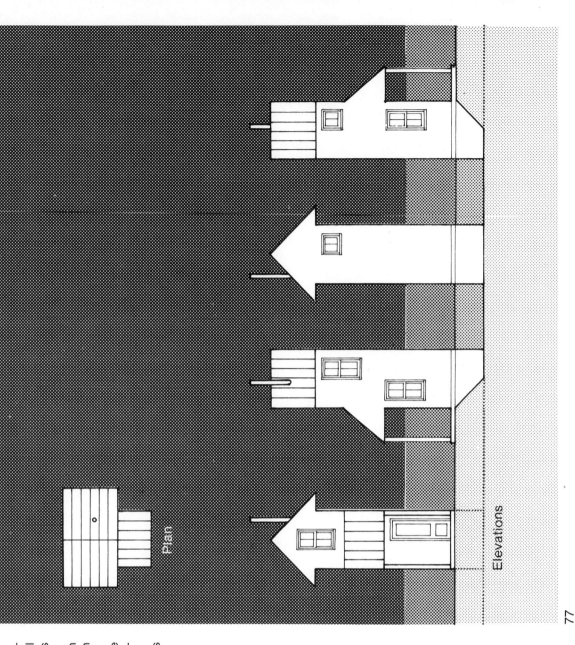

Plan

Elevations

77

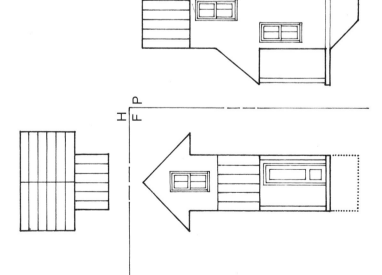

76

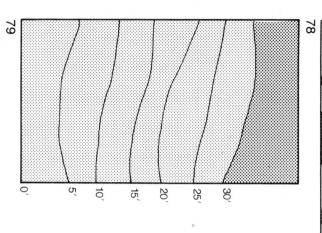

78

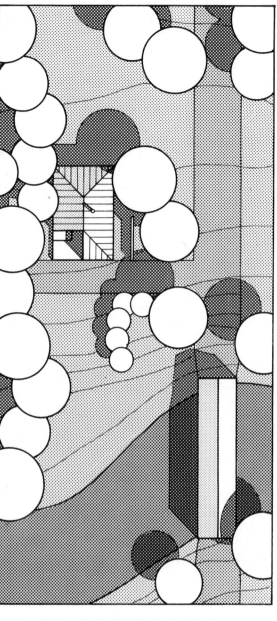

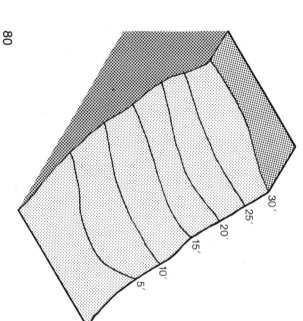

79

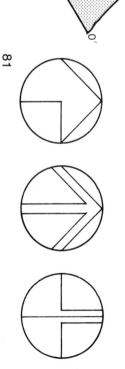

80

81

Site Plans

Site plans (78) depict buildings in the context of their natural environments. Site plans typically illustrate the natural physical topography of the terrain: trees, slope of the land, roads, sidewalks, ground cover, rivers and lakes.

Site plans are usually larger in size than the plans, elevations, and sections included with them in a presentation when all are drawn at the same scale. Designers often use an engineer's scale ruler to reduce the size of the site plan and proportionally balance its impact in relation to the other drawings in a presentation. A reduced site plan usually depicts a building in roof plan and often includes shadows cast by the building and trees to give a sense of their three-dimensional quality.

A site plan that is drawn at the same scale as the other presentation drawings often depicts the grade-level floor plan within the context of the site rather than a roof plan.

By convention a site plan is usually oriented so that north is at the top of the drawing. North arrows can be drawn in a number of ways, three of which are illustrated (81). The center arrow, an easy one to draw, makes its point with a 90° angle, and the width of its parts is 1/7 the circle's diameter.

Contour Lines

Contour lines are used on site plans to abstractly depict the natural slope of the land; each contour line represents a constant land elevation (79, 80). Contour lines are drawn at regular intervals and are expressed in feet above sea level. The closer the contour lines, the steeper the slope of the terrain.

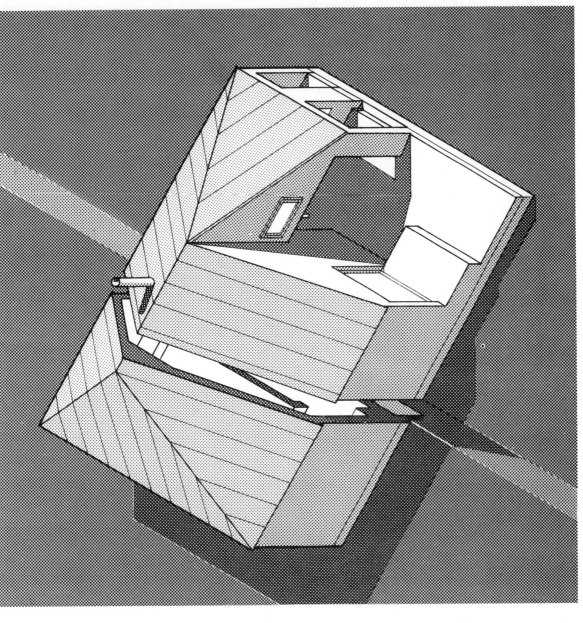

83

Sections

Section drawings depict interior elevations of buildings.

Imagine a building that is sliced into two parts, one of which is removed (83). The section drawing is an elevation view looking directly into the remaining part of the building (82).

Section cuts and drawings are usually made at a significant interior location and are usually drawn at one of two scales: $1/8'' = 1'-0''$ or $1/4'' = 1'-0''$.

As a rule a section line with arrows shows where a section is cut and the direction from which it is viewed.

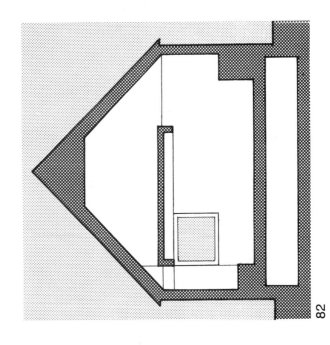

82

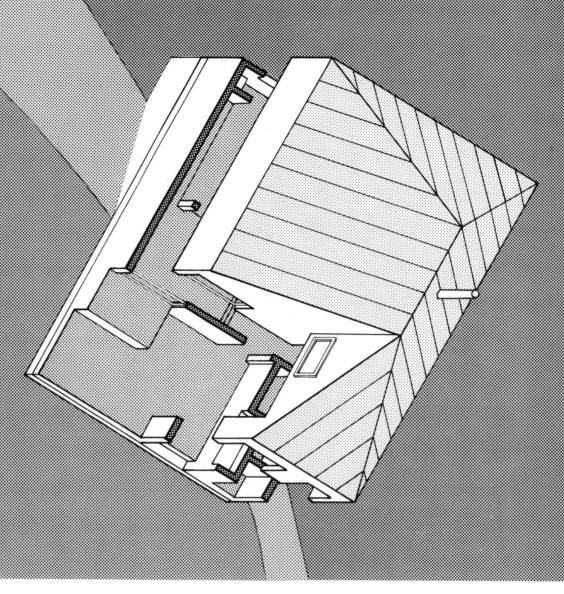

Floor Plans

Floor plans show the interior plan-view organization of build-ings.

Floor plans are theoretically horizontal sections cut laterally through a building (84). The upper part is removed, and the re-sulting view downward is called the floor plan.

Dashed lines are used to depict major architectural features that occur above the cut line through the building.

The addition of furniture to a plan helps to give a sense of scale and defines different areas of use.

Floor plans for each of the floors in a building are usually drawn at either 1/8" = 1'-0" or the 1/4" = 1'-0" scale and are oriented with north at the top of the page.

The illustration to the right (86) depicts a first-floor plan and a second-floor plan. A roof plan is shown below (85).

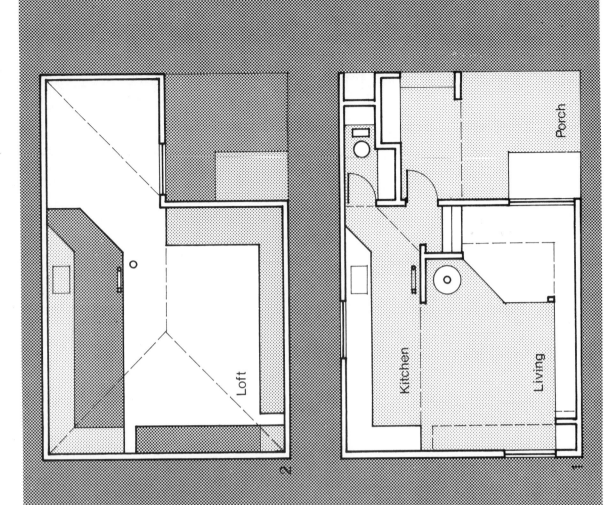

86

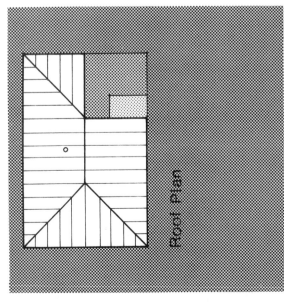

Roof Plan

85

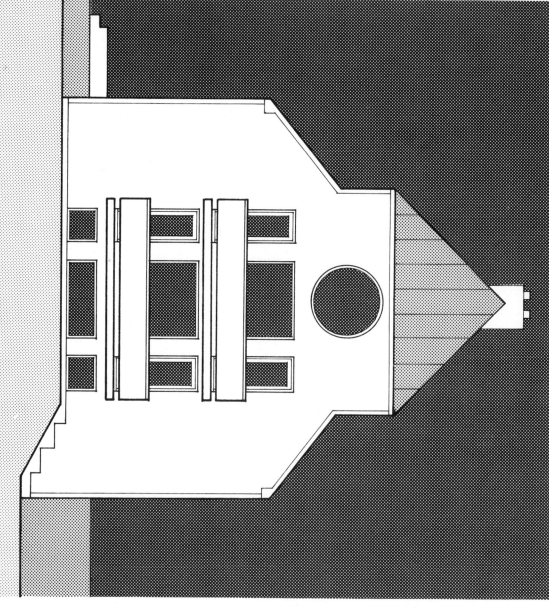

Exterior Elevations

Exterior elevations used as presentation drawings depict a building's exterior features: its height, form massing, texture, material of construction, and type, size, and location of door and window openings (87, 88).

An exterior elevation shows a building in relation to its ground plane. Whether a building is firmly rooted in the ground, supported on poles, or dug into the ground, the ground line is an important reference line that should be consistently drawn in each of a building's elevations.

A sense of depth can be achieved in an elevation by using both shade and shadows and variations in the line weight.

Variation in line weight is helpful in an elevation drawing that does not contain shade and shadow. Heavier, thicker lines appear to advance or to be closer than lighter lines, which have a tendency to recede in a drawing. Line weight can be used effectively to articulate the relative depth of surfaces.

Shade and shadow can be used in two ways in an elevation.

1. They can depict the actual play of light on a building's form — the light from a true specific source and the shade and shadow cast accordingly.

2. They can be used to articulate a building's form in all elevations. Shadows are cast downward and to the right from a light source at the upper left, regardless of the elevation's true orientation.

Elevations are labeled by reference to the compass point that they face. A north elevation of a building, for example, faces to the north. A viewer looking at that elevation would have his back to the north.

People, trees, and cars can be depicted in exterior elevations to enhance the sense of scale.

Exterior elevations are generally drawn at the 1/8" = 1'-0" or the 1/4" = 1'-0" scale.

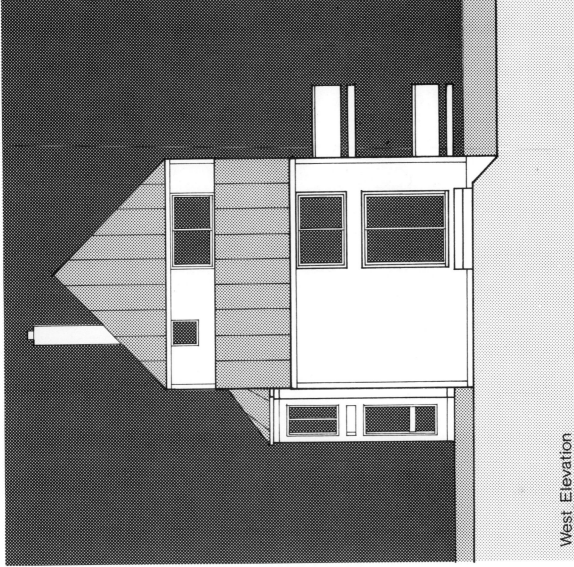

West Elevation

88

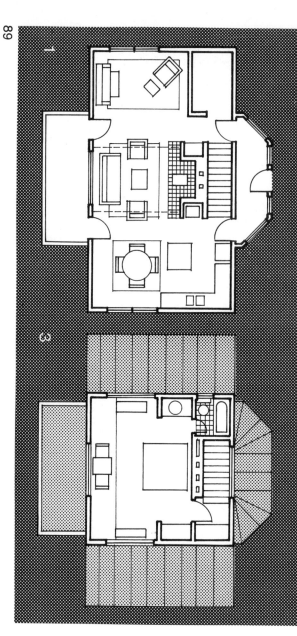

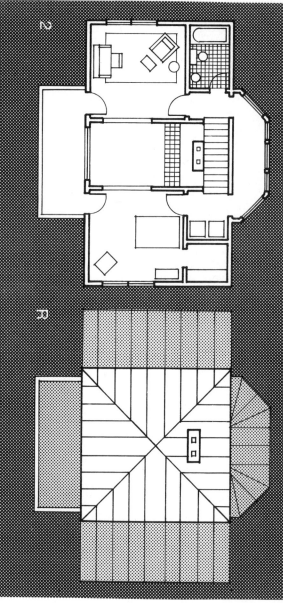

The addition of furniture to a floor plan helps to provide a sense of scale and defines different areas of use (89).

Interior Elevations

Interior elevations are similar to section views of a building and are used by interior designers to illustrate the interior features of a building.

Interior elevations do not show the heavy-profile cut line that is drawn in a section view but rather concentrate on the boundary lines of interior walls.

Interior elevations are commonly drawn at either the ⅛″ = 1′-0″ or the ¼″ = 1′-0″ scale. If detail demands a larger drawing, a ½″ = 1′-0″ scale is used.

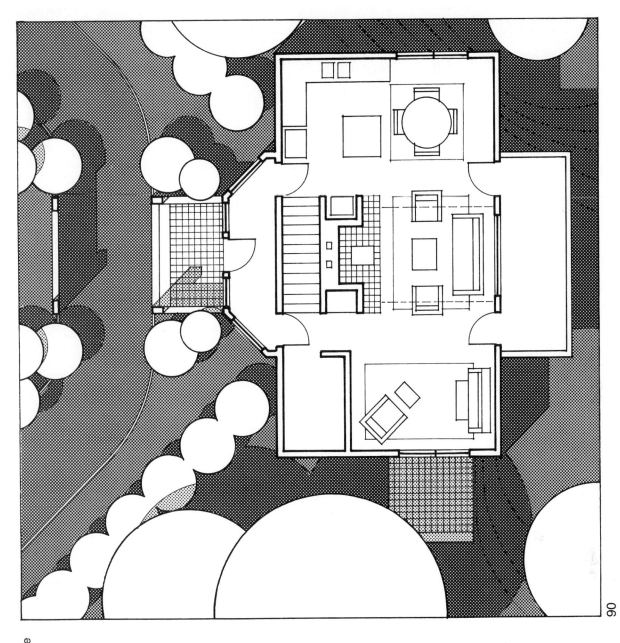

90

The first floor plan is often presented in the context of the site plan (90).

Paralines

Paralines are a type of single-view drawing with a common visual theme: Parallel lines in paraline drawings remain parallel to each other; they do not appear to converge to vanishing points, as do parallel lines in perspective.

Paralines are easier and faster to construct than perspectives which makes them useful for quickly illustrating three-dimensional ideas, especially in the early stages of the design process. Paralines are also effective as schematic illustrations in presentation drawings and as substitutes for bird's eye perspectives.

The first portion of this chapter describes methods and concepts for constructing orthographic and oblique paraline projections of buildings directly from plans and elevations. The second portion of the chapter establishes the typical rules and conventions for constructing paraline drawings without projecting from plans and elevations.

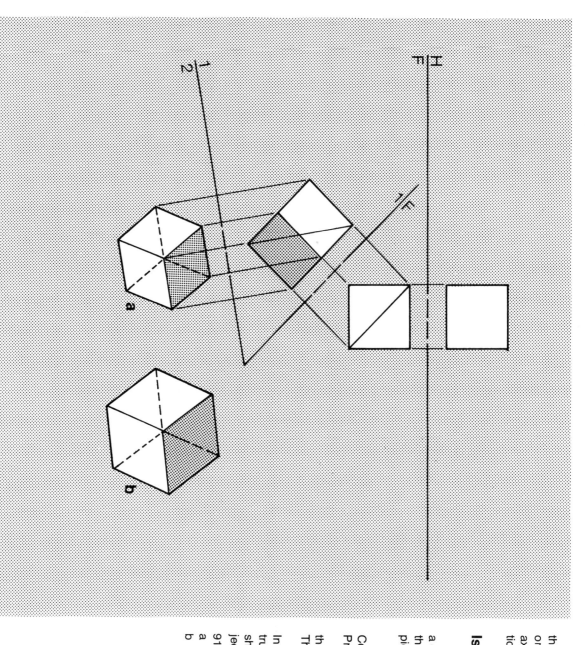

Isometric Projection

Isometrics, dimetrics, trimetrics, and transmetrics belong to the family of axonometric paralines. All axonometrics are forms of orthographic projection. As a result the various types of axonometric paralines can all be derived from the plan and elevation views of an object or building.

The figure below (92) pictorially shows the isometric image of a cube on the picture plane. To qualify as an isometric projection, the real cube's diagonal must be oriented perpendicular to the picture plane.

To project an isometric view:

1. Draw a fold line perpendicular to a diagonal of the cube. Construct this fold line to extend off the plan or elevation view. Project the cube into this view.

2. Draw a fold line perpendicular to a diagonal of the cube in the newly constructed view. Project the cube into this new view. The resulting image is an isometric projection of the cube.

Do not confuse isometric projections with isometric drawings. In an isometric drawing the edges of a cube are measured at their true scales, whereas in an isometric projection they measure shorter than true length. Compare the sizes of the isometric projection and the isometric drawing (91).

91
a Isometric projection
b Isometric drawing

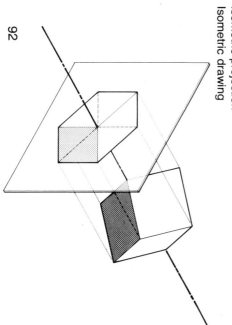

92

91
a Isometric projection
b Isometric drawing

Dimetric Projection

The three forward edges of an isometric cube all foreshorten equally. By comparison only two of the three forward edges of a dimetric cube form the same angle with the picture plane and therefore only two of its forward edges foreshorten equally. The third edge remains longer or shorter than its companions (93).

To project a dimetric view:

1. Project a 45° auxiliary or inclined view off the plan or elevation view of a cube.

2. Project a second inclined view off the newly constructed view. Orient the fold line so that it is not perpendicular to the cube's diagonal. The resulting image is a dimetric projection.

Trimetric Projection

The three forward edges of a trimetric cube form varying angles with the picture plane. As a result each each of its leading edges foreshortens at a different rate.

To project a trimetric view:

1. Project an auxiliary or inclined view off the plan or elevation view of a cube. Orient the fold line for this projection at an angle other than perpendicular to a diagonal of the cube.

2. To obtain a trimetric projection, project an inclined view off the newly constructed view.

Transmetric Projection

Isometrics, dimetrics, and trimetrics are three-dimensional axonometric paralines. The transmetric projection is neither three-dimensional nor two-dimensional. It falls somewhere in between, slightly less than three-dimensional yet slightly more than two-dimensional. All views projected directly off the plan or elevation view are transmetric projections.

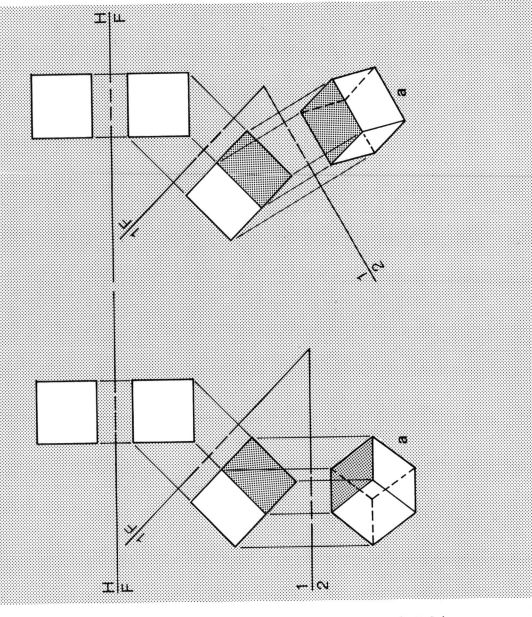

93

93
a   Dimetric projection

Oblique Projections

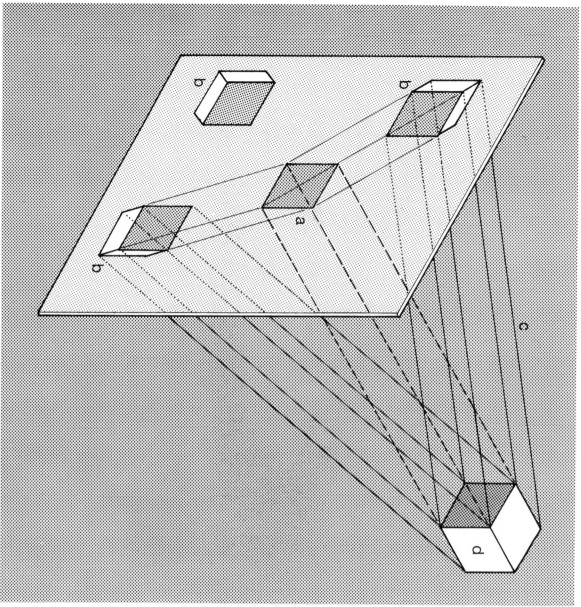

The oblique image of an object is beamed to the surface of the picture plane along parallel projectors that are oriented at angles other than 90° to the picture plane. This nonperpendicular arrangement of projectors results in the following characteristics.

Two or three faces of a cube oriented parallel to the picture plane can be seen in the same view. This would not be possible if the cube were orthographically projected: in this case only one face of the cube would reveal itself on the picture plane. In a sense obliques peek around corners, catching glimpses of faces and sides that could not be seen orthographically.

Planes that are oriented parallel to the picture plane project their true size images on the surface of the picture plane (94).

Rectangular planes that are perpendicular to the picture plane, such as the sides of the cube (94), appear as parallelograms on the picture plane. Varying the angle that oblique projectors form with the picture plane varies the size and shape of these parallelograms.

94
a Orthographic projection
b Oblique projection
c Projector rays
d Actual object

Receding Lines

Object edges that are perpendicular to the picture plane project on the surface of the picture plane as receding lines. In the case of a cube oriented parallel to the picture plane (95) the edges that suggest its depth in an oblique projection are its receding lines.

Varying the oblique angle formed between projectors and the picture plane varies the length of receding lines. The opposite is also true: varying the length of receding lines varies the oblique angle between parallel projectors and the picture plane. As a result a set of oblique projectors can be found for any orientation and length of a receding line. This makes it possible to construct the third dimension in oblique drawings without having to project from plans and elevations. Receding lines are used to construct depths directly within the oblique drawing.

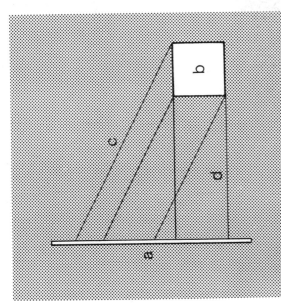

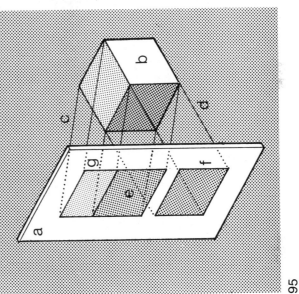

95

96

81

95, 96

a Picture plane
b Actual object
c Oblique projectors
d Orthographic projectors
e Oblique projection
f Orthographic projection
g Receding line

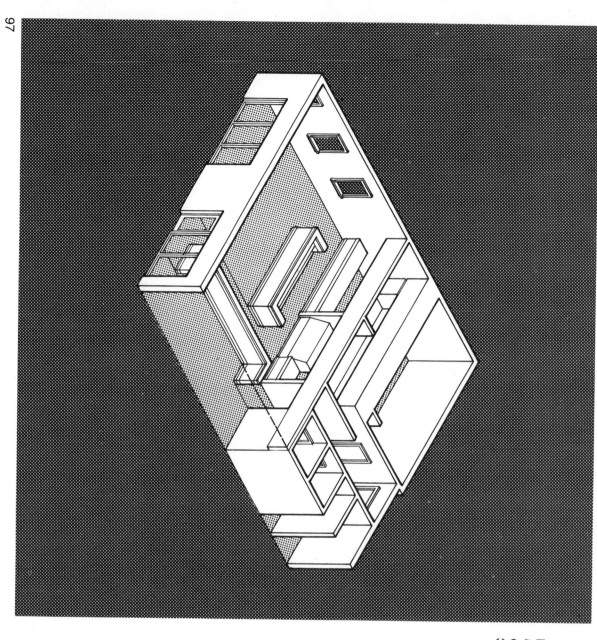

Isometric Drawings

Isometric drawings are based on 30° angles (97). Their three principal axes of measurement include two ground-plane axes and a vertical-height axis. These axes collectively define three edges of an isometric cube. Isometric ground-plane axes both tilt 30° above the horizontal, and their height axis is a vertical line.

Begin an isometric drawing by constructing its three major axes (98). In laying out isometric lines, make measurements only along routes parallel to the three principal axes and use the same architectural scale to measure in each of the three major directions.

The construction of lines not parallel to any of the three major axes, isometric circles, and curves and irregular shapes is discussed later in this chapter (pages 93, 94, and 92, respectively).

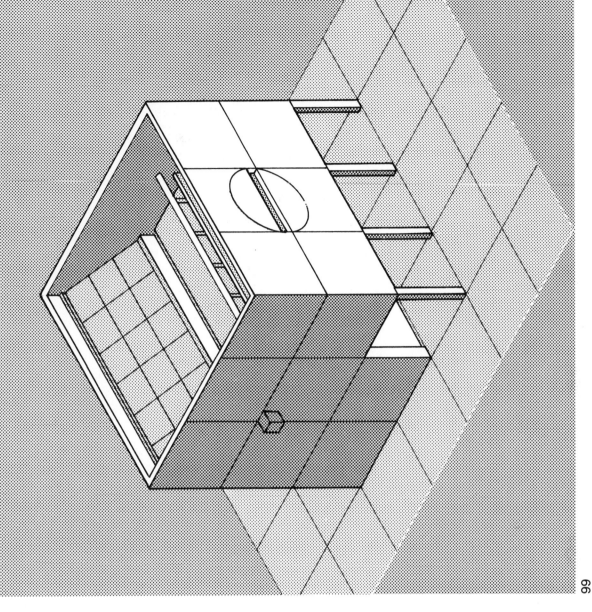

99

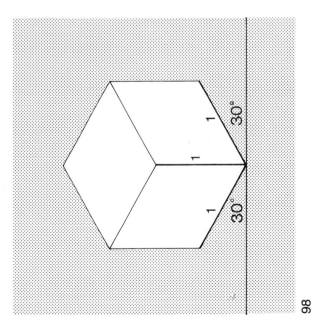

98

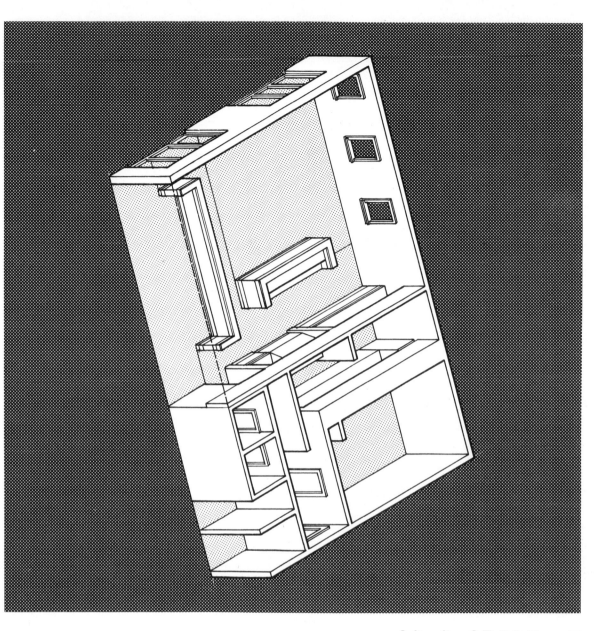

100

Dimetric Drawings

Three typical dimetric setups are shown here (101, 102, 103). For each setup two of the three major axes are constructed at the same scale. To correctly proportion a dimetric drawing, measure in the direction of an axis using an architectural scale that is proportional to the whole number or fraction indicated for that direction.

For all forms of dimetric drawings make scale measurements along routes parallel to the three principal axes (100).

The construction of lines not parallel to any of the three major axes, dimetric circles, and curves and irregular shapes is discussed later in this chapter (pages 93, 95, and 92, respectively).

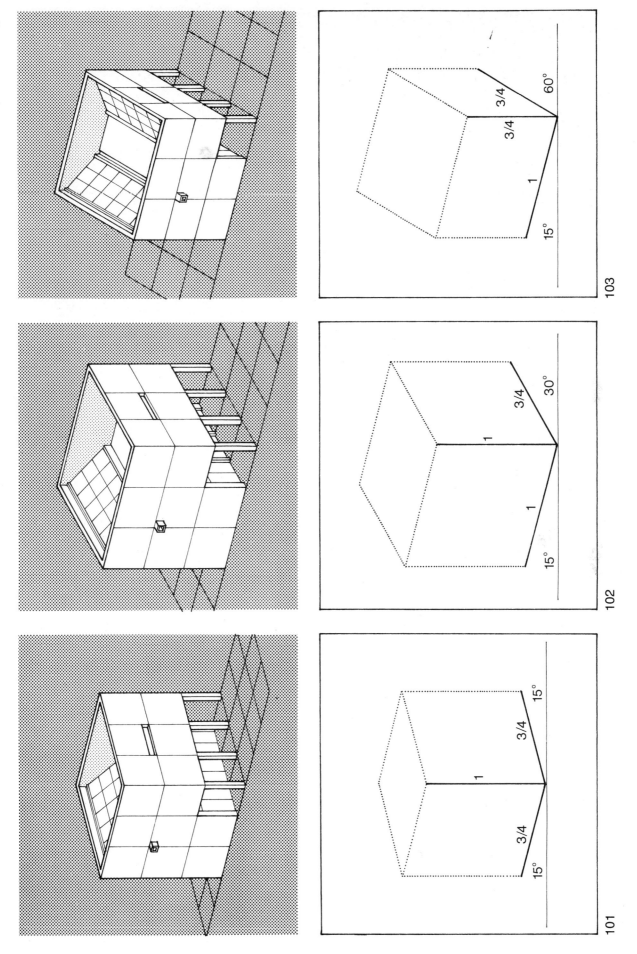

101

102

103

104

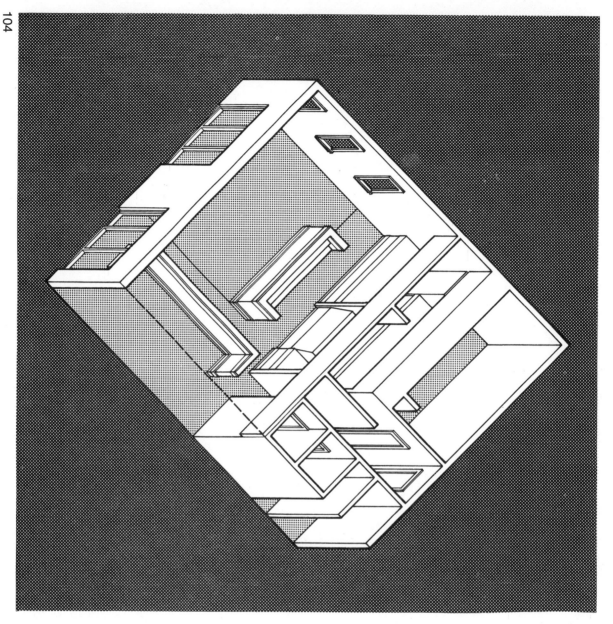

Plan Obliques

The plan view of a building retains its true size and shape in a plan oblique. For this reason the building plan can be used directly to construct the paraline. The plan is usually tilted at an angle, and receding lines are drawn as verticals (104).

Three variables affect the appearance of plan obliques (105):

1. The orientation of the plan

2. The direction of the receding lines

3. The scale ratio between receding lines and the plan view

The following notation describes a specific plan oblique:
30°-135°-1:¾ plan oblique

The first figure in the notation describes the orientation of the plan view. Rotate the given orientation of a plan clockwise to achieve this orientation.

The second figure describes the direction of the receding lines. To fix the direction of receding lines, measure clockwise from the top of the drawing sheet. Measure this figure in degrees. Receding lines point away from the top of the building.

The two numbers at the end of the notation describe the ratio of the scale of the plan view to the scale used for the receding lines. The whole number in the notation refers to the scale of the plan.

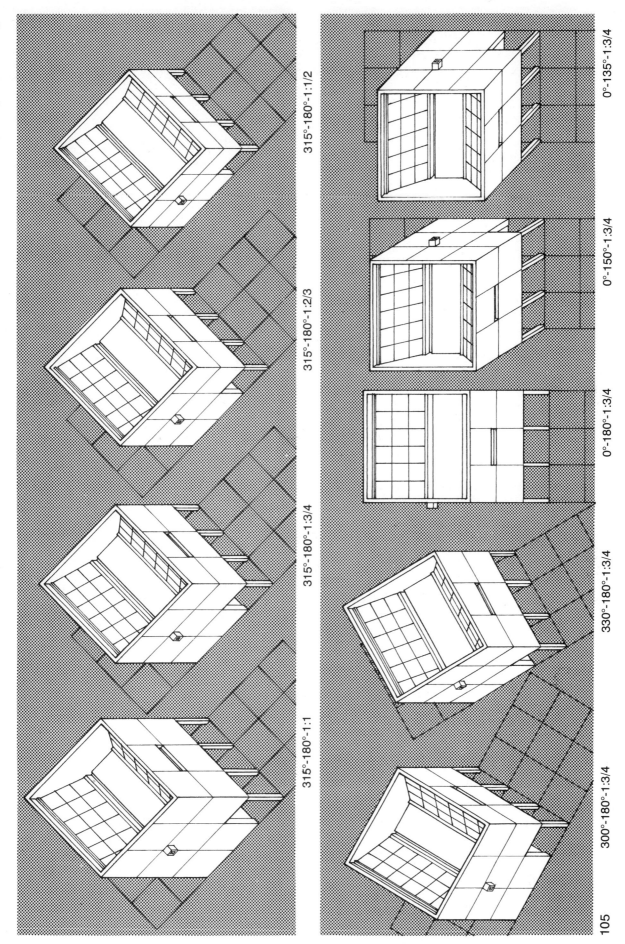

315°-180°-1:1/2

315°-180°-1:2/3

315°-180°-1:3/4

315°-180°-1:1

0°-135°-1:3/4

0°-150°-1:3/4

0°-180°-1:3/4

330°-180°-1:3/4

300°-180°-1:3/4

105

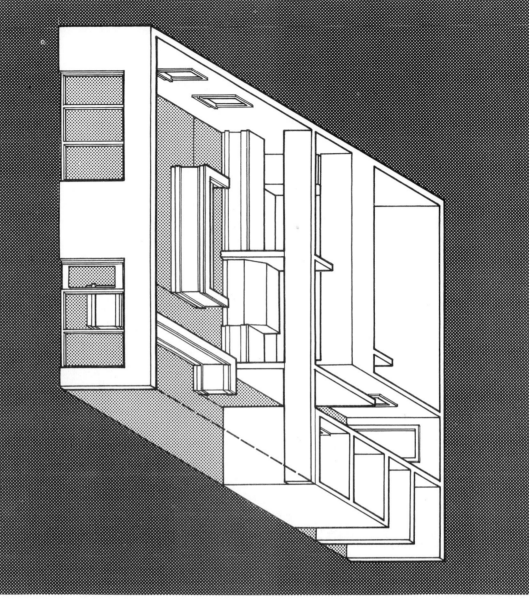

Elevation Obliques

Building elevations retain their true size and shape in elevation obliques. Oblique paralines can thus be constructed directly from elevation views. Receding lines are usually drawn at 30°, 45°, or 60° angles to the elevation, which is oriented in its normal upright position. Depths are measured along receding lines (106).

Two variables affect the appearance of elevation obliques (107):

1. The direction of the receding lines

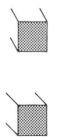

2. The scale ratio between receding lines and true size elevation

The following notation describes a specific elevation oblique:

45° — 1:¾ elevation oblique

The first number in the notation describes the direction of the receding lines. To fix this direction, measure the specified number of degrees clockwise from the top of the sheet — or due north. Receding lines point away from the front face of the building.

The two numbers at the end of the notation express the ratio of the scale of the elevation to the scale used for the receding lines. The whole number in the ratio refers to the scale of the elevation.

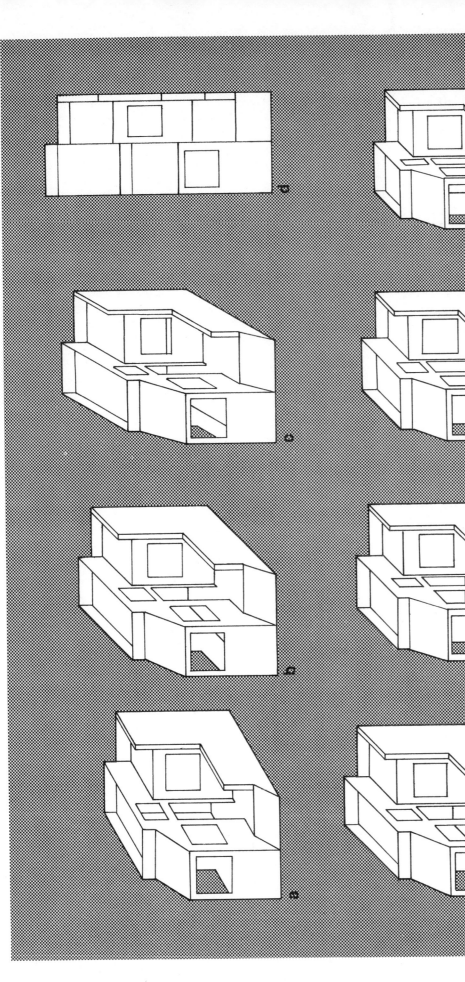

107

a 60°-1:1
b 45°-1:1
c 30°-1:1
d 0°-1:1

e 45°-1:1
f 45°-1:3/4
g 45°-1:2/3
h 45°-1:1/2

108

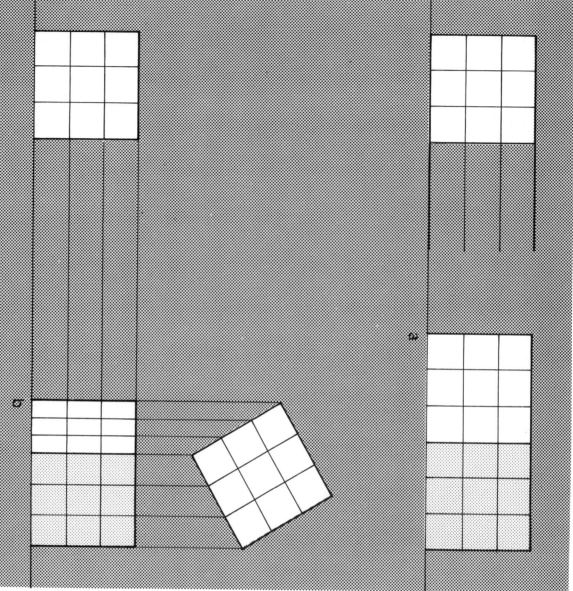

108, 109
a Transoblique
b Transmetric

Transparalines depict only two orthogonal building surfaces in a single view. This is one less than the normal paraline, which usually shows three surfaces in the same view.

There are two types of transparalines: transobliques and transmetrics. Two transparaline views of a cube are shown here (108). The upper cube is a transoblique: one face is featured at its true size and shape, while the other may be shown either full-scale or foreshortened in width. The lower cube is a transmetric: both faces are foreshortened to less than their true widths.

Transobliques are drawn with true-size plans or elevations. The plan transoblique communicates awkward and ambiguous views of buildings; the elevation transoblique is fairly easy to understand, especially when it is modeled in shadows.

To construct an elevation transoblique, begin with an elevation view of a building and make depth measurements along horizontal receding lines. Elevation transobliques appear more natural if their receding lines are foreshortened and measured at 2/3 or 3/4 the scale of the elevation.

To construct a transmetric, place the building plan and elevation off to the side and above the space provided for the drawing. Construct the transmetric view of the building by projecting heights horizontally from the elevation and transferring vertical edges straight down from the plan. The drawing on the opposite page (91) is an elevation transmetric depicting an old house.

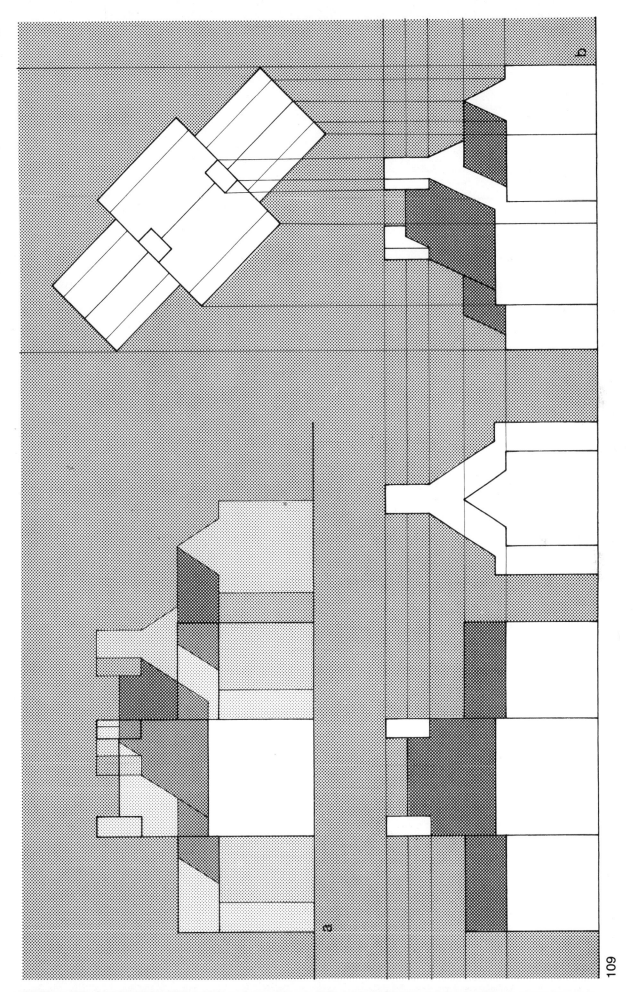

110

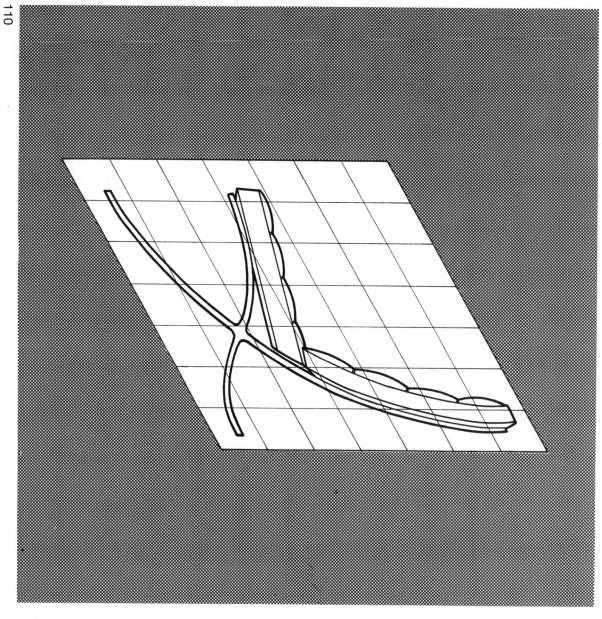

Free-form Shapes

Grids are used to transfer the true sizes and shapes of circles and curves into paraline drawings. The finer the texture of the grid, the more accurate the transfer.

To draw a paraline curve:

1. Construct a grid over the plan or elevation view of the circle or curve (111).

2. Construct the same grid in paraline.

3. Locate coordinates of intersection between the grid and the free-form shape and transfer these coordinates to the paraline.

4. In the paraline grid complete the irregular shape by connecting the transferred points (110).

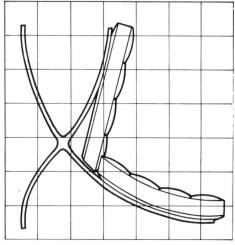

111

Nonaxial Lines

Nonaxial lines are not parallel to any of the three major paraline axes. With the exception of the true-shape planes in plan and elevation obliques (112), nonaxial lines cannot be measured at their true scale in a paraline drawing.

For all nonaxial lines other than the lines contained in oblique true-shape planes locate their endpoints and connect them.

When several nonaxial lines are parallel to each other, apply the following rule: parallel nonaxial lines remain parallel in paralines (113).

113
a Nonaxial lines

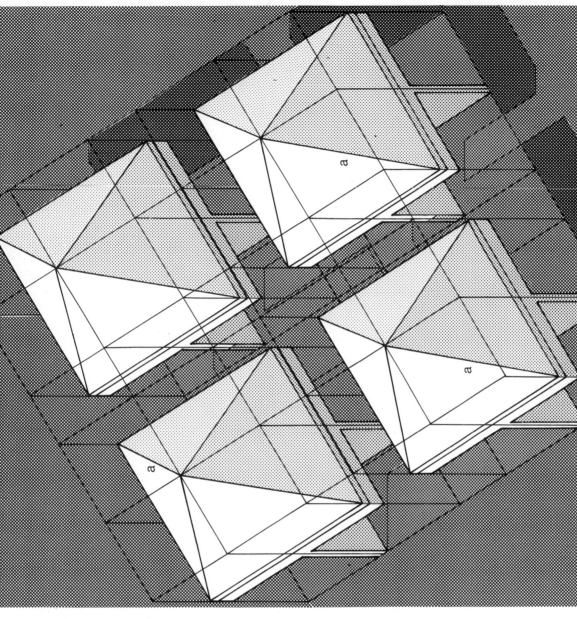

113

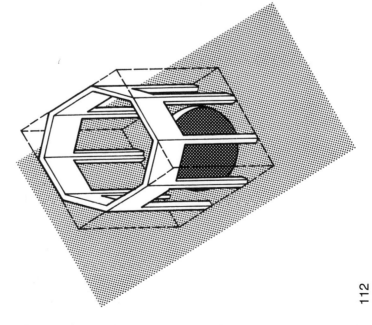

112

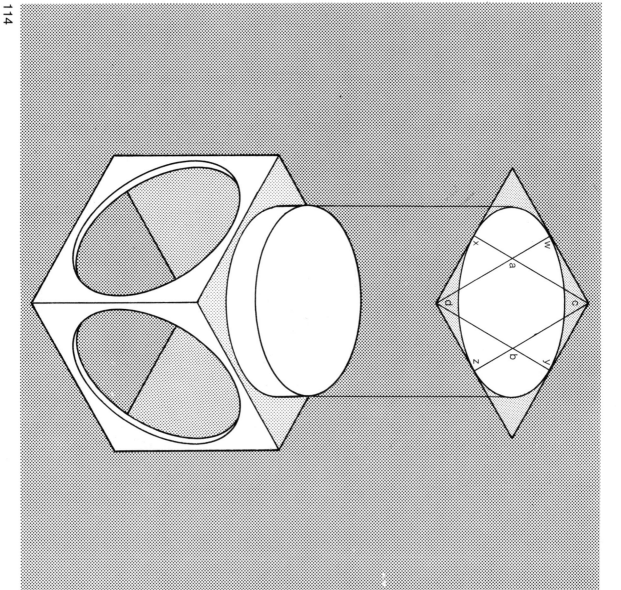

Circles

Isometric Circles

To draw an isometric circle (114):
1. Construct an isometric square.
2. Use a 30°-60° triangle to form a double-cross pattern.
3. Draw arcs wx and yz. Use points a and b as centers for these arcs.
4. Draw arcs wy and xz. Use points c and d as centers for these arcs.

Oblique Circles

Circles retain their true size and shape in the true-size planes of oblique drawings (115). For this reason obliques are often pre-ferred to isometrics and dimetrics in situations where several cir-cles appear in the same plan or elevation view of a building.

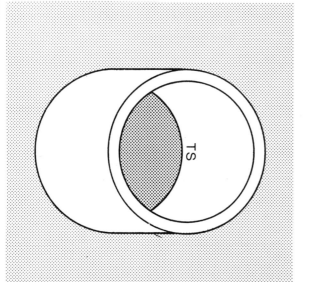

Other Constructed Circles

To construct circles whose encompassing squares have sides of equal length in paraline (116):

1. Divide the encompassing square of the circle into four equal parts.

2. Draw perpendiculars from the midpoints of two adjacent edges. These perpendiculars must be at right angles to their respective edges.

3. Use the intersection of the perpendiculars as the center for a constructed arc.

4. Follow the procedure above to find a similar arc on the opposite side of the square.

5. To complete the circle, use points c and d as the centers for the two remaining smaller arcs.

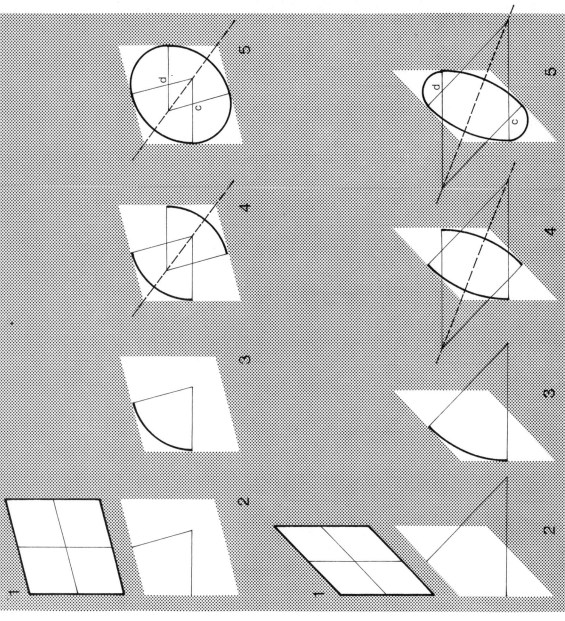

116

117

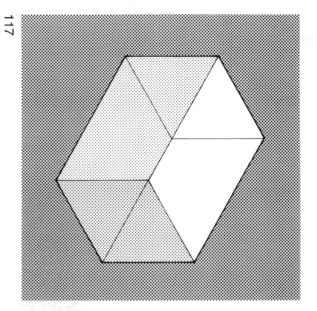

118

119

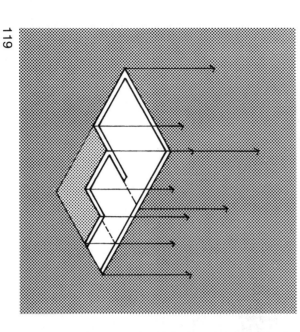

120

Constructing Paralines

There are two basic approaches to the construction of paralines.

1. Construct a paraline box that is large enough to contain the entire building and subdivide it to find the building contained within (117, 118).

2. It is sometimes easier to construct the entire floor plan or elevation of a building in paraline and then to project up or back to find heights or depths (119, 120).

Paralines have many uses in the design process. Below are a few applications.

Exploded-view Paralines

Remove the outer skin of the building and pull the floor levels apart to emphasize the internal functional relationships (122).

Structure-enclosure Diagrams

Isolate the basic structure and enclosure elements of the building to emphasize important overall spatial relationships (122).

Worm's-eye-view Paralines

Cut away the base of the building and turn it upside down to produce a view looking toward the ceiling (121).

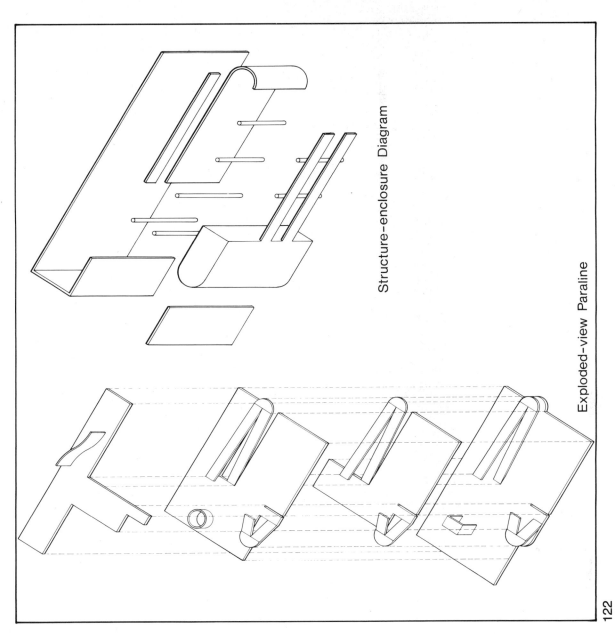

Structure-enclosure Diagram

Exploded-view Paraline

122

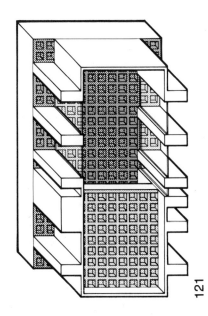

121

Perspectives

Perspectives are the most realistic type of representational design drawing. Architects and designers frequently use perspectives both as design-development and as design-presentation drawings.

Design-development perspective drawings are generally quick freehand sketches that attempt to capture the character of a space: its scale, basic light and shadow patterns, and textural qualities.

Perspectives used in presentation drawings are precisely constructed and carefully rendered to depict the building and its environment as realistically as possible.

The execution of a correct and precise perspective drawing requires a knowledge of several drawing-construction methods. A particular type of perspective drawing may more clearly show the character of a building design.

A well-constructed perspective drawing is only the beginning of quality rendering. A meaningful perspective is carefully composed and includes people, vegetation, cars, and furniture, which animate and give life to the drawing. It should also be remembered that a good perspective drawing does not necessarily make a bad design better.

This chapter defines a vocabulary and illustrates the four basic methods of drawing one- and two-point perspectives: two-point common method, one-point common method, one-point magic or measuring-line method, and two-point magic-circle method.

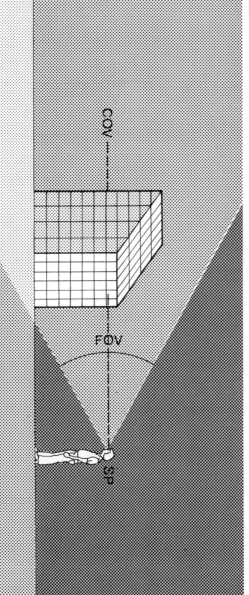

Elevation

124

Plan

123

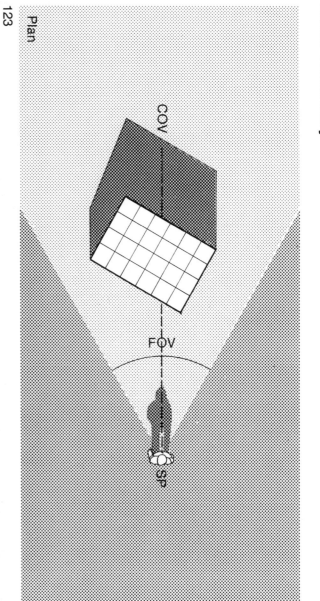

Station Point (SP)

The station point locates the fixed position of the viewer (123, 124).

Center of Vision (COV)

The center axis within the viewer's field of vision is called the center of vision (123, 124).

Field of Vision (FOV)

The viewer's plan (123) and elevation (124) field of vision bound the environment captured within the perspective drawing. Elements located beyond the boundaries of the plan or elevation field of vision do not appear within the frame of the finished perspective drawing.

A horizontal slice through the apex of the pyramid of vision (discussed at right) defines the plan field of vision. A similar slice taken vertically through the apex of the pyramid of vision defines the elevation field of vision.

Pyramid of Vision (POV)

The pyramid of vision resembles a regular pyramid tipped sideways with its apex at the eye of the viewer (125). The pyramid's open rectangular end extends indefinitely, consuming more and more of the environment as it moves away from SP. A finished perspective drawing depicts the view through the tip of the pyramid; the boundaries of this view are the walls of the pyramid of vision.

Picture Frame (PF)

Picture frames are analogous to the wooden frames around oil paintings. Their purpose is to heighten awareness of the perspective field by framing it (125).

The picture frame lies at the intersection of the pyramid of vision and the picture plane. A view through the apex of the pyramid of vision is recorded in perspective within the rectangular boundaries of the picture frame on the picture plane.

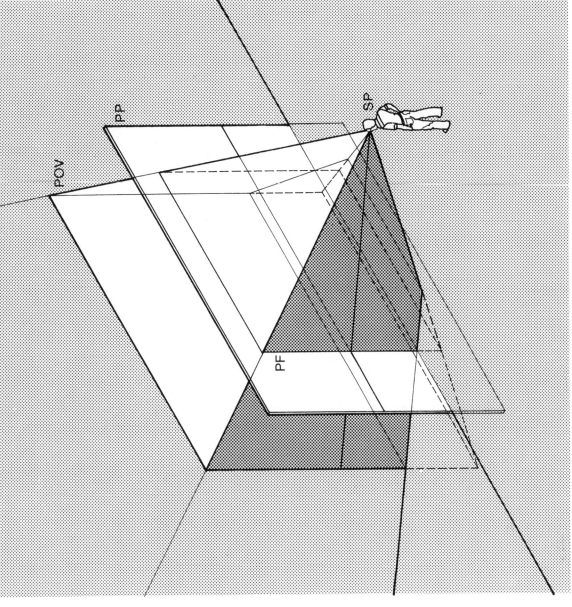

125

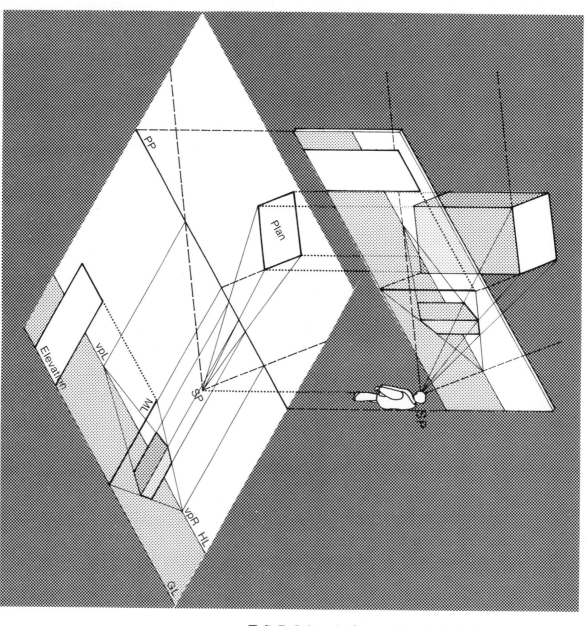

PP

Plan

Elevation

vpL

ML

SP

vpR   HL

GL

SP

Picture Plane (PP)

Picture planes are flat, two-dimensional surfaces that record the projected perspective images of buildings and environments. A picture plane always aligns perpendicular to the viewer's center of vision.

The picture plane is the only true-size plane in the perspective field. Elements located behind the picture plane project to its surface smaller than true scale; elements located between the viewer and the picture plane project to its surface larger than true scale (126, 127).

Measuring Line (ML)

All measuring lines are located on the picture plane, which is the only true-size plane in the perspective field. Measuring lines are thus the only true-scale lines in a perspective drawing.

Although various orientations are possible, measuring lines are typically constructed as vertical or horizontal lines. Common-method perspectives employ vertical measuring lines; measured heights from an elevation drawn on the picture plane are transferred to these vertical measuring lines before they are projected into perspective (126, 127).

Line of Sight (LOS)

A sight line is a straight line radiating from the station point (126, 127).

Ground Line (GL)

The ground line lies at the intersection of the picture plane and the ground plane (126, 127).

Horizon Line (HL)

The horizon line lies at the intersection of the picture plane and a horizontal plane through the eye of the viewer (126, 127).

Vanishing Point (VP)

Points at which parallel lines appear to meet in perspective are called vanishing points. In theory the vanishing point for a set of parallel object lines is located at the point where a sight line parallel to the set of object lines intersects the picture plane (126, 127).

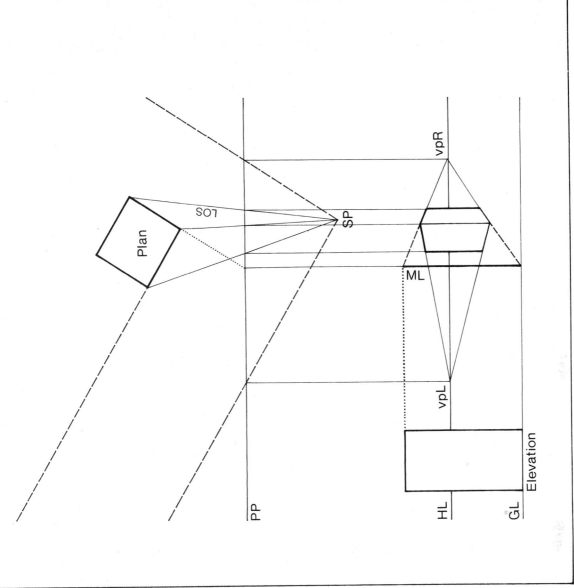

127

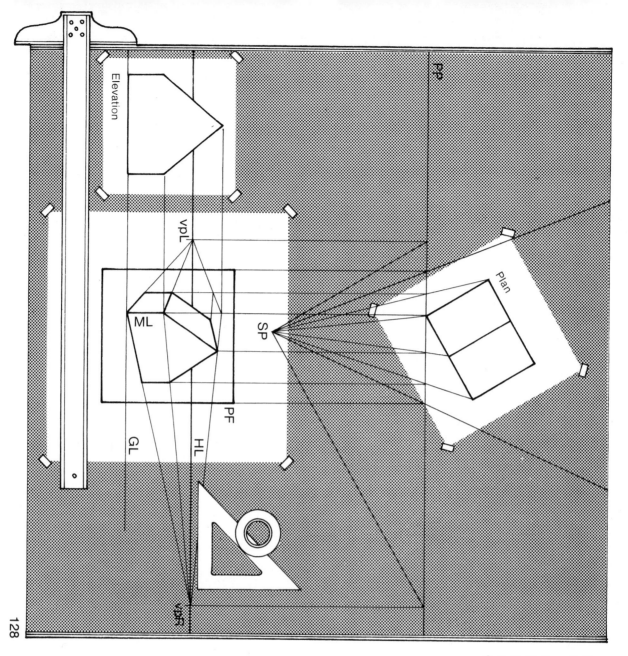

This is a good method for beginning students because no steps are mysteriously hidden beneath its surface; all relationships in the perspective construction are evident.

The two-point common method for drawing perspectives requires a building plan and an elevation. Both must be drawn at the same scale. All the building's important height measurements must be included in the elevation. A composite of all important roof, floor-plan, and site information should be included in the plan drawing.

Two-point Common Method

A completed two-point common-method perspective is shown with a typical board setup (128) and as a solution to a graphics workbook problem (130). The many lines describing a finished perspective construction are often confusing. To clarify the meaning of these lines, separate layers of information are peeled away and explained on the following pages. Explanations include procedures for locating the station point, finding the picture plane and horizon line, locating vanishing points, using measuring lines, and transferring vertical edges from the plan view.

The station point, picture plane, and horizon line should be constructed first. The order of assembly for the rest of a perspective is not important and does not affect the final product.

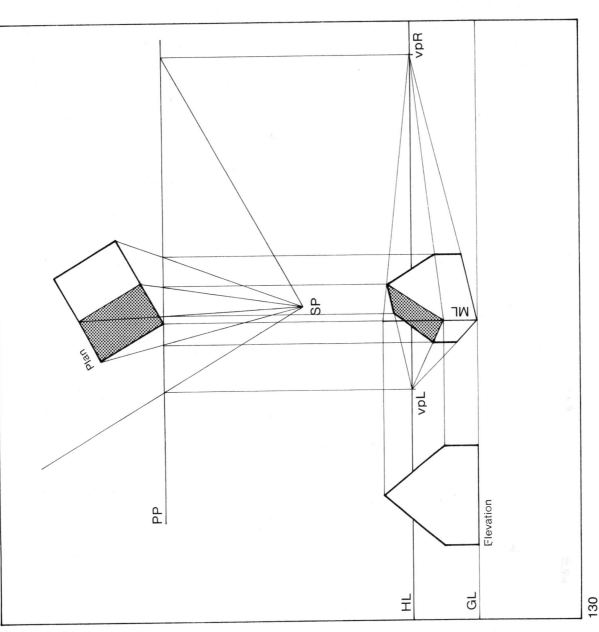

130

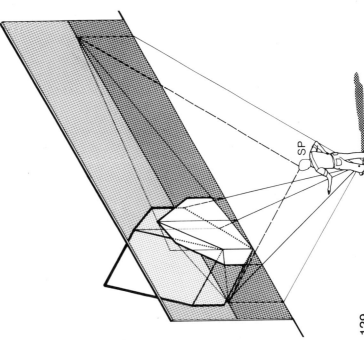

129

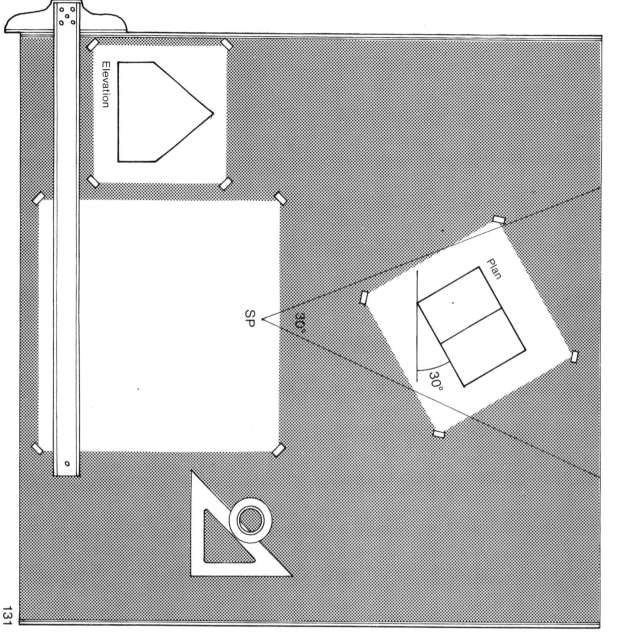

131

The Plan

Locate the plan above the space where the perspective is to be drawn. Tilt the plan at an angle. A 30° or 45° angle is typical for most perspectives. Avoid angles less than 30°, as vanishing points are likely to fall off the end of the drawing board. Orientation of the plan affects the perspective image (133).

The Elevation

Locate the elevation to the left of the area where the perspective is to be drawn (131).

The Station Point

Position the station point below the plan view of the building (131). Here are some guidelines for selecting a location for the station point.

1. Keep the building within a 30° field of vision.

2. Aim the viewer's center of vision toward the building's center of interest.

3. Avoid common alignment of building edges along site lines radiating from the station point.

Varying the distance from the station point to the building affects the perspective image.

Two-point Common Method

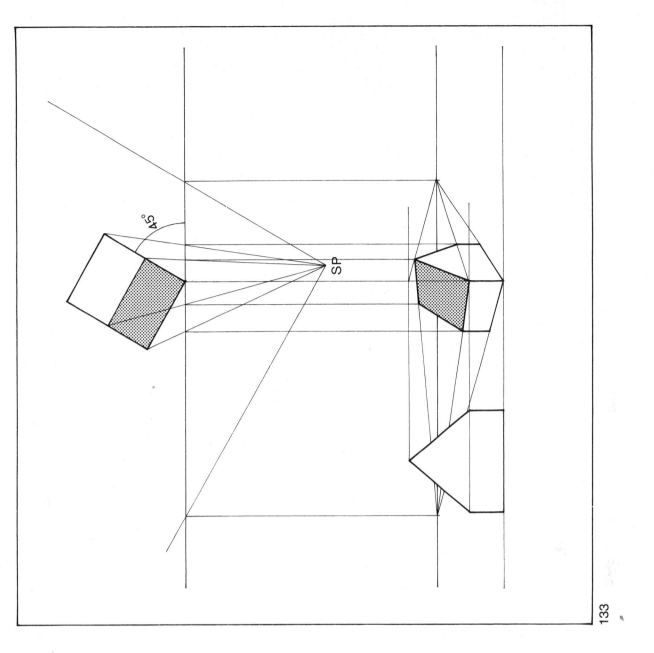

133

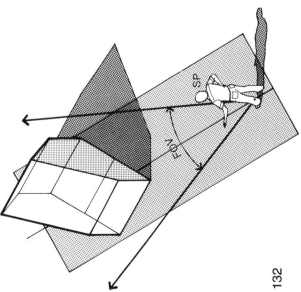

132

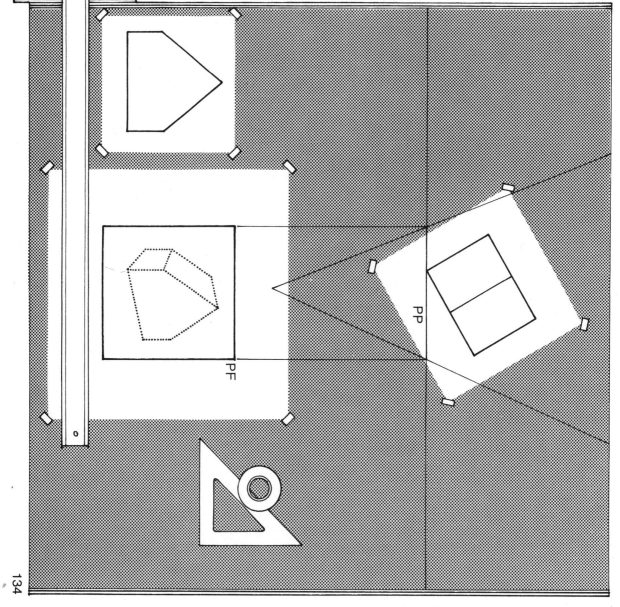

Picture Plane

Draw the edge view of the picture plane horizontally through the leading corner of the plan (134). This is the typical placement for the picture plane. Other placements are shown here (137).

Locating the picture plane in positions other than through the leading edge of the building affects the size of the perspective drawing. The perspective image grows larger as the picture plane is shifted away from the station point, much as moving a slide screen away from a slide projector enlarges the size of the slide's projected image on the screen.

Picture Frame

To find the left and right edges of the perspective picture frame, draw lines vertically down from the two points where field-of-vision lines intersect with the picture plane in plan (134). The upper and lower edges of the perspective picture frame can be positioned anywhere. Draw them after the perspective is constructed.

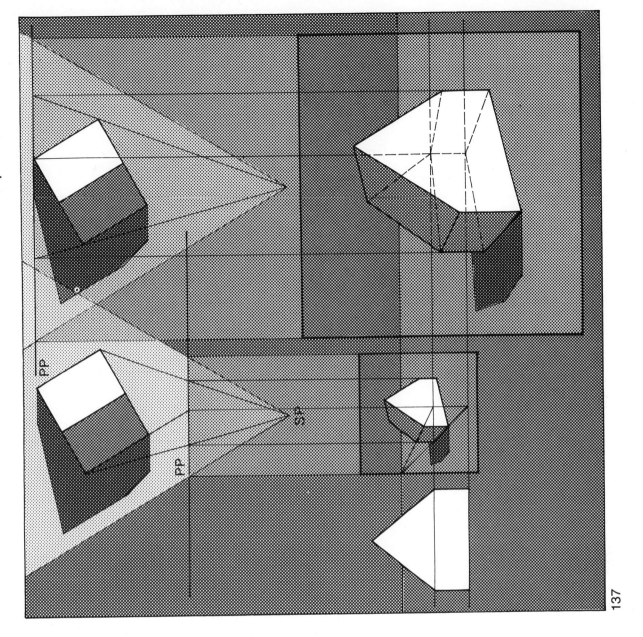

137

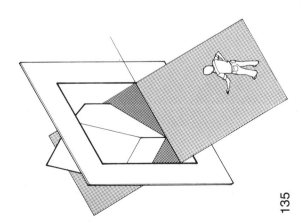

135

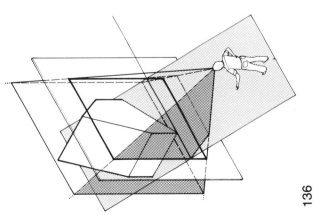

136

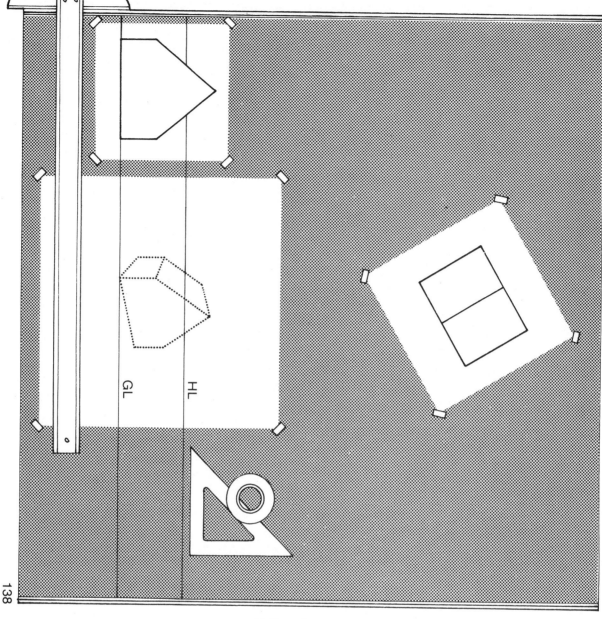

138

Ground Line

The ground line lies at the intersection of the picture plane and the ground plane. A ground-line contour in perspective captures the profile where the picture plane slices through the building in plan. The height of this ground line must coordinate with heights in the elevation. In the case of this perspective setup (138) the ground line is a horizontal line extending through the base of the elevation.

Horizon Line

The horizon line is a horizontal line that corresponds to the eye level of the viewer or station point. It can be constructed anywhere above the ground line (138). To enhance perspective realism, the horizon line is normally located at a natural viewing height—one that corresponds to eye level for a standing or seated viewer. Locate the horizon line 5'-0" above the ground plane for a standing view or 3'-6" above the ground plane for a seated view. Measure this height at the scale of the elevation and vertically up from the ground line.

When the horizon line is positioned higher than the elevation, the constructed perspective view is called a bird's-eye perspective (141).

Two-point Common Method

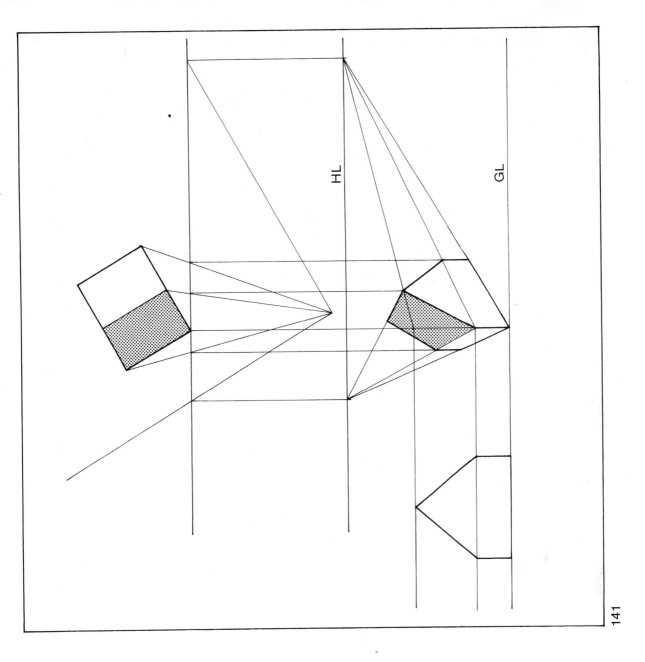

141

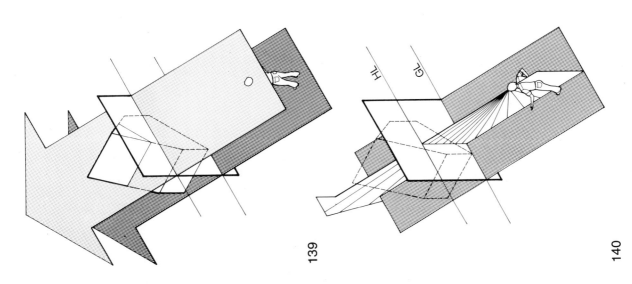

139

140

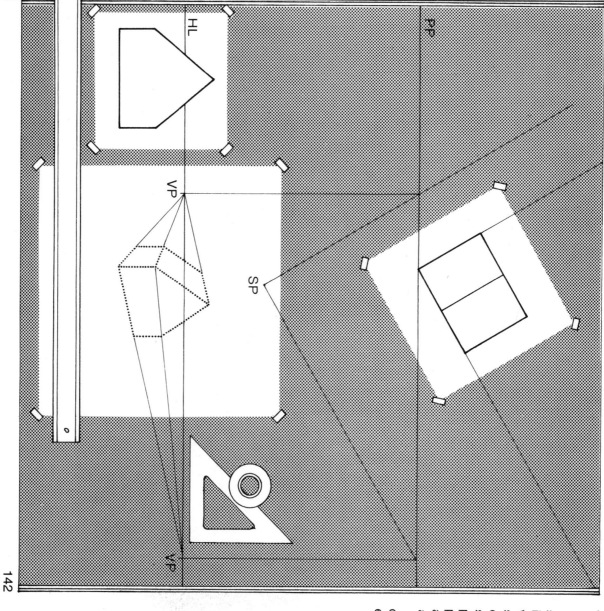

Vanishing Points

Sets of parallel lines that are not parallel to the picture plane share common perspective vanishing points. Most of these vanishing points appear on the horizon line. To find the location of a vanishing point on the horizon line, draw a site line through the station point parallel to the plan direction of the parallel object edges in question and transfer the point where this site line intersects the picture plane vertically down to the horizon line. This procedure works for all sets of parallel building edges that are also parallel to the ground plane (142, 145). Sets of parallel lines that are not parallel to the ground plane, such as the sloping edges of a gable-roofed house, are discussed later (page 172).

Sloping edges, especially when only a few lines are involved, can be drawn in perspective by locating their end points. This eliminates the need to construct additional vanishing points.

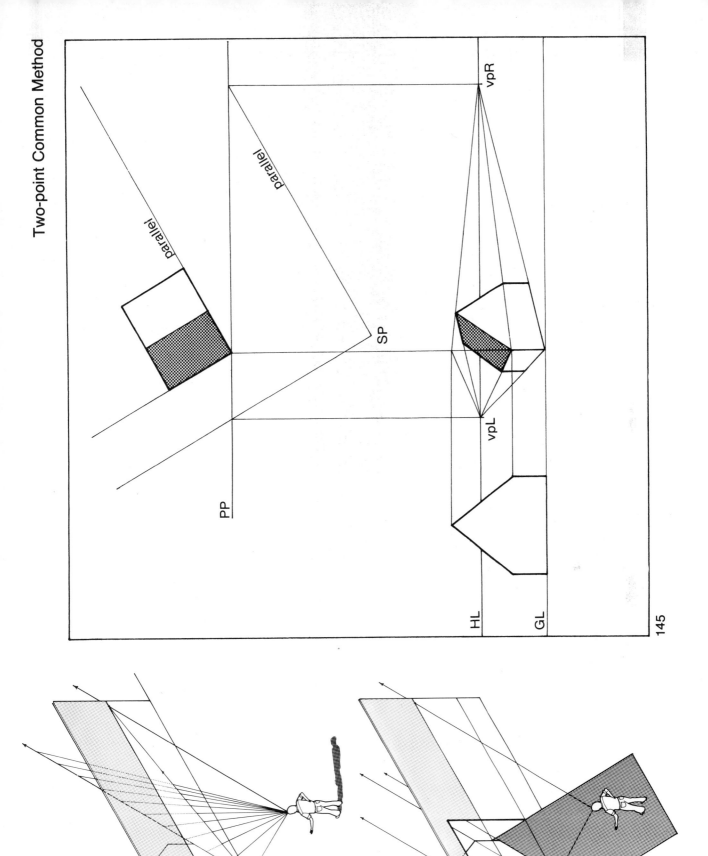

Two-point Common Method

parallel

parallel

PP

SP

HL

GL

vpR

vpL

143

144

145

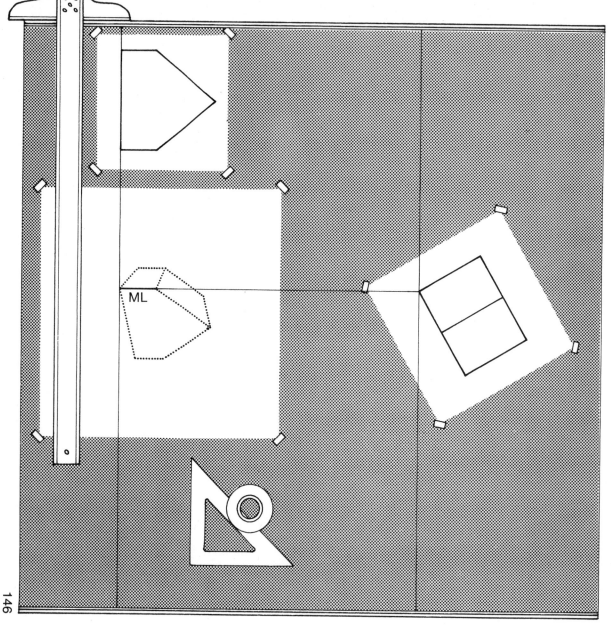

Measuring Lines

In a perspective drawing lines and edges that are contained on the picture plane's surface remain in the scale of the plan from which the perspective is projected. These lines and edges, called measuring lines, are the only true-scale elements in a perspective drawing.

The following measuring-line rules apply to all common-method perspectives.

1. Draw measuring lines as points on the picture plane in plan and as vertical lines in perspective. Points in plan must coincide with vertical lines in perspective (146).

2. Transfer elevation heights only to vertical measuring lines.

3. Project true heights on measuring lines into the perspective along known routes toward vanishing points.

To find the perspective height of a vertical building edge that is not contained on the picture plane, transfer its height from the elevation view to a vertical measuring line and project this true height into perspective along known vanishing-point routes until the edge in question coincides with its location in the perspective as projected from the plan view.

The leading edge of the building is most often used as a measuring line (146). Transfer elevation heights to this edge and project into the perspective.

Two-point Common Method

A building plan is sometimes located entirely behind the picture plane with no edges touching its surface. To find measuring lines, extend walls of the building forward to meet the picture plane (148). Imagine that these walls are temporary brick-fence extensions of the building. Use these "brick fences" to project true heights back toward the building. When the drawing is completed, tear down the "fences."

The building plan can also be positioned to overlap the picture plane. In such situations points of intersection between the plan and the picture plane are measuring lines.

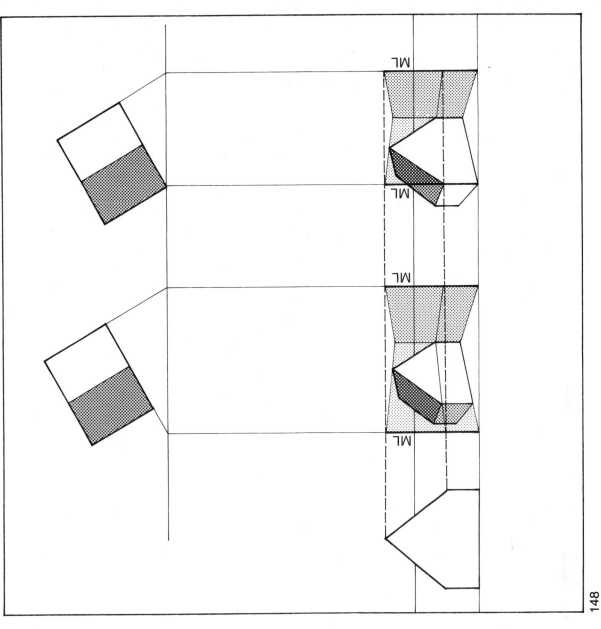

148

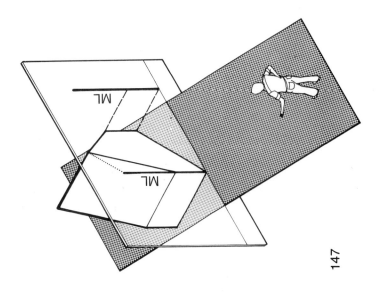

147

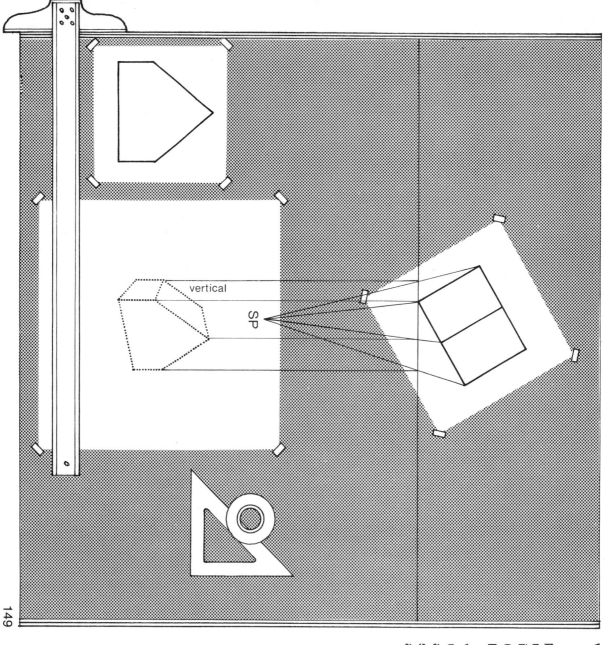

149

Vertical Edges

To pinpoint the location of the building's vertical edges in the perspective drawing, draw site lines from the station point to significant corners of the building. Project the points where site lines intersect the picture plane vertically down into the perspective (149). Use measuring lines and vanishing-point routes to find the perspective heights of vertical edges.

As a matter of procedure, do not project all the building's vertical edges into the perspective view at the same time. This usually results in a wilderness of vertical lines. Instead frame out and construct the larger parts of the perspective before the smaller (152). Transfer vertical edges down into the perspective as they are needed.

Two-point Common Method

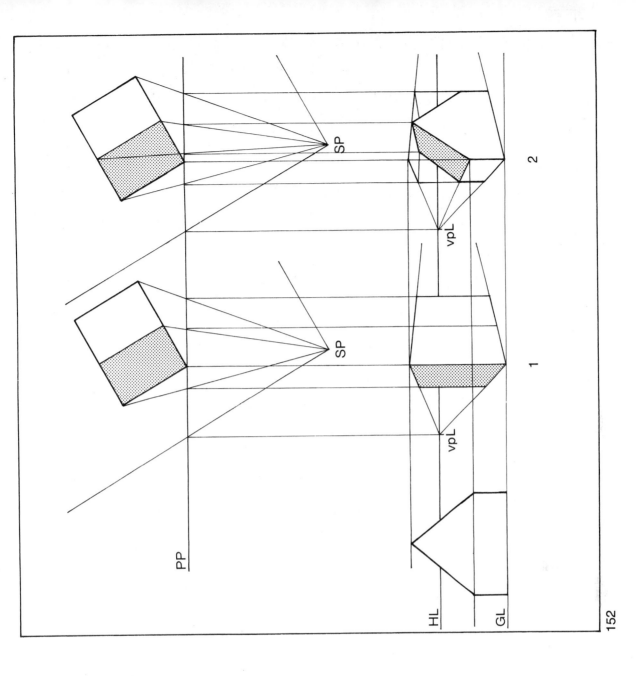

PP

SP

SP

vpL

vpL

HL

GL

2

1

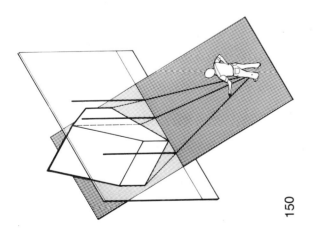

150

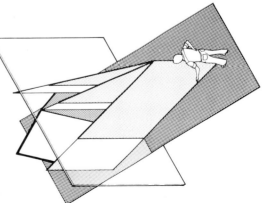

151

152

One-point Common Method

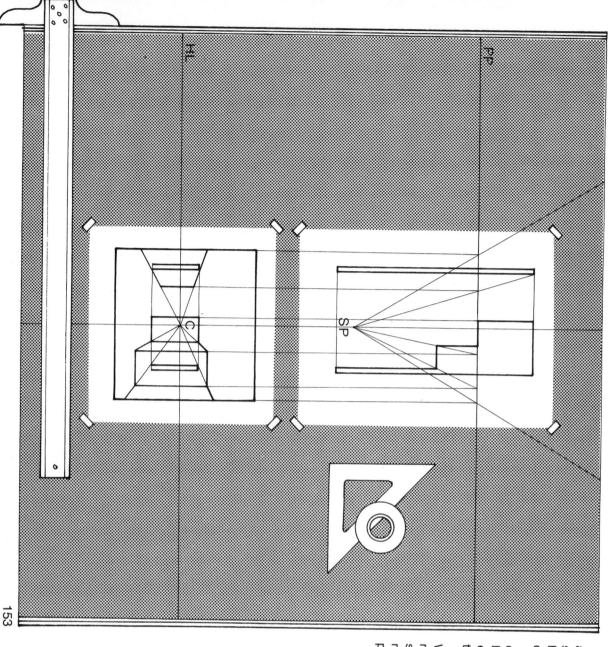

This method of drawing perspectives requires a building plan and a building elevation or section that are both drawn to the same scale. The elevation or section must contain important height information. Roof, floor plan, and site form should be included in the plan drawing.

To set up a one-point common-method perspective using the direct projection approach, place the elevation or section directly below the plan. Tape a sheet of tracing paper over the top of the elevation or section (153) and construct the perspective on the tracing paper.

A variation on this setup is called the offset one-point method. With this variation the elevation or section is not positioned directly below the plan. It is instead located off to the side as in the setup for a two-point common-method perspective. True-height measurements are transferred from the elevation or section to the perspective drawing.

One-point Common Method

Identical perspective constructions are shown here (153, 155). One looks like a typical graphics workbook problem; the other lies in the context of a design experience. Prearranged setups are useful for describing perspective constructions (155). The drawing board in the background (153) furnishes a design-experience setting for these perspective constructions.

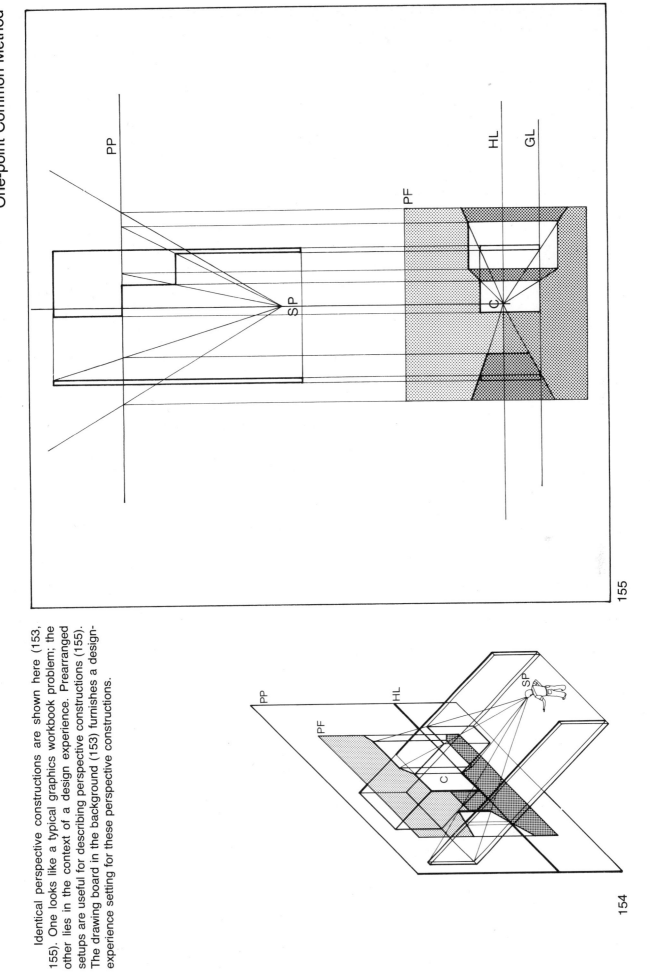

155

154

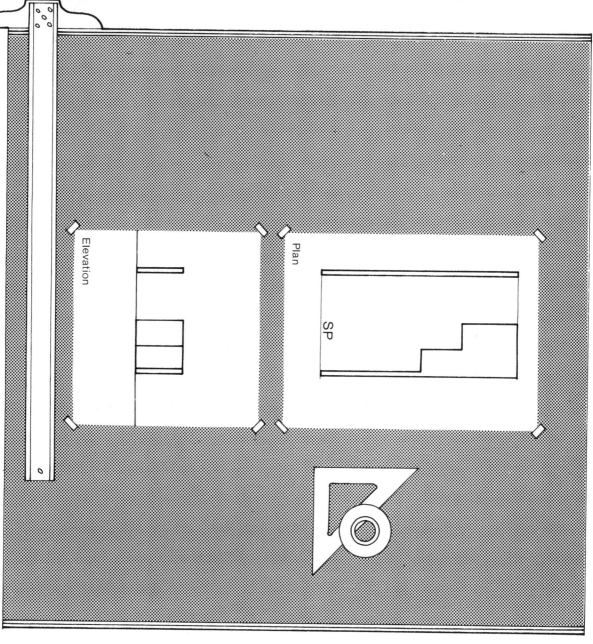

156

The Plan

Position the plan directly above the space provided for the perspective. Orient the plan so that one set of its axes is parallel to the viewer's center of vision (156).

The Section or Elevation

Place the section or elevation directly below the plan. Tape a sheet of tracing paper over the section or elevation. Draw the perspective on the tracing paper (156).

The Station Point or Viewer

Locate the station point in plan (156). Here are some guidelines for positioning the station point.

1. Keep the environment within a 45° to 90° field of vision.

2. Aim the viewer's center of vision toward the perspective's center of interest.

3. Avoid common alignment of building edges along site lines radiating from the station point.

Variables

Across the upper perspective drawings (158) the station point gradually moves closer to the picture plane. The other elements remain unchanged. The resulting perspective image is affected in two ways: the size of the perspective shrinks because the width of the field of vision on the picture plane decreases as SP moves closer to the picture plane, and the perspective view changes. The middle wall parallel to the station point's line of sight appears deeper as it drifts toward the fringes of the perspective field.

Across the lower perspectives (158) the size of the visual field changes. Narrowing the visual field is similar in effect to cropping a photograph. What remains of the larger perspective is the same in the remaining view except that there is less of it.

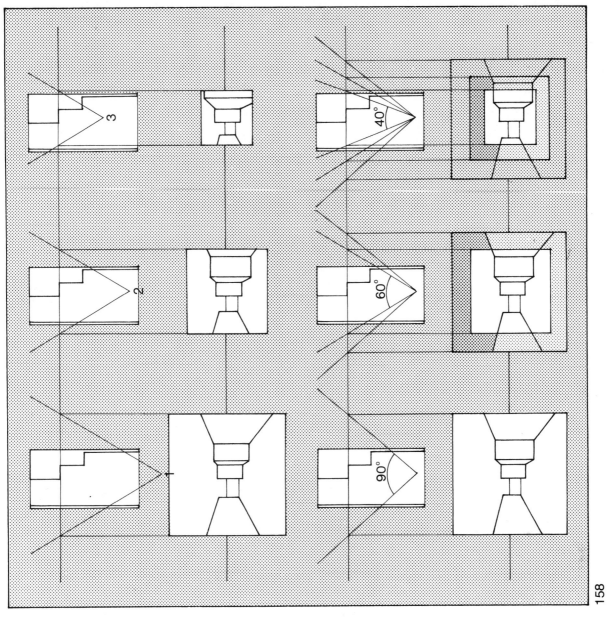

158

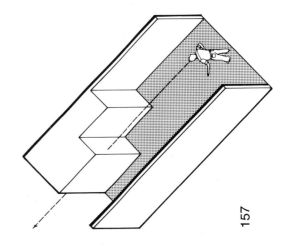

157

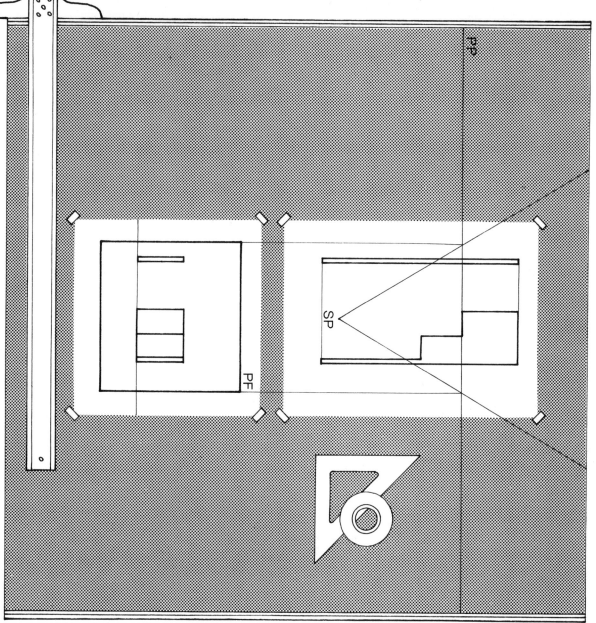

159

Picture Plane

Construct the plan view of the picture plane perpendicular to the viewer's center of vision. The picture plane is typically situated in one of three locations:

1. for exterior perspectives along the leading plane of the principal building.
2. for interior perspectives along the rear wall of the space.
3. for perspectives with no clearly defined major building or rear wall along a wall far enough from the station point to assure an adequately sized drawing (159).

Picture Frame

The picture frame is like a window in the picture-plane wall (161). Use it to contain perspective drawings or to gauge how much of the perspective field the drawing is to include. The two points of intersection between the plan field of vision and the picture plane mark the vertical edges for the picture frame (159). Locate the picture frame's horizontal edges to suit the needs of the finished perspective drawing.

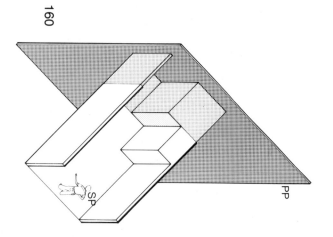

160

PP

One-point Common Method

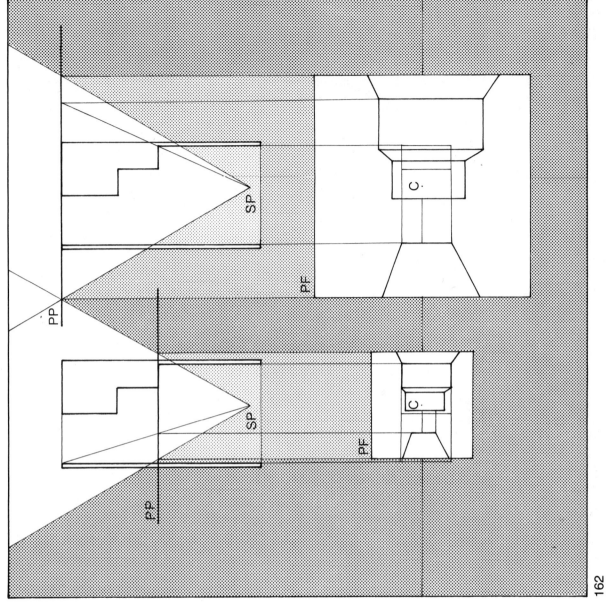

162

Variations

Varying the location of the picture plane affects the size of the perspective drawing. As the picture plane moves away from the station point, the size of the perspective drawing increases (162).

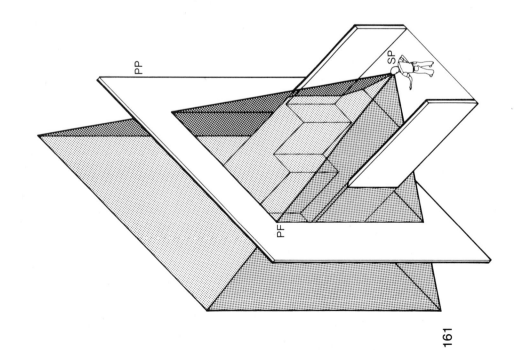

161

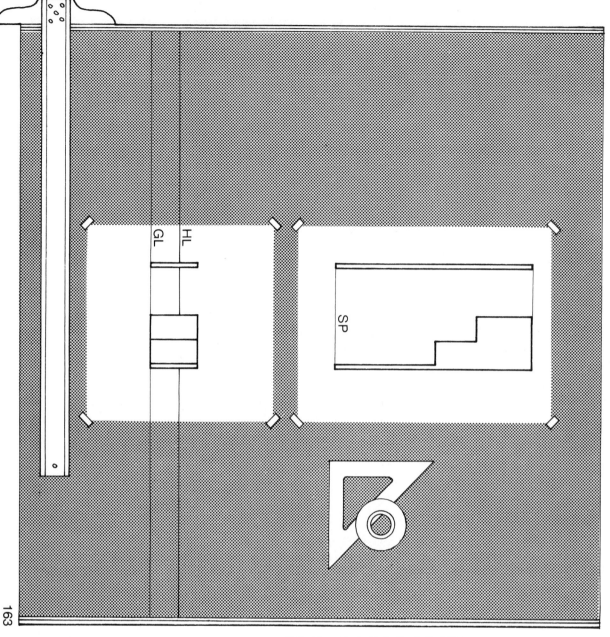

Ground Line

The ground line lies at the intersection of the picture plane and the ground plane. The ground line for the elevation or section is also the ground line for the perspective (163).

Horizon Line

The horizon line defines the meeting of ground and sky in perspective. Draw the horizon line as a horizontal line (163). The height of the horizon line above the ground line, measured at the scale of the elevation or section, corresponds to the height of the viewer or station point. The higher the horizon line is constructed above the ground line, the more the resulting perspective view is directed down at the environment. For example, if the horizon line is drawn 30' above the ground line, the perspective view of the environment will appear as if viewed by a sparrow from the branch of a tree or by a businessman from the sill of a third-story window.

To enhance the realism of a perspective, place the horizon line or eye level at a height that would be natural for viewing the depicted space—3'-6" above the ground line for a seated view, 5'-0" above the ground line for a standing view.

One-point Common Method

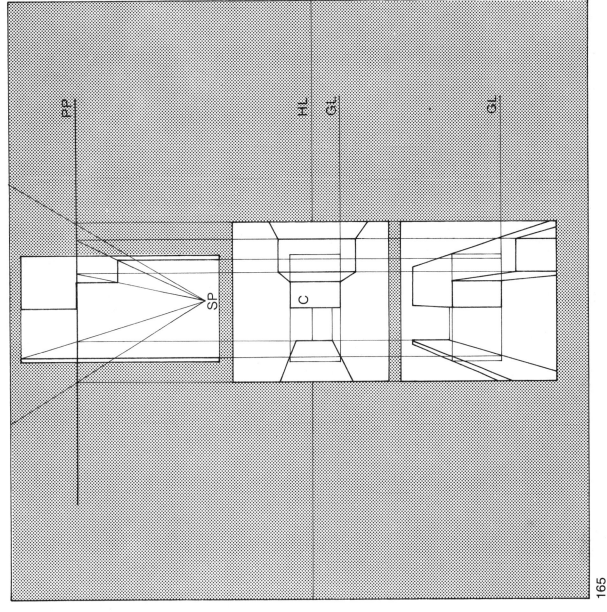

165

Variations

Shifting the position of the horizon line affects the viewer's vertical viewing angle. The upper perspective construction at right (165) depicts a normal viewing angle for a standing observer. The lower construction is a bird's-eye perspective. Bird's-eye perspectives show roofs. To draw a bird's-eye view, situate the horizon line above the building's elevation.

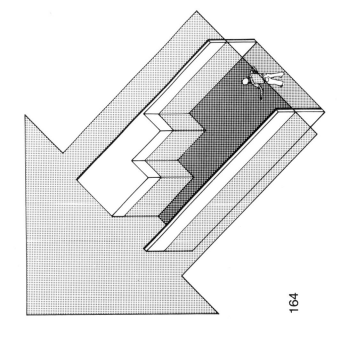

164

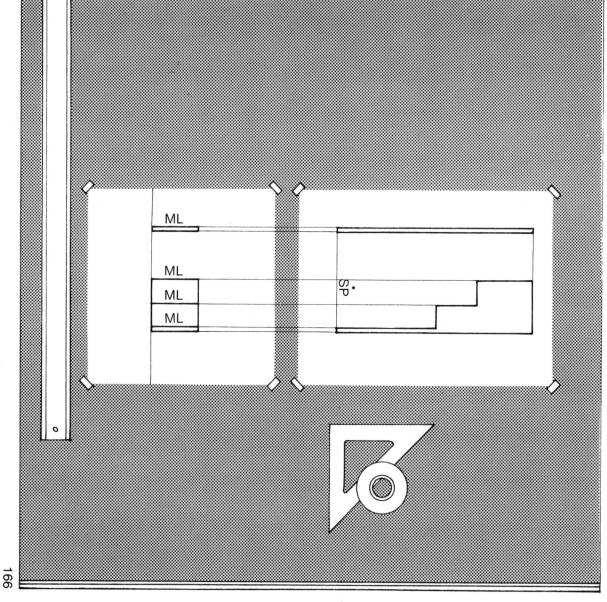

166

Measuring Lines

Measuring lines must be located on the picture plane. All lines defining the elevation or section in a one-point direct-projection setup are measuring lines (166). In fact, the entire elevation or section is a measuring plane. Any line contained in this view, regardless of its orientation or shape, can be used as a measuring line. Typically, however, only vertical measuring lines are used to construct one-point perspectives.

To find the perspective height of a vertical building edge that is not contained on the picture plane, determine its true height on the picture plane. The point view of this edge in plan and its true height-or-measuring line—in section or elevation—lie along a common vertical line. Use C, the center vanishing point (page 128), to project this true height into the perspective. The edge's height in perspective coincides with its true perspective location as sighted by SP in plan and projected down into the perspective.

The elevation or section view for a direct-projection one-point common-method perspective is used as a measuring plane (167). It is occasionally useful to take advantage of the fact that the entire elevation or section is a measuring plane. For example, a circle on the picture plane projects into perspective as a circle, retaining its true shape but not its true size. This phenomenon is explained in more detail later (page 134).

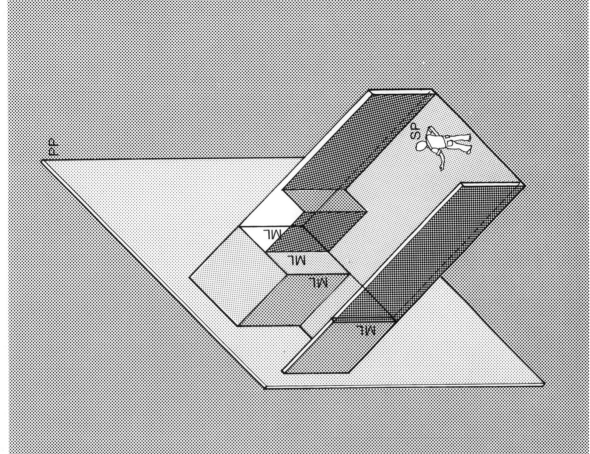

167

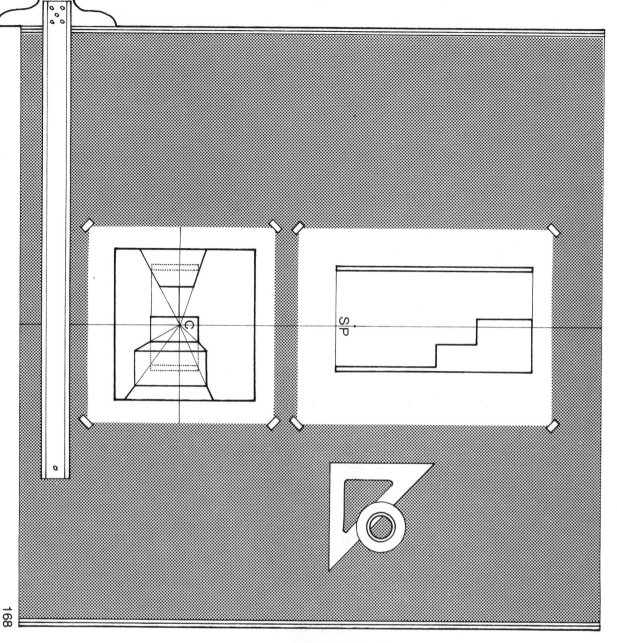

168

Vanishing Points

The distinctive feature of a one-point perspective is its single central vanishing point (168). Rectangular buildings are deliberately set up with all edges and surfaces oriented parallel or perpendicular to the picture plane in order to achieve that feature.

Building edges and surfaces that are oriented perpendicular to the picture plane vanish toward C, which is the only vanishing point in a one-point perspective.

To locate C, draw a vertical line from the station point to the horizon line. C lies at the point where the vertical line and the horizon line meet. The one-point arrangement of building and picture plane also results in a set of parallel building edges with no vanishing point of its own. A ray through the station point that is parallel to building edges that are themselves parallel to the picture plane never meets the picture plane. No vanishing point can be located. Building edges that are parallel to the picture plane appear as parallel lines in perspective.

One-point Common Method

Vertical Edges

The following procedure fixes the perspective locations of vertical building edges (169).

1. Draw sight lines from the station point to significant corners of the building.

2. Project their intersections with the picture plane vertically down into the perspective view.

For complex perspectives avoid transferring all the vertical edges of the building into the perspective view at once. This results in a confusion of vertical lines. As a rule, frame out and complete the bigger parts of the perspective before the smaller.

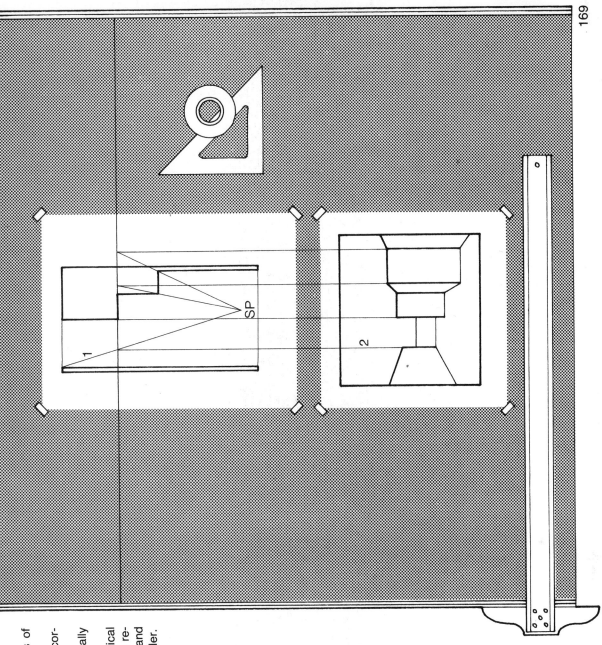

169

170

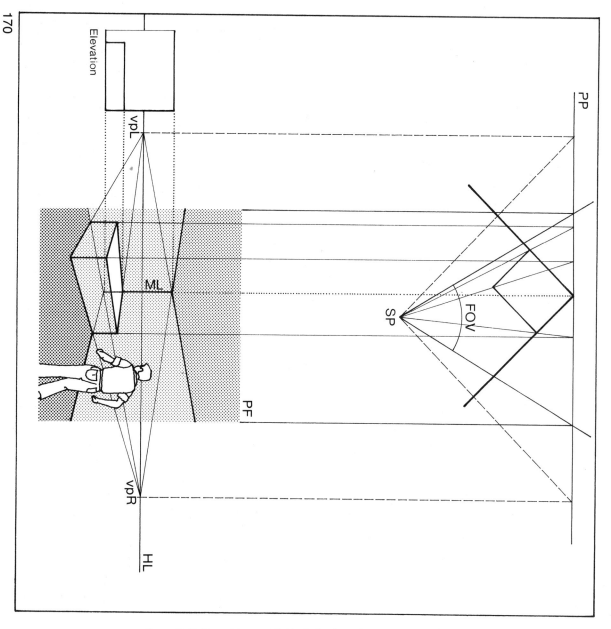

PP

Elevation

vpL

ML

SP

FOV

PF

vpR

HL

The setup and procedure for constructing two-point interior perspectives (170) is similar to the method used for drawing exterior perspectives.

1. Set up the plan and elevation. Orient the plan at a convenient angle. Locate the elevation or section off to the side of the perspective.

2. Locate SP. If possible, keep SP within the plan of the room and avoid a field of vision greater than 90°. Familiar objects such as doors, sofas, and double-hung windows appear distorted when they are located toward the fringes of a perspective with a 90° field of vision. If all important elements within the room cannot be included within the field of vision when SP is located inside the room, locate SP outside the space. Imagine that the viewer—or SP—has x-ray vision and can see through walls to the inside of the room.

3. Locate the picture plane in plan. The picture plane typically contains the furthest corner of the room.

4. The picture frame lies at the intersection of the field of vision and the picture plane. Two finished-effect options are possible with the picture frame: either draw a distinct frame around the finished perspective, creating a snapshot effect (170), or subtly imply the boundaries of a picture frame around the finished perspective drawing, creating a cameo effect.

5. Locate vanishing points.

6. Locate vertical edges of the space as required, drawing large objects first.

7. Transfer true-height measurements from the section or elevation to vertical measuring lines. When the picture plane passes through the far corner of the depicted space, the far corner is used as the measuring line (170).

8. Project true heights from measuring lines into the perspective.

Unattached Objects

The pillar (171) is an example of an unattached object in the sense that it is not connected to a wall. To find the pillar's intersection with floor and ceiling in perspective, follow these directions.

1. In the plan view extend a face of the pillar to the wall. This extension is represented by a dashed line.

2. Construct the intersection of the dashed line and the wall in plan as a vertical line on the same wall in perspective. Construct a plane in perspective that coincides with the dashed line in plan, making its height equal to the height of the pillar.

3. Locate the forward vertical edges of the pillar along the dashed plane by transferring the sighted locations of both vertical edges down from the plan.

4. The receding face of the pillar can be found by projecting its top and bottom toward the left vanishing point and transferring the sighted location of its rear vertical edge down from the plan.

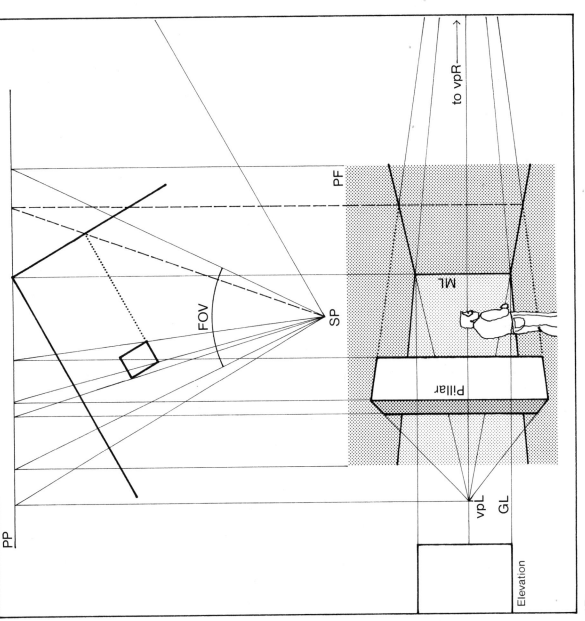

Interior Two-point Common Method

171

Elevation

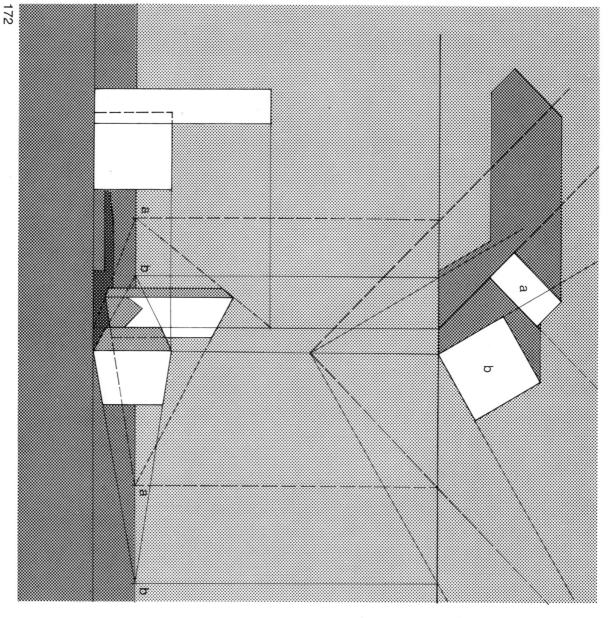

172

Multiple Vanishing Points for Horizontal Edges

To locate the vanishing points for many horizontal edges that are oriented at various angles to the picture plane (172), follow these rules.

1. In the plan view draw sight lines parallel to each set of parallel edges. Mark where these sight lines intersect the picture plane.

2. Transfer points of intersection vertically down to the horizon line. Each intersection on the horizon line represents the location of a vanishing point for a particular set of parallel edges.

Picture Frame

Portions of buildings, fences, trees, cars, and shrubbery that lie outside the boundaries of the plan field of vision do not appear within the perspective picture frame (173).

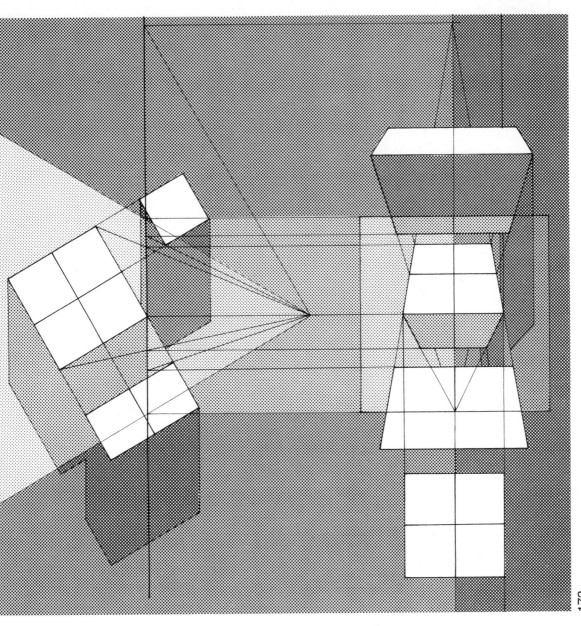

173

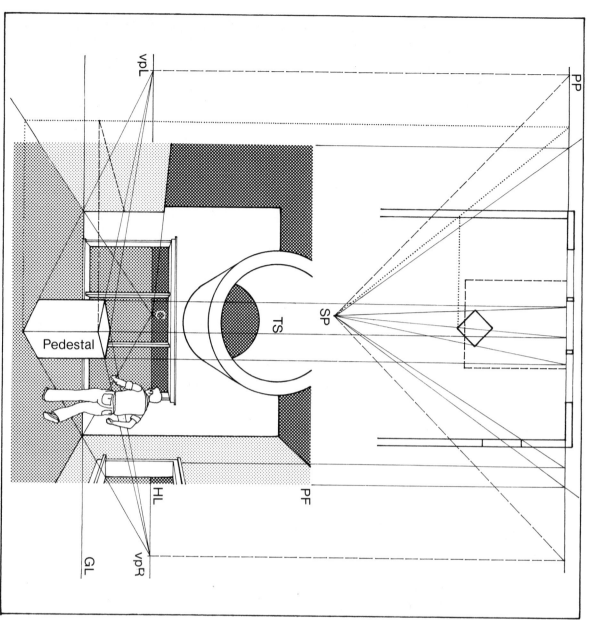

One-point Complex Perspective

This one-point perspective (174) contains unusual constructions.

1. In the foreground of the perspective the pedestallike block is oriented at a 45° angle to the picture plane. Construct the pedestal as a miniature two-point within the framework of the larger one-point.

2. The pedestal is not attached to the wall. Its height and precise location in perspective can be found by constructing imaginary dashed lines and planes.

3. The forward rim of the elevated truncated culvert is a true circle in perspective. Planar shapes—including circles—that are parallel to the picture plane retain their true shape but not their true size when projected from C.

One-point Magic Method

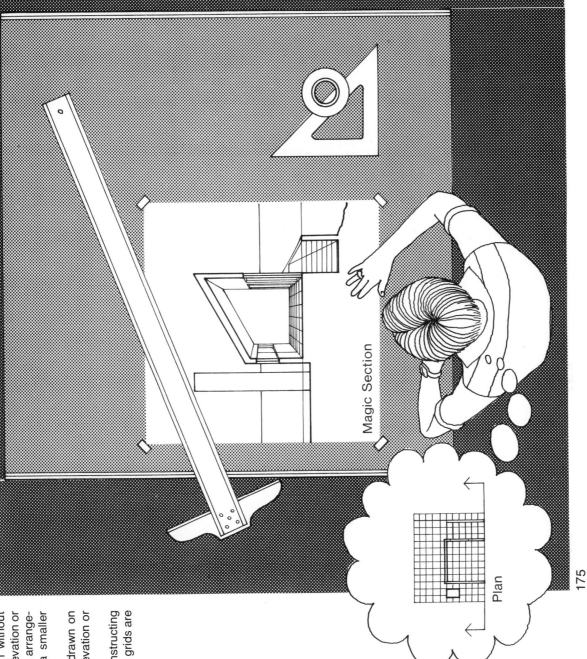

Magic Section

Plan

175

Precision magic one-point perspectives are drawn without projecting from a plan view. Only a drafted and scaled elevation or section is required for the setup. The advantages of this arrangement include a saving in drafting-board space and a smaller number of construction lines to draw.

A one-point magic-method perspective is usually drawn on tracing paper that is taped over the top of the scaled elevation or section (175).

The following pages describe procedures for constructing magic interior, exterior, and section perspectives. Magic grids are also discussed.

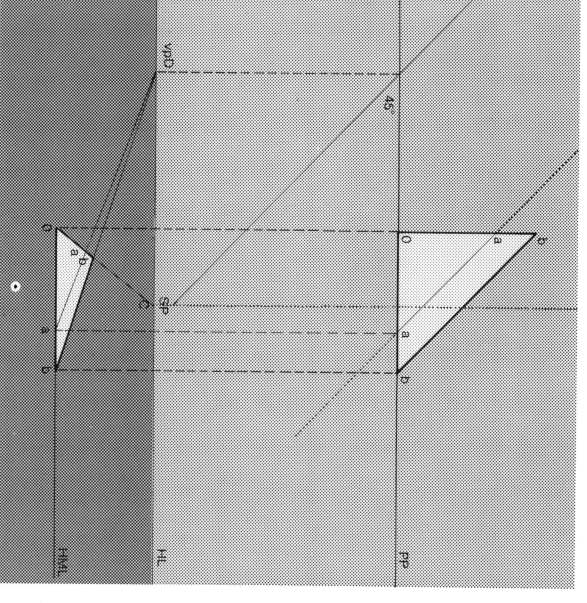

176

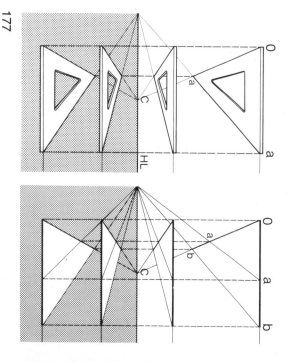

177

Technique

All magic one-point perspectives use the same technique for finding accurate perspective depth measurements without projecting from the plan. The technique derives from the following rule of geometry: two sides of a 45° right triangle are equal in length.

Adapting this geometry to magic perspectives, one of the two equal sides of the triangle is set up as a horizontal measuring line (HML), while the other equal side is set up to vanish toward C. The hypotenuse—or long side—of the triangle vanishes toward vpD, which is the vanishing point for a set of horizontal lines oriented at a 45° angle to the picture plane (176).

Finding depths in perspective involves constructing 45° triangles in perspective (177). Desired perspective depths are measured at the scale of the elevation or section along the HML. From the HML these depths are transferred into perspective by constructing triangles whose hypotenuses vanish toward vpD. By definition the measured length of the HML side of the triangle always equals the perspective length of the side that vanishes toward C.

Basic Setup

The procedure for setting up a typical magic one-point perspective (178) is as follows.

1. Begin with a section or elevation.

2. Construct the horizon line. Locate C somewhere toward the middle of this horizon line.

3. Locate vpD—the vanishing point for lines oriented at a 45° angle to the picture plane—to the left or right of C. Position vpD on the horizon line. The location of SP in plan can be deduced from the location of vpD by applying the following rule: the distance from C to vpD is equal to the distance from C to SP. In other words the perpendicular distance from SP to the picture plane is equal to the distance from vpD to C. As a rule moving vpD closer to C increases the apparent depth of the depicted space. The interior of the cube appears deeper in one view because the station point is positioned closer to the cube. As SP moves closer to the cube, vpD moves closer to C. In theory, vpD can be located anywhere to the left or right of C. Its position merely affects the apparent depth of the space.

4. Construct a horizontal measuring line (HML). The HML is typically located along the ground line. This is not the only possible location for HMLs. In the example (178) the forward edge of the ceiling is the HML. When the ground line is very close to the horizon line, the HML is usually located somewhere well above or below the ground line. This is done in order to obtain wider angles of intersection for triangulating depths.

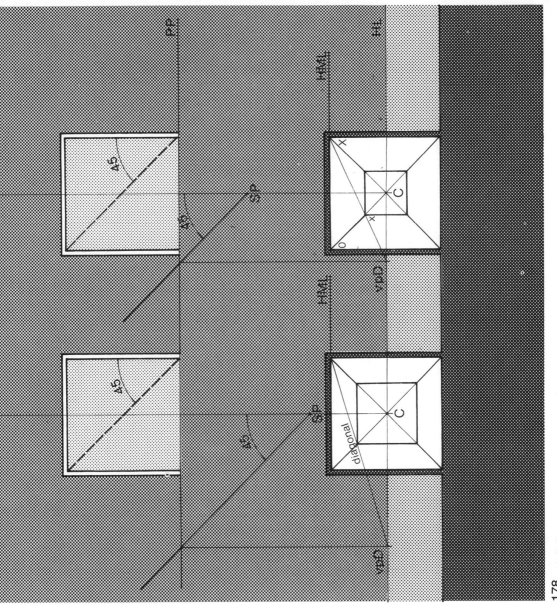

178

One-point Magic Method

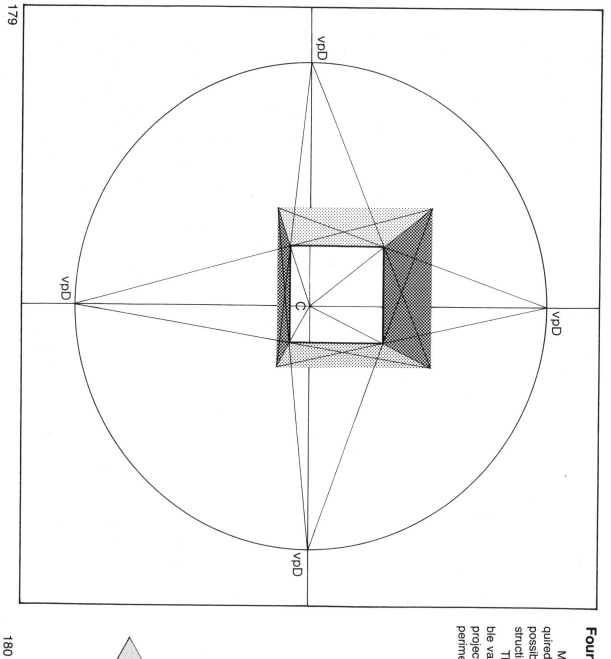

179

Four Diagonal Vanishing Points

Magic perspectives have four vpDs. While only one is re-quired to find perspective depths, knowing that four locations are possible increases the designer's flexibility in setting up and con-structing perspectives.

The drawing (179) shows the interior of a cube. All the possi-ble vanishing diagonals for the interior surfaces of the cube are projected to their respective vpDs. The four vpDs lie along the perimeter of a circle whose center is at C.

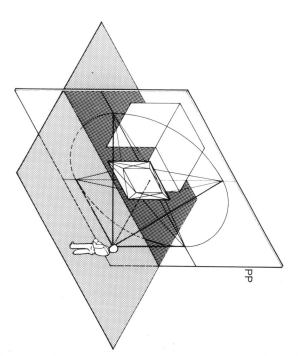

180

Depth Measurements

The following is a typical procedure for finding perspective depth measurements.

1. Measure a desired perspective depth from point 0 along HML. Make this measurement at the scale of the section or elevation.

2. Use vpD to transfer this measurement to perspective line OC. The location of this measurement on line OC marks the desired perspective depth.

3. Transfer the perspective depth on line OC into the depicted space. For example, perspective depths can be transferred up along the vertical plane defining the left wall and horizontally across the floor plane to locate the depth of the box resting on the floor (182).

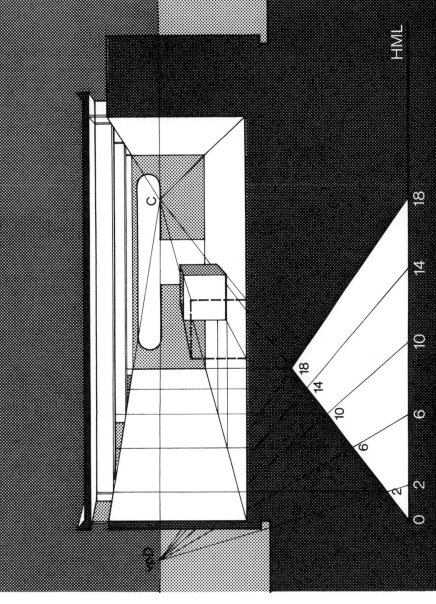

182

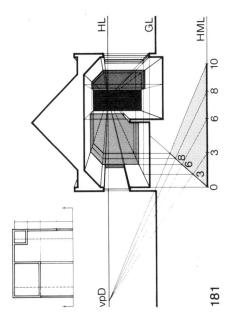

181

139

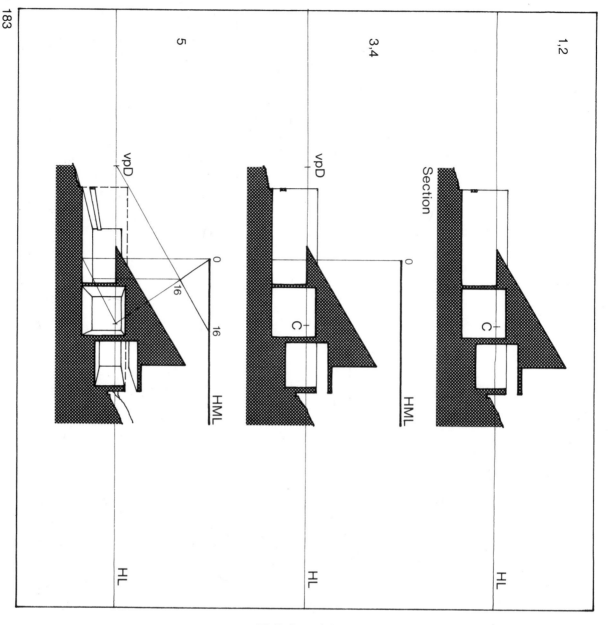

1,2

3,4

5

Section

vpD

vpD

0

16

16

0

C

C

C

HML

HML

HML

HL

HL

HL

Magic Sections

Magic sections are one-point perspective sections (184). The plane of the section cut is used as the picture plane. Depths are projected back into perspective from this plane. Here is the procedure for constructing a magic section (183).

1. Begin with a scaled section view of the building or environment.

2. Construct the horizon line. Locate C toward the middle of the horizon line.

3. Locate vpD to the left or right of C on HL. As a rule of thumb keep the distance between vpD and C at least as great as the width of the building section.

4. Construct HML. Here the HML is located above the horizon line. Other locations for HML include positions on or below the ground line.

5. Project the section back toward C. To find perspective depths, measure distances along HML at the scale of the section and then transfer distances into perspective using vpD. Their intersections with OC mark their depths in perspective.

6. Once perspective depths are located on line OC, the rest of the problem involves transferring depths around the same perspective depth planes until intersections with lines and edges projecting back toward C are made.

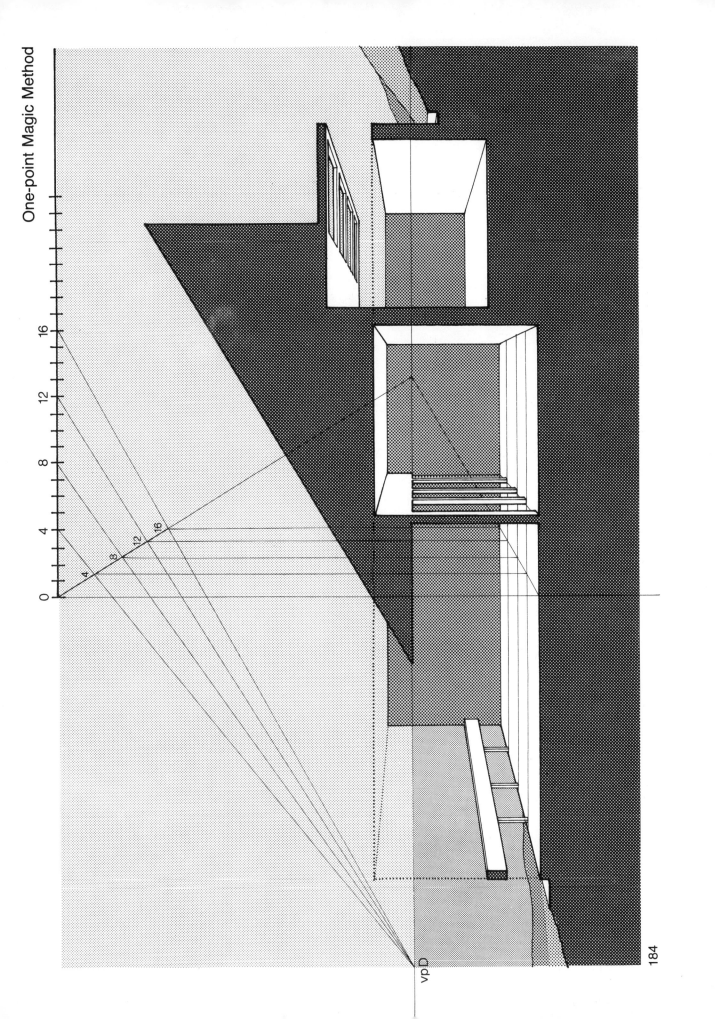

185

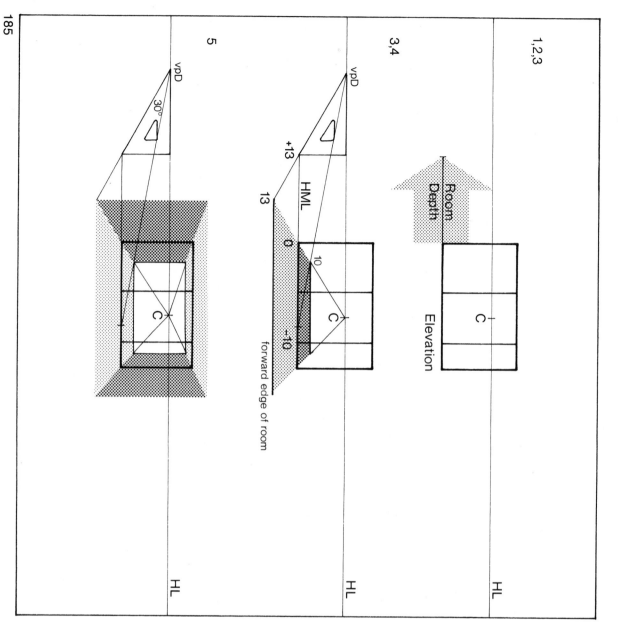

Magic Interiors

30° Method

The location of vpD controls the apparent depth of interior spaces. The 30° method (186) is designed to locate vpD so that distortion toward the foreground fringes of interior one-point perspectives is held to a minimum. For one-point magic interiors the plane of the back wall serves as the picture plane. The 30° method does not employ a picture frame and does not take into account the location of the station point—which is often not positioned within the depicted room. Here is the typical procedure for constructing magic interiors using the 30° method (185).

1. Begin with a drafted and scaled elevation.

2. Construct the horizon line. Locate C toward the middle of the horizon line.

3. Locate vpD on HL. To do this, extend the ground line from the lower-left corner of the elevation. Measure the depth of the room along the extended ground line. For example, if the room is 20′ deep, measure 20′ from the corner of the elevation along the ground-line extension. Draw a 30° angle from the end point of this measured depth. VpD is located at the point where this angle intersects the horizon line.

4. Use the elevation's ground line as the HML. Transfer depths from HML to line OC. Depths measured to the left of 0 on HML result in forward depth projections. Depths measured to the right of 0 on HML project back into perspective and behind the picture-plane wall.

5. The rest of the construction involves transferring depths vertically and horizontally within the same perspective depth planes until intersections with lines and edges projected from C are made.

One-point Magic Method

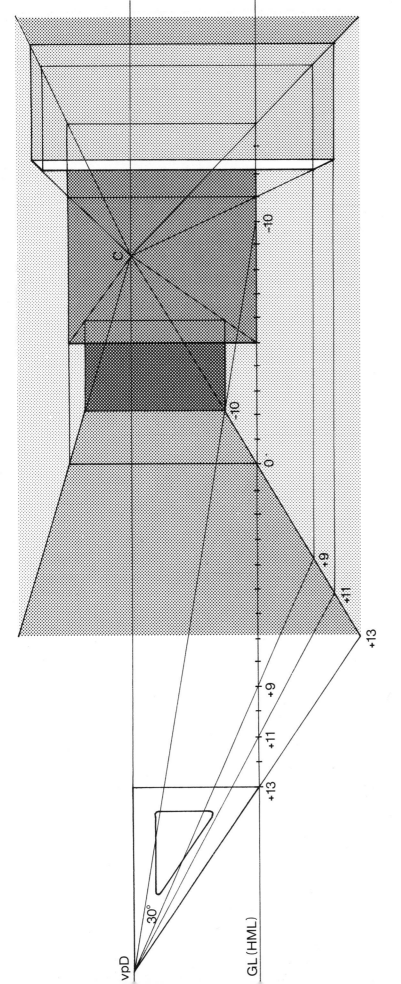

One-point Magic Method

144

187

VpD = SP Method

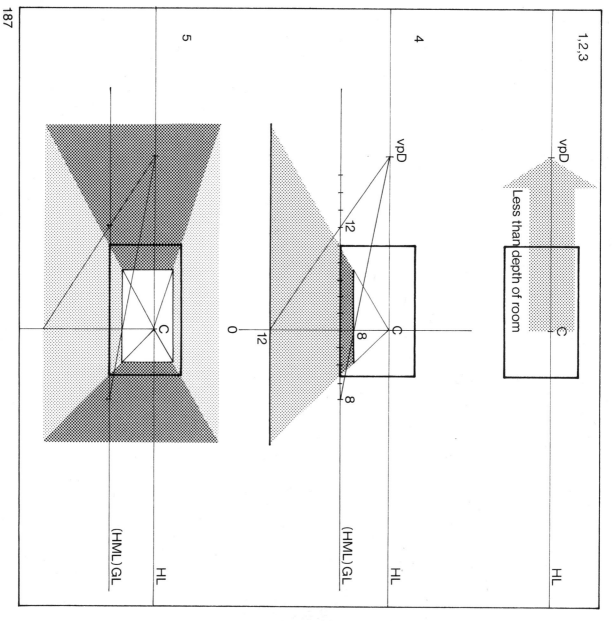

As a rule of thumb use the 30° method for small or shallow spaces such as bedrooms, closets, and views across narrow corridors. Apply the vpD=SP method (188) to large or deep spaces such as auditoriums, lecture halls, and views down long corridors. The vpD=SP method locates the SP within the boundaries of the depicted room. Here is the procedure for drawing vpD=SP magic interiors (187).

1. Begin with a drafted and scaled interior elevation.
2. Draw a horizon line. Locate C toward the middle of the horizon line.

3. Locate vpD. At the scale of the elevation measure along the horizon line from point C. Measure a distance that does not exceed the distance from the picture-plane wall to the foreground wall of the depicted room. This places SP within the room. For example, if the plan dimensions of the room are 15' x 15', the distance from C to vpD should not exceed 15', or the station point would be located outside the room.

4. The following method for finding perspective depths is used. Let the ground line serve as the HML. Draw a vertical line through C. This line fixes point 0 on HML. To project depths in front of the picture plane, measure to the left of 0 on HML. Use vpD to transfer measured distances to their perspective depths along the vertical line through C. To project depths behind the picture-plane wall, measure to the right of 0 on HML. Use vpD to transfer measured distances into perspective along the vertical line through C.

5. The rest of the construction involves transferring depths vertically and horizontally within the same perspective depth planes until intersections with corresponding lines and edges projected from C are made.

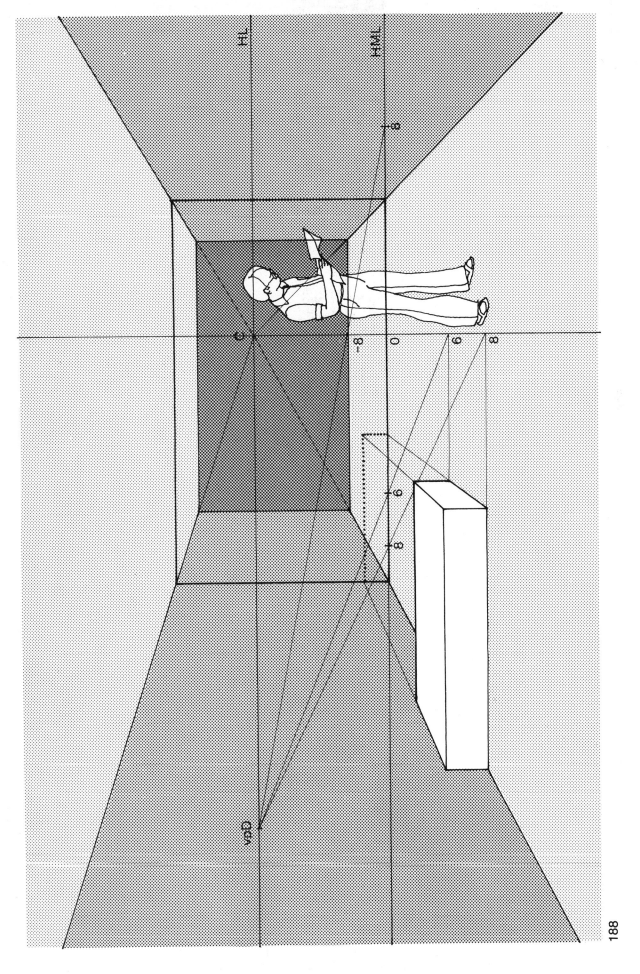

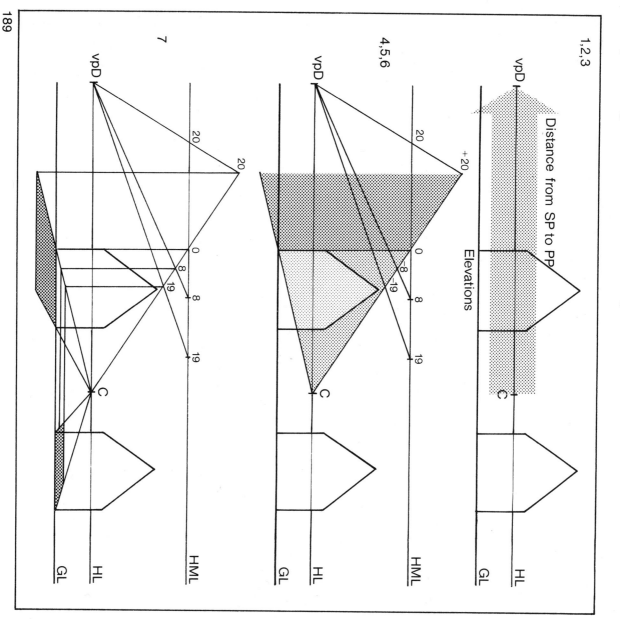

Distance from SP to PP

Elevations

1,2,3

4,5,6

7

vpD · · ·

+20

20

0
8
-19

C

HL

GL

HML

vpD

20

0
8
19

C

HL

GL

HML

vpD

20

20

0
8
19

0
8
19

C

HL

GL

HML

Magic Exteriors

The elevation view of the exterior building and environment is the plane of projection, or picture plane, for magic-exterior perspectives (190). Elements drawn in elevation that are not contained on the picture plane are projected to their respective depths in perspective. Here is the typical procedure for constructing magic exterior perspectives (189).

1. Begin with a drafted and scaled elevation view of the building and its surrounding environment.

2. Construct a horizon line. Locate C on the horizon line.

3. Locate vpD on the horizon line. Follow this rule to locate vpD: the distance from C to vpD is equal to the distance from C to SP. Measure this distance at the scale of the elevation.

4. Construct HML. Here HML is located above the elevation.

5. Locate point 0 along HML. Point 0 is typically located on a vertical line that contains an important vertical building edge, in this case the rear edge of the left building.

6. Make depth measurements at the scale of the elevation along the HML. Measure to the right of point 0 to project depths behind the elevation and measure to the left of point 0 to project depths in front of the elevation. Use vpD to transfer measurements on HML to their perspective depths along line OC.

7. The rest of the construction involves transferring depths vertically and horizontally within the same perspective depth planes until intersections with corresponding lines and edges projected from C are made.

8. This step is optional: draw a picture frame around the perspective. Keep the vertical edges of the picture plane inside vpD. Measure equal distances on both sides of C to locate the picture frame's vertical edges. Locate the horizontal edges anywhere.

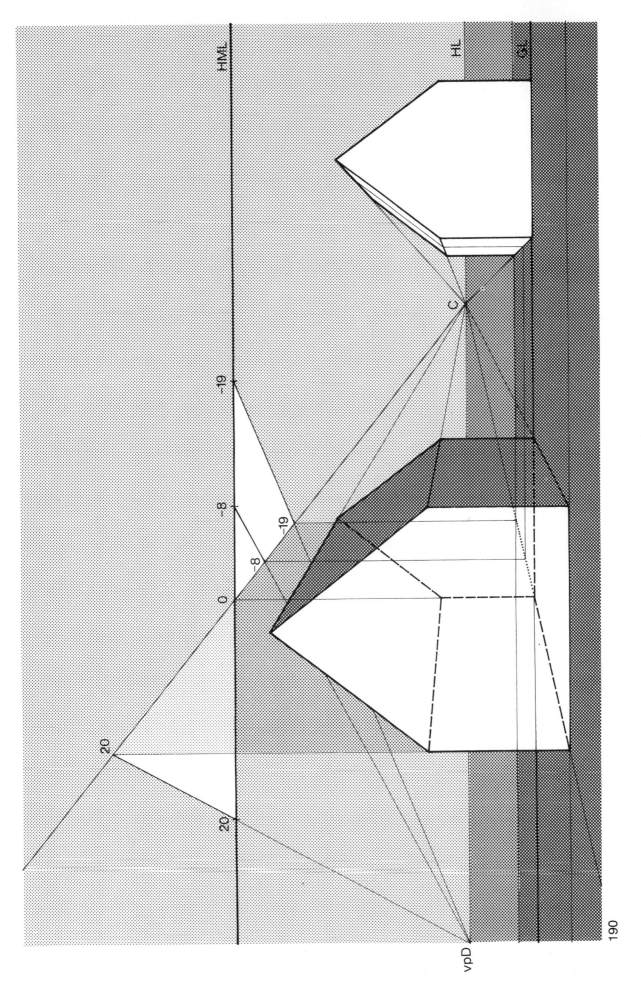

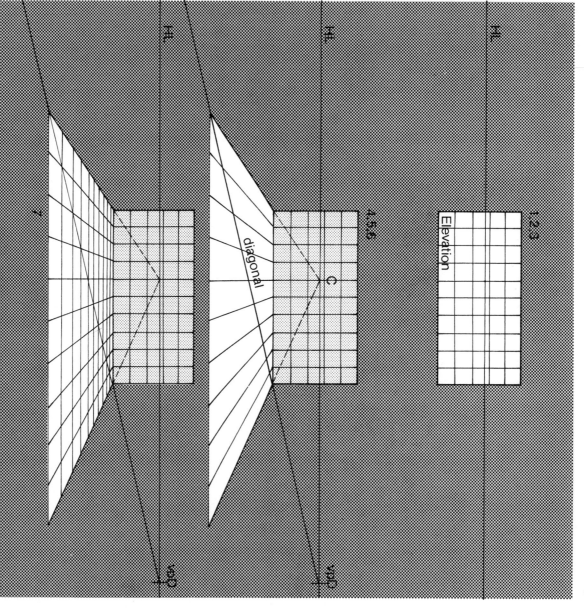

Magic Grids

Magic grids are frequently used to draw one-point interior, exterior, and section perspectives. They are especially handy for sketching spaces. Once constructed, a basic grid can be used over and over again for rooms of similar size. If perspective grids have a drawback, it is that objects such as chairs, sofas, and ottomans are awkward and difficult to locate precisely within the framework of grid lines. Such objects are usually eyeballed into position—guessed within a few inches of their true location in perspective. Here is a typical procedure for constructing a magic grid (191, 192).

1. Begin with an interior elevation of a room.

2. Grid the elevation. Grid spacing depends largely on the size and scale of the room in a house, a small office building, or a branch bank, a 1' grid spacing is typical. Finer grid spacings generate more accurate results, but the extra time required to construct them is not worth the additional effort.

3. Locate the horizon line—typically 5'-0" above the ground line for a standing viewer or 3'-0" above the ground line for a seated viewer.

4. Locate C and vpD on the horizon line. Place C toward the middle of the horizon line. A reasonable distance from C to vpD is at least 1½ times the width of the elevation.

5. Use C to project grid lines on the floor plane toward the foreground of the perspective.

6. Use vpD to construct a diagonal across the floor plane.

7. Draw horizontal lines through points where the diagonal intersects ground lines radiating from C. This creates a network of squares on the floor plane.

8. Project the floor plane's horizontal grid lines completely around the space, drawing vertical grid lines on vertical walls and horizontal grid lines on horizontal ceilings. For rectangular-shaped elevations these grid lines should form a series of rectangular hoops marching back into perspective.

9. To complete the perspective grid, construct lines radiating from C on the ceiling and both wall planes. Draw these lines through the intersection of elevation grid lines with elevation edges.

10. On the floor plane of the grid construct the plans of objects such as chairs, sofas, and partitions. Project these objects up to their heights in perspective. Use the horizontal grid lines on walls to find specific heights.

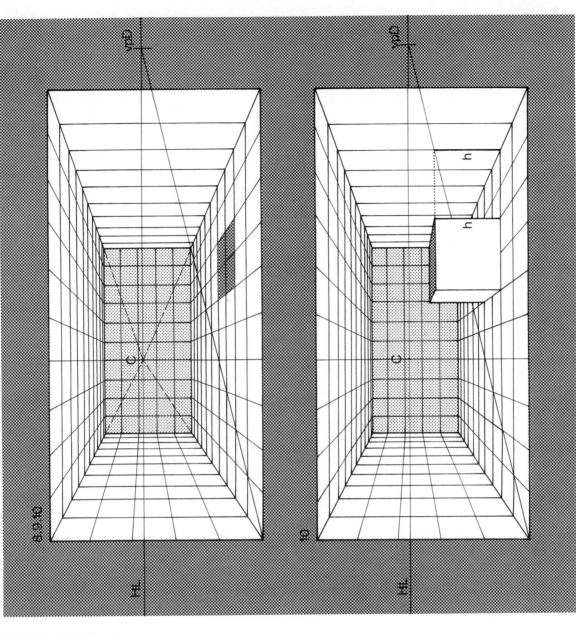

192

193

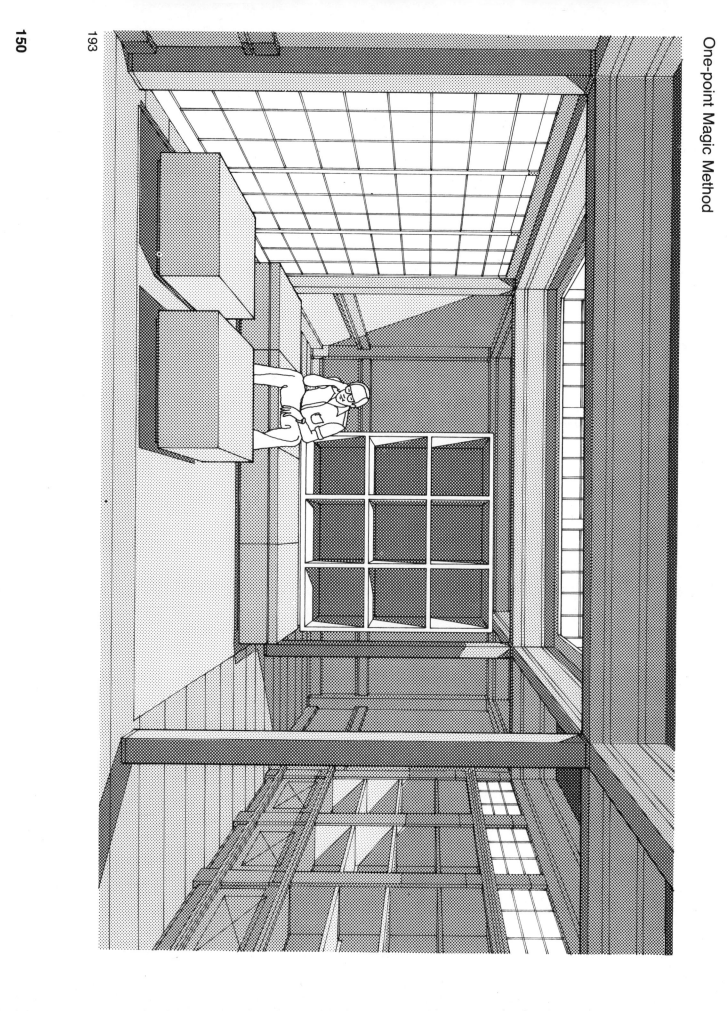

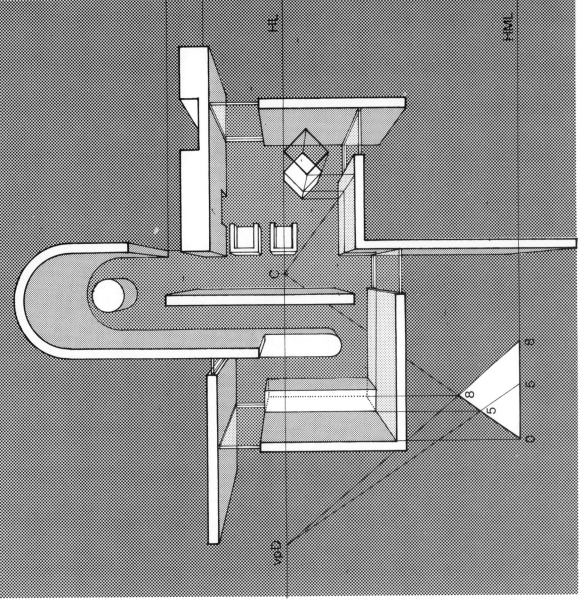

194

Magic-grid Picture Frames

The forward perimeter of a completed perspective grid in effect resembles a section taken through the room. By constructing a picture frame over the perspective grid this effect can be changed from a perspective resembling a section view to a perspective that works like a snapshot or photograph. In a snapshot the four edges of intersection between floor, wall, and ceiling planes that vanish toward C would probably not line up with the corners of the picture frame. While the difference is subtle, the effect is noticeable.

Fabricate the picture frame anywhere over the completed perspective. Snip or erase portions of the perspective that spill over the edge of the picture frame (193).

Magic Plans

The concepts and techniques for developing magic one-point plans are identical to those for developing other types of magic perspectives. To construct magic one-point plan perspectives, deal with the plan as if it were an elevation or section (194).

1. Begin with a drafted and scaled plan view.
2. Locate C somewhere toward the center of the plan. Draw a horizon line through C. The purpose of this horizon line is to help construct the perspective. It should be erased after the perspective is completed.
3. Locate vpD on the horizon line. Keep the distance between vpD and C at least as great as the width of the plan.
4. Project the plan back toward C, using HML and vpD to find perspective depths along line OC.'

151

One-point Magic Method

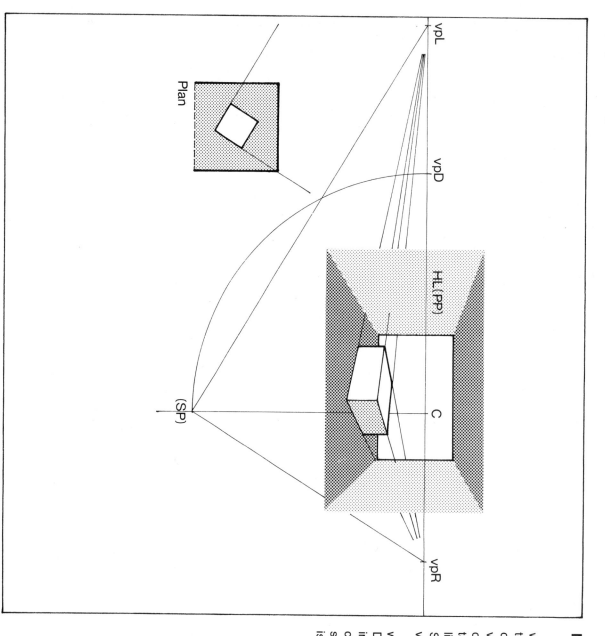

Plan

vpL

vpD

HL(PP)

C

(SP)

vpR

Multiple Vanishing Points

To find the vanishing points for two-point objects contained within one-point magic perspectives, layer a plan setup over the top of the perspective (195). Let the horizon line in perspective coincide with the picture plane in plan. In effect this amounts to a very compact and efficient setup for a one- or two-point common-method perspective. To locate SP in plan, take advantage of the fact that the distance from C to vpD along the horizon line is equal to the distance from SP to the picture plane in plan. Swing an arc with C as its center through vpD until it intersects a vertical line extending down through C. Label this intersection SP.

Handle the plan setup, which includes SP and PP, as if it were the plan view for a two-point common-method perspective. Draw sight lines parallel to the object edges in question until they intersect with the picture plane. Since the picture plane in plan coincides with the horizon line in perspective, the points where sight lines intersect the picture plane locate the positions of vanishing points on the horizon line.

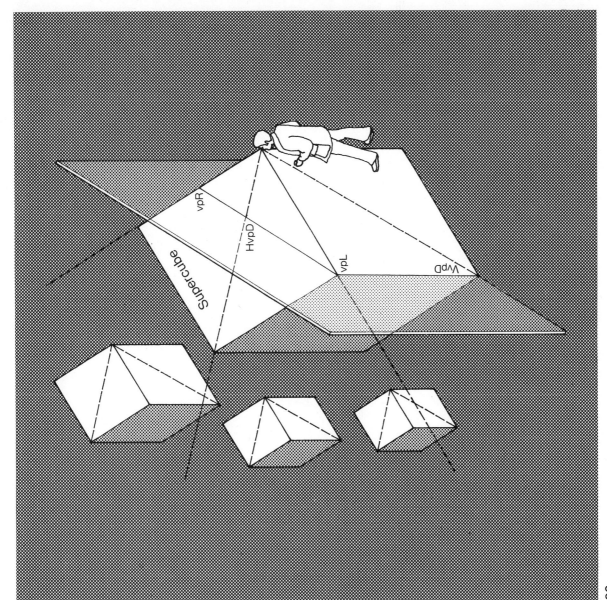

196

This method allows for precise perspective constructions of buildings and environments without projecting from drafted plans or elevations. It is quickly set up and requires less drafting-board surface than common-method perspectives.

The gist of the method involves the following steps: a minimum of four vanishing points are plotted in the perspective setup before anything is drawn in perspective; using the plotted vanishing points, a perspective cube is constructed; the perspective cube is subdivided or multiplied to render the finished perspective form of the building or environment.

The four vanishing points required to set up and construct perspective cubes include a left and right vanishing point on the horizon line (vpL and vpR) and horizontal and vertical diagonal vanishing points (HvpD and VvpD).

The supercube concept (196) explains the locations of these vanishing points. The intersection of the supercube and the picture plane pinpoints vanishing-point positions. One of the supercube's corners is the station point, while one of its vertical edges hinges on the picture plane—line vpL-VvpD. The supercube's orientation can vary from nearly parallel to the picture plane to a 45° angle with the picture plane. Regardless of its orientation, the supercube defines the vanishing points for sets of similarly oriented cubes in the perspective field.

The following pages include the technical constructions required to implement the supercube concept and three methods for setting up and constructing two-point magic perspectives.

Technical Constructions

Four vanishing points are required to draw a magic cube in perspective. They include a left and a right vanishing point and horizontal and vertical diagonal vanishing points. Three of these vanishing points are located on the horizon line. The geometric construction for establishing the relationship between these three vanishing points is illustrated here (197).

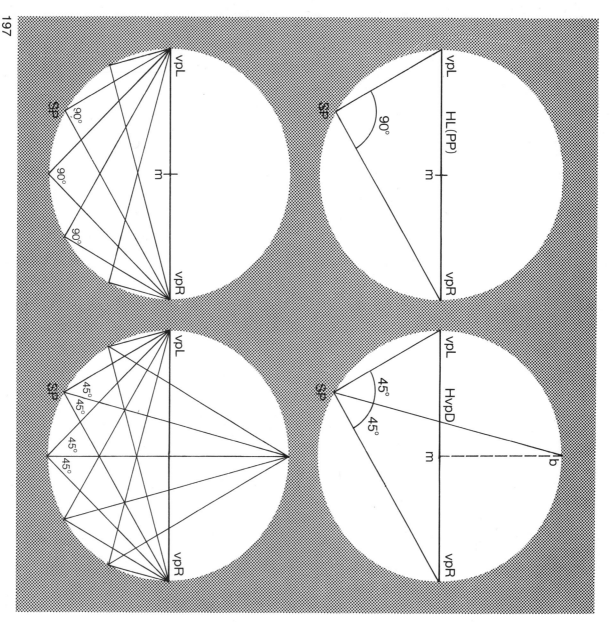

Right-angle Construction

If point SP is located anywhere on the circumference of the circle, site lines from SP to vpL and vpR will form a right angle.

Bisecting the Right Angle

If a vertical line is drawn from point m, the midpoint of the circle, to point b, the line connecting b and SP bisects the right angle. The intersection of line b-SP and the horizon line marks the location for HvpD.

Plan and Perspective Views

In the setup for a two-point common-method perspective the plan is drawn above the perspective. Intersections of sight lines with the picture plane in plan are projected down into the perspective view. The magic method condenses this process: to economize space, the plan view is layered over the perspective view so that the picture plane in plan coincides with the horizon line in perspective.

Two-point Magic Method

Setup

Here is the procedure for setting up a typical two-point magic-method perspective (198).

1. Draw a horizon line. Construct a light vertical line through the horizon line to indicate the center of interest of the drawing.

2. Locate vpL and vpR, the left and right vanishing points, anywhere to the left and right of the center of interest. Position them on the horizon line.

3. Use midpoint m on the horizon line to construct a circle through vpL and vpR. Point m is located halfway between vpL and vpR. Draw a vertical line through point m intersecting the circle at top and bottom. Draw line SP-b. The intersection of SP-b with the horizon line marks the location of HvpD—the vanishing point for a set of horizontal diagonal lines—on the horizon line.

4. Construct lines SP-vpR and SP-vpL.

5. Use vpL and vpR as center points to construct arcs from SP to vertical lines extending through vpL and vpR. Each intersection of arc and vertical line marks the location of VvpD—the vanishing point for a set of vertical diagonal lines. Only one VvpD is required to draw the perspective even though two are illustrated. Four such VvpDs are possible (199).

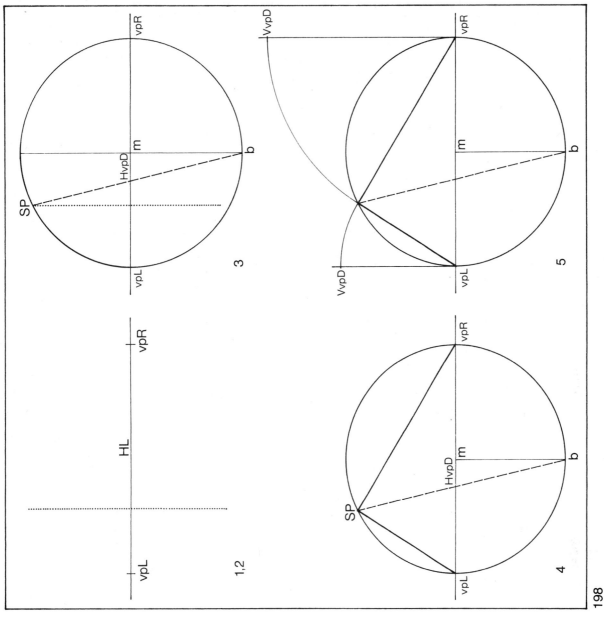

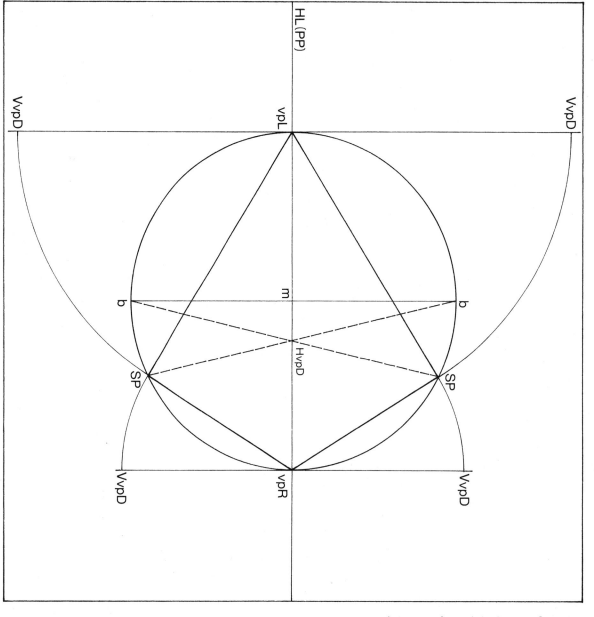

Diagonal Vanishing Points

Although only one VvpD is required to construct a two-point cube, four locations are possible (199). These VvpDs can be used to construct all the diagonals on the vertical faces of a two-point perspective cube. To find all four VvpDs, swing two arcs, one with center point at vpL and the other at vpR, through SP. Their intersections with vertical lines extending through vpL and vpR mark the locations of the four VvpDs.

Two Station Points

The location of SP on the rim of the great circle can be plotted above or below the horizon line—or both. If both SPs are plotted, they must lie along a common vertical line.

Constructing a Magic Cube

Here is how to draw a two-point magic cube in perspective.

1. Begin with the two-point magic-method setup described previously (page 155).

2. Construct the leading vertical edge of the cube (200). Use this edge as the measuring line. To minimize distortion, it should closely line up with a vertical through SP. Scale the edge and decide how it relates to the horizon line.

3. Draw a leading vertical face of the cube. For example, extend the top and bottom of the cube's leading edge back toward vpL. Use VvpD to construct a diagonal across this face of the cube. Its intersection with an edge vanishing toward vpL marks the vertical rear edge of this face.

4. Draw a square on the ground plane. Use HvpD, the vanishing point for horizontal diagonals, to locate the back corner of the square.

5. Complete the cube. Horizontal edges of the cube vanish toward vpL or vpR. Diagonals establish the depth of faces.

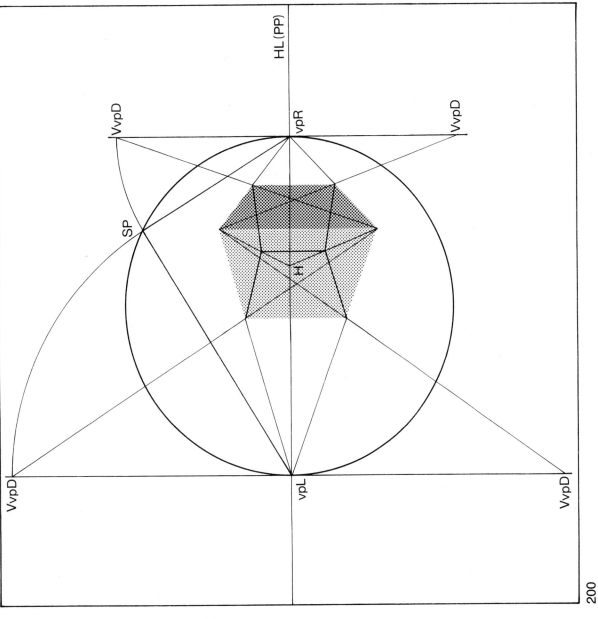

200

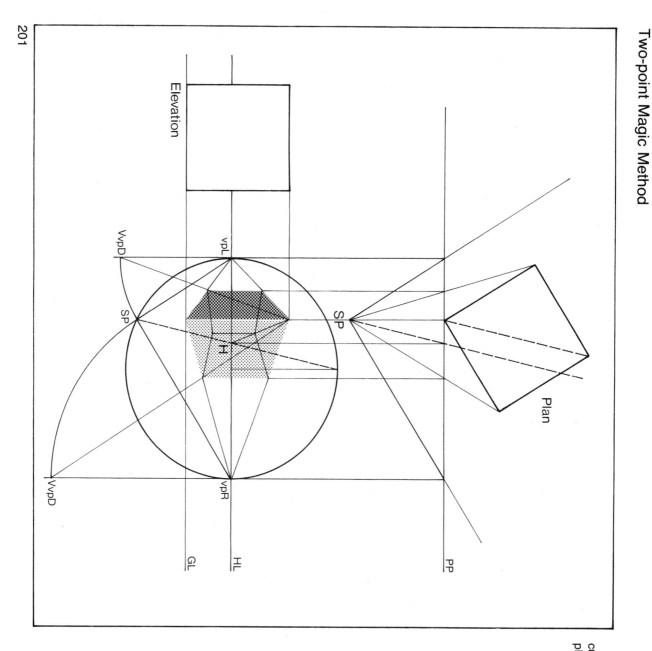

Elevation

Plan

VvpD

vpL

SP

SP

H

VvpD

vpR

GL

HL

PP

To show the precision of the magic-method approach, the cube (page 157) is worked backward so that it projects from a plan and elevation (201).

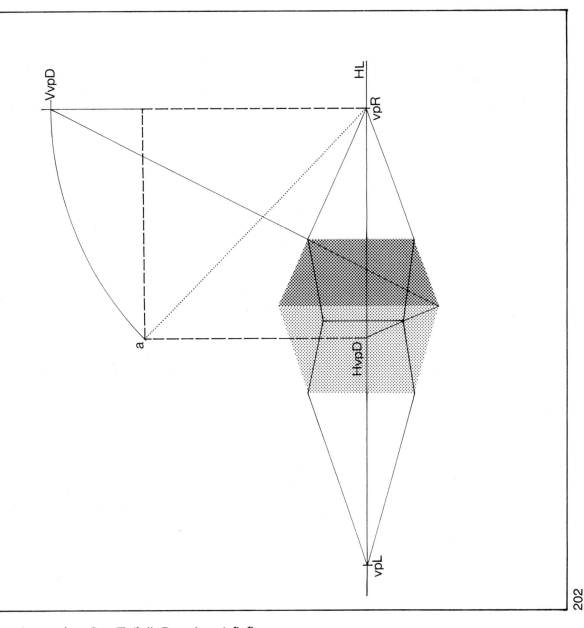

45° Shortcut

The perspective setup can be simplified when cubes are oriented at a 45° angle to the picture plane (202).

1. Construct a horizon line.

2. Locate HvpD—the vanishing point for horizontal-diagonals—toward the middle of the horizon line.

3. Locate vpL and vpR at equal distances from HvpD on the horizon line.

4. To locate VvpD, construct the square with corner labeled A. The base of the square is line HvpD-vpR. With vpR as its center, swing an arc through point A. The point where this arc intersects a vertical line extending through vpR marks the location of VvpD.

5. Construct a cube in perspective. To prevent distortion, center this construction midway between vpL and vpR.

Horizontal edges of the cube vanish toward vpL and vpR. The diagonals to squares oriented parallel to the ground plane vanish toward HvpD. The diagonals to vertical faces of the cube that orient toward vpR vanish toward VvpD.

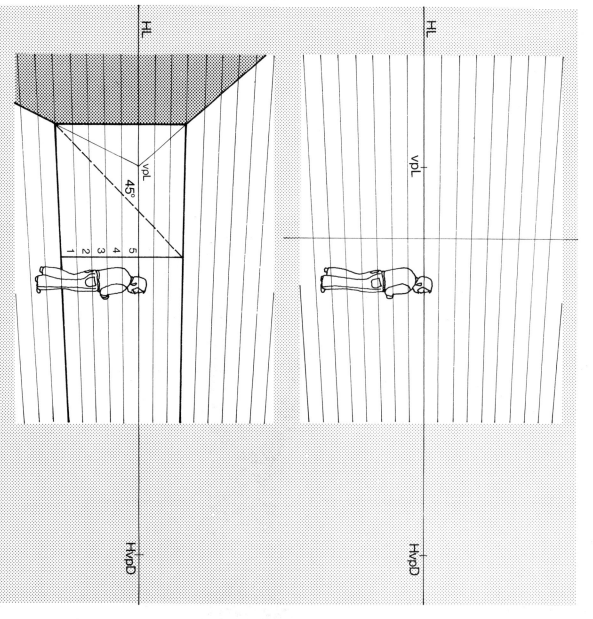

Sketch Method

The size of the drawing-board surface often restricts the range of workable plan orientations for two-point exterior and interior perspectives. This is because plan views that are not oriented parallel to the picture plane often contain one vanishing point that falls well beyond the edge of most drafting-board surfaces.

Several perspective methods and devices are designed to compensate for this far-away vanishing point. The magic two-point sketch method (203, 204), while not precise, handles the problem of the remote vanishing point with a technique of constructing sets of tapering lines. Here is the setup and procedure for drawing an interior magic two-point sketch-method perspective.

1. Draw a horizon line. Construct a light vertical line through the center of this horizon line.

2. Construct two vertical edges to define the left and right boundaries of the perspective. Locate these edges at equal distances from the center vertical.

3. Locate vpL on the horizon line. Position vpL slightly less than halfway from the center vertical to the left perspective boundary.

4. Locate HvpD on the horizon line. Make the distance from the center vertical to HvpD at least as great as the total width of the perspective.

5. Construct a set of lines that tapers toward the far-away right vanishing point. Use a calipers to do this. Set the calipers for a specific increment of height—usually 1' or 2'. Walk the calipers up and down from the horizon line along the left vertical edge of the picture frame. Slightly close the calipers and walk up and down from the horizon line along the right vertical edge of the picture frame. Connect the calipered points together to form a set of lines that gradually tapers toward the far-away right vanishing point.

6. Construct a measuring-plane wall that vanishes toward vpR. Use the spacing of the tapered lines as a guide for the height of this wall.

7. Draw a wall that vanishes toward vpL.

8. With a 45° triangle draw a diagonal across the measuring-plane wall. This forms a square on the wall.

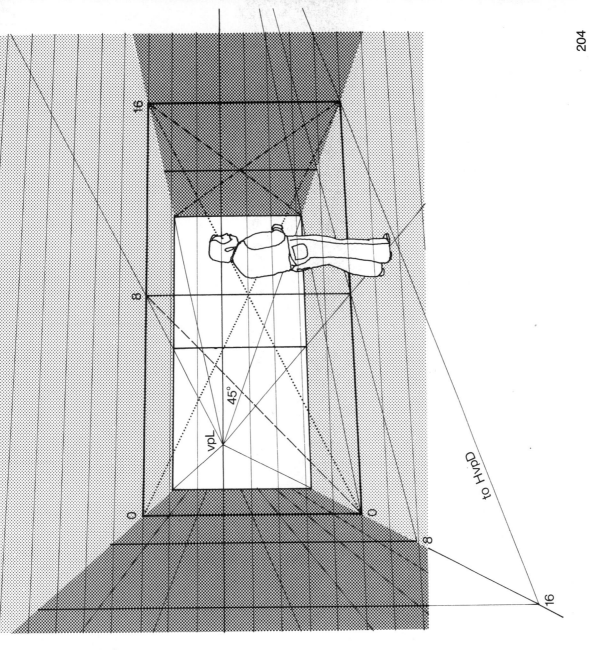

9. Transfer the width of the square on the measuring-plane wall to the wall vanishing toward vpL. Use HvpD to draw a diagonal through the base of the square. Its intersection with the base of the wall vanishing toward vpL marks the perspective depth of the square.

10. To locate other walls and other depths, use the halfway method (page 169).

11. To locate objects such as tables and chairs in perspective, draw their silhouettes on the ground plane. Project these silhouettes up to their perspective heights.

204

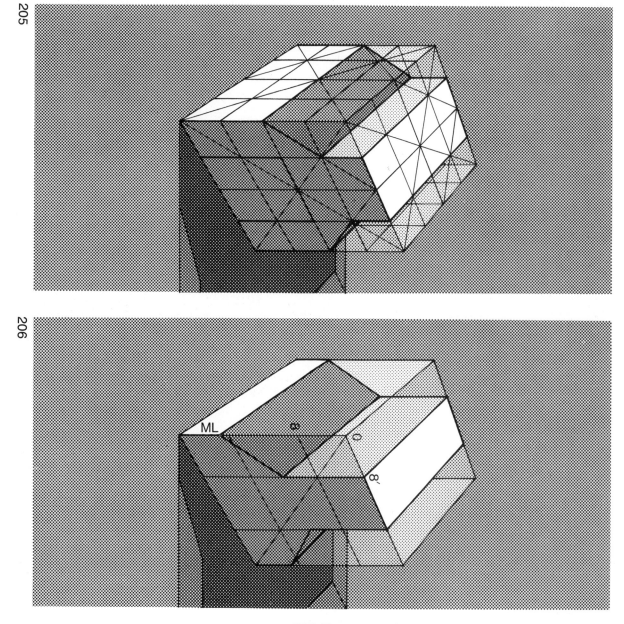

205

206

Subdividing and Extending the Cube

To render the finished form of a building or environment within the context of two-point cubes, subdivide or extend these cubes, applying one of the following techniques. Detailed explanations are given later (pages 168, 169).

Halfway Subdividing Technique

Construct grids on the faces of the cube. Locate the building within the fabric of these grids (205).

Proportional-division Subdividing Technique

To measure specific perspective depths on the two leading faces of a cube, let the front vertical edge of the cube serve as a measuring line (206).

From point 0, construct diagonals on the two faces that recede from the measuring line. Beginning at point 0, scale desired perspective depths along the measuring line. Project depths back toward vpL or vpR. Their intersections with face diagonals pinpoint specific perspective depths. Construct vertical lines through these pinpointed locations.

Extending Technique

Extend cubes by doubling the width of their faces. To double the width of the cube, find the midpoint of an edge. Construct a diagonal through this midpoint. The intersection of the diagonal with an extended edge of the face marks the doubled length of the face (207).

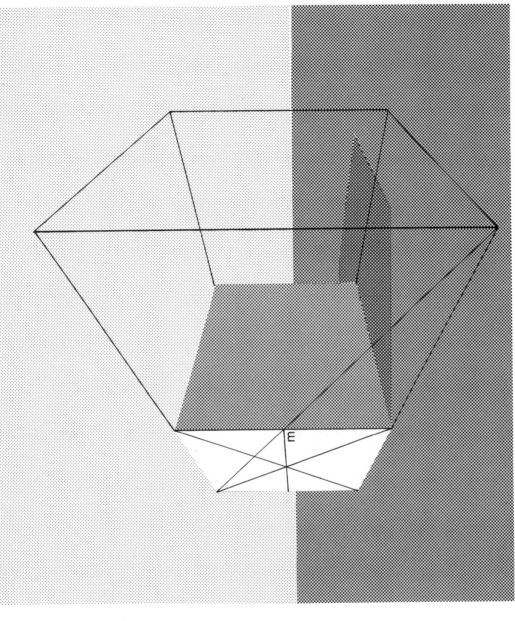

207

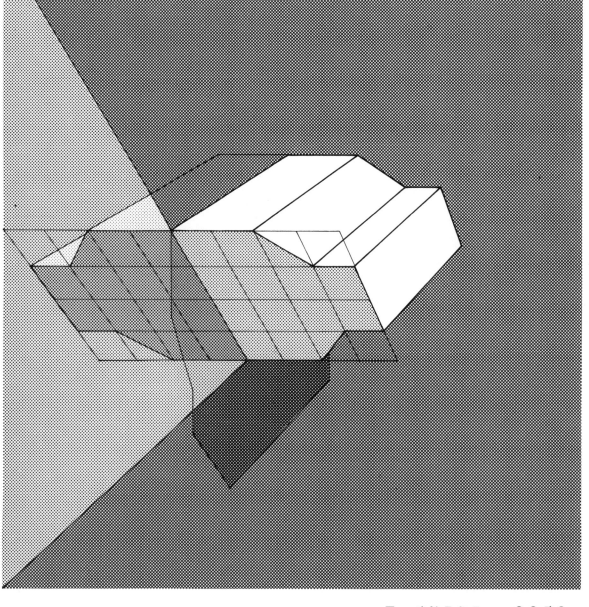

The following general rule applies to all reflection drawings: objects reflect symmetrically across the plane of reflective surfaces. Mirrors, windows, and placid mountain lakes are examples of reflective surface planes. Here is the typical procedure for drawing a building's reflection in perspective.

1. Think of the building as a pattern of points.

2. Project each point perpendicularly across the plane of the reflective surface. A simple point and its reflection must be located at equal distances from the reflective surface. When projectors do not vanish in perspective, measure true scale distances (208, 209). For projectors that vanish in perspective measure perspective distances.

3. Connect the reflected points together to form the completed pattern of the building's reflection (208).

Extending the Plane of Reflection

A point and its reflection must be located at equal distances from the surface of the reflective plane. The plane of the reflective surface must sometimes be extended in order to find the reflection of points.

The U-shaped object (209) rests on a bank that is higher than the reflective surface. To find its reflection in the pool, extend the base of the structure down to a temporary extension of the reflective surface plane. Project points across the extended surface of reflection. Connect the reflected points to form the pattern of the reflected object in the pond.

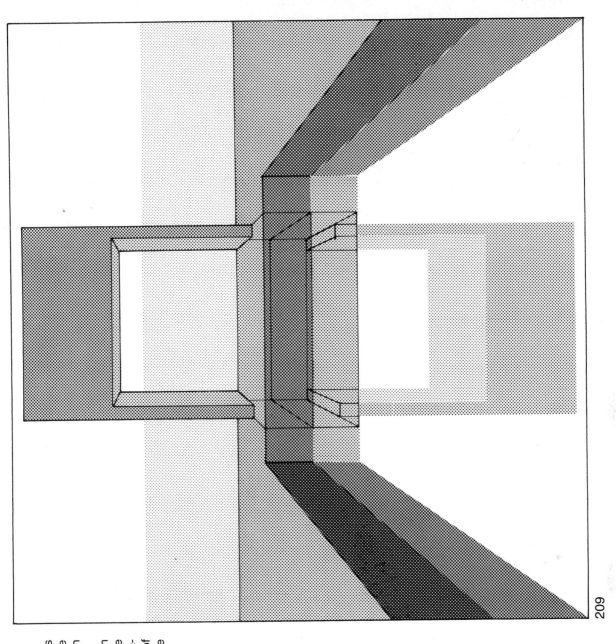

209

166

212

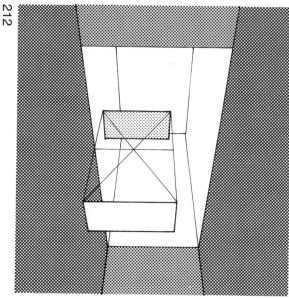

210

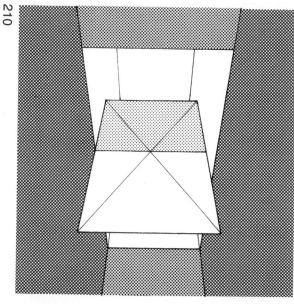

213

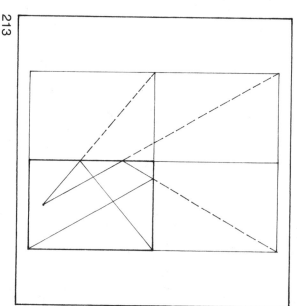

211

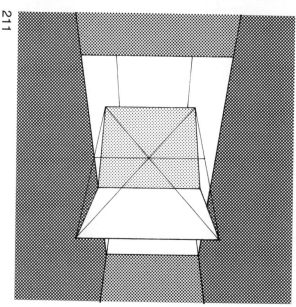

Vertical Reflective Surfaces

The reflections of three planes are illustrated here (210-212). In each case points defining the planes were reflected perpendicularly across the plane of the mirrored vertical surface. The reflective depth of each point was found by using the halfway proportioning method.

Double Reflections

The reflection of a space with two mirrored walls is shown here (214). The room appears four times as large as its actual size.

Two of the three rooms in reflection are easily found by applying the basic procedure (page 164). The third reflected room—the room that lies along the ceiling diagonal—is the result of a double reflection. The room and its reflections are depicted in plan view (213). In this plan site lines from SP to real corners of the room bounce or reflect off mirrored surfaces in the same manner as bank or cushion shots in pocket billiards, always forming equal angles on both sides of the bounce. The site lines for the reflected images of the room that extend straight back and to the left are like single-cushion billiard shots. For double reflections site lines from SP make two equal-angled bounces—one off each mirrored surface—before reaching the real corners of the room.

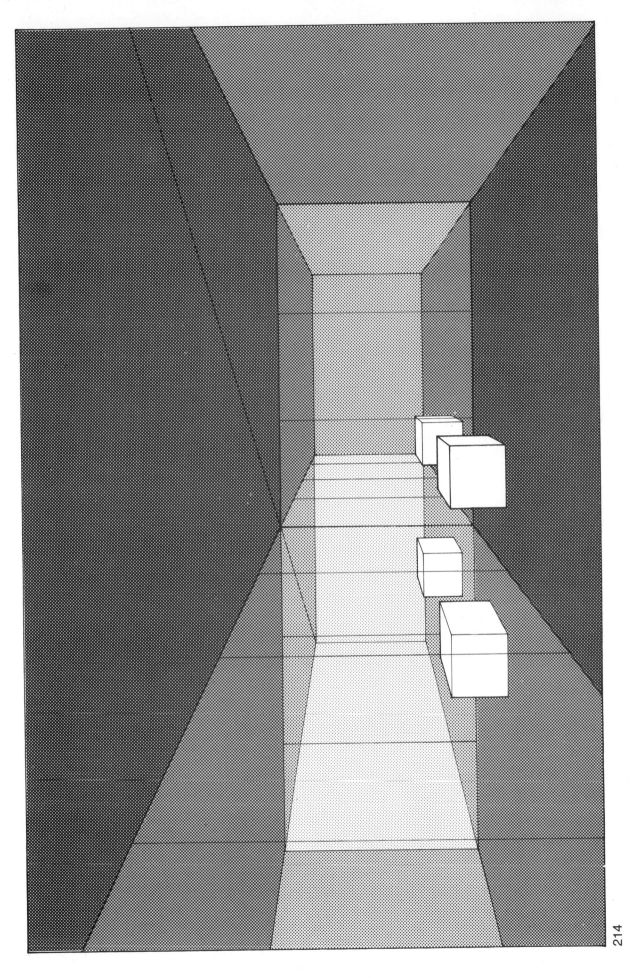

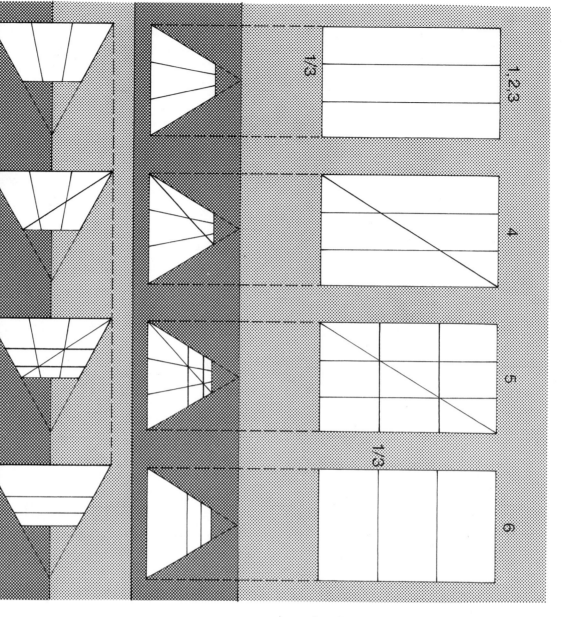

215

1,2,3   4   5   6

1/3   1/3

Proportional Divisions

Here is how to proportionally divide perspective lines into several equal or unequal parts (215).

1. Begin with a rectangular plane in perspective. Two of its edges must not vanish in perspective.

2. Divide the leading edge of the plane into several equal or unequal parts.

3. Project these divisions back toward the vanishing point.

4. Draw a diagonal through the rectangle.

5. Construct lines parallel to the leading edge of the rectangle through points where the diagonal intersects the vanishing lines.

6. The perspective depth of these lines is proportional to the divisions along the leading edge of the rectangle.

For square rectangles perspective depths equal the distances marked off on the frontal edge of the square.

Halving and Doubling Perspective Depth

Here is how to halve the perspective depth of a plane (216).

1. Begin with a rectangular plane.
2. Draw diagonals.
3. Draw a line through the intersection of the diagonals.
4. This line divides the plane into halves.

Here is how to double the depth of a plane (217).

5. Completed halved plane.
6. Draw diagonals.
7. Draw a line through the intersection of the diagonals.
8. Draw a diagonal from a corner of the plane through the point where the line through its diagonals meets an edge of the plane.
9. The intersection of this diagonal and an extended edge of the plane marks the doubled depth of the plane in perspective.
10. Completed doubled plane.

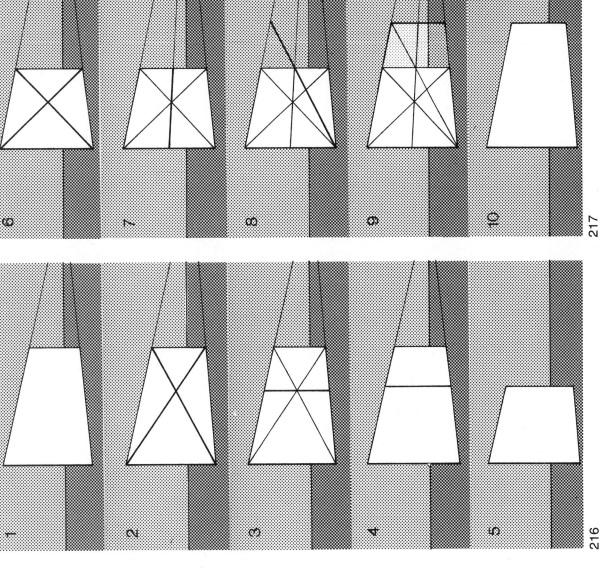

216

217

169

Twelve-point-perspective Circle

Big perspective circles can be quickly plotted in perspective using the twelve-point-circle technique. Here is how to construct a twelve-point circle in perspective (218).

1. Divide a square containing the circle into sixteen smaller squares.

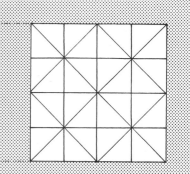

2. Draw lines from each of the four corners of the surrounding square to the far corners of the smaller squares. Draw eight lines in all. The first intersection of a line from a corner with the edge of a smaller square marks a point on the circle. Eight such intersections are possible.

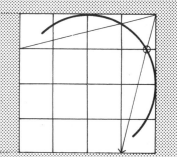

3. The remaining four points on the circle are located at the midpoints along the sides of the surrounding square. These are the four points where the circle is tangent to the square.

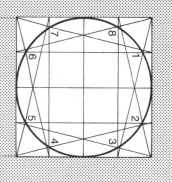

4. After each of the twelve points defining the circle is plotted, connect the points together with a smooth and continuous curve.

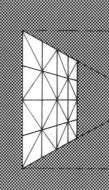
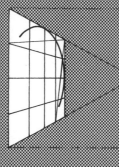
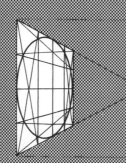
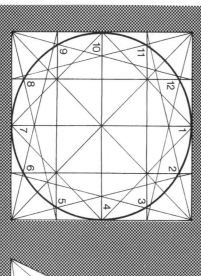
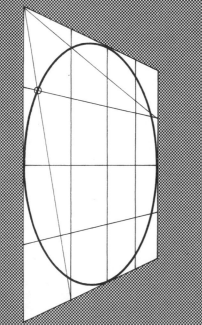

Compact Perspective Setup

To reduce the size of the work area required for drawing one- and two-point common-method perspectives, crowd the plan and elevation under the sheet used for the perspective drawing (219).

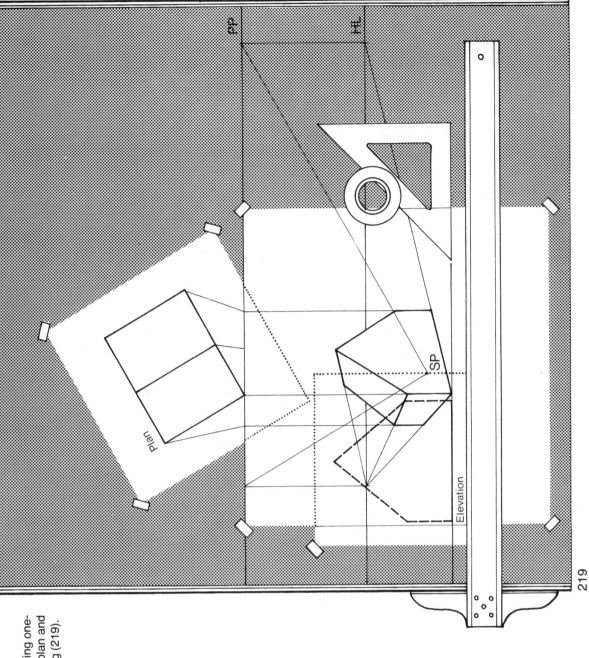

219

Vanishing Points for Sloping Lines

The vanishing point for sloping or nonhorizontal parallel object lines is located above or below the horizon line. Here is the procedure for finding the vanishing point for a set of parallel sloping lines (220).

1. Find the vanishing point for the plan direction of the sloping lines. Locate this vanishing point on the horizon line. Label it vpH.

2. Draw a light vertical line through vpH. The vanishing point for the sloping lines lies somewhere along this vertical.

3. With point X as its center, swing an arc from SP to point M on the picture plane. Transfer point M to the horizon line.

4. Construct a ray, measured at the true vertical angle of the sloping lines, from point M on the horizon line to the vertical line through vpH. Measure this true vertical angle above the horizon line for lines that slope up as they go back into perspective. Measure the true vertical angle below the horizon line for lines that slope down as they go back into perspective. The intersection of the true vertical angle with the vertical line through vpH marks the location of the vanishing point, labeled vpS, for the sloping lines.

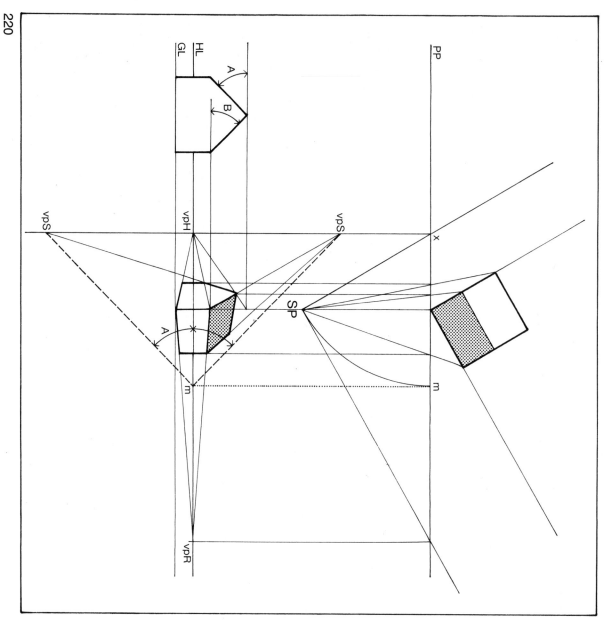

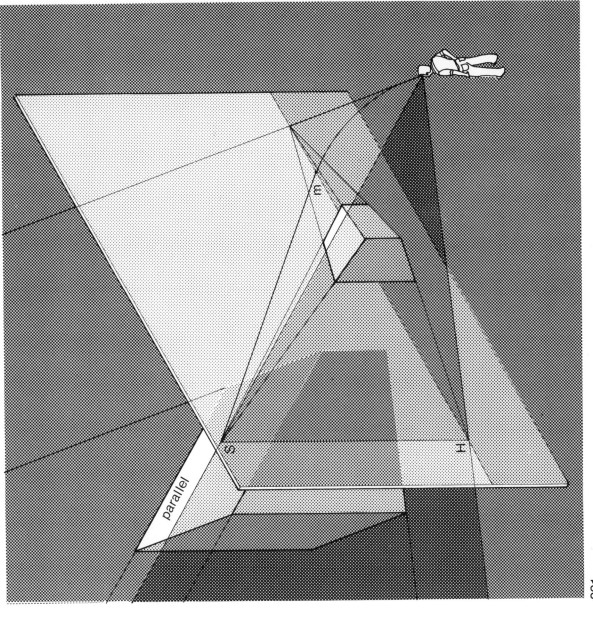

221

The procedure for finding the vanishing point for sloping edges is based on the revolving-hinge principle. The site line through SP that is parallel to the sloping edges of the shed-roof garage intersects the picture plane above the horizon line (221). This intersection marks the vanishing point for the garage's sloping edges.

In the procedure for constructing the vanishing point for sloping edges this vanishing point is located by revolving the triangular wedge with its tip at SP about the vertical trace through vpH, which serves as its hinge, until it meets the picture plane. Since the triangle retains its true size and shape through the swing, the true vertical angle of the sloping light rays is not affected in its revolved shift to the surface of the picture plane, where it can be measured directly.

173

Shadows

Shadow is the silent sidekick of light. It sneaks down stairs, slides across walls, and hides under things. An integral part of our perception of the world, shadow is everywhere.

An understanding of light and shadow fundamentals is a vital tool in architectural design and presentation.

In the design phase a building's light and shadow behavior should be considered. For example, in some climates shadows cast by buildings into public areas such as plazas create a cold and uncomfortable atmosphere. In a warmer climate a building's shadow may conversely be a welcome relief to a midday pedestrian. Shadow patterns also influence a building in terms of solar design.

In the presentation stage shadows cast on plan and elevation drawings enhance the illustion of depth. For example, drawings with shadows are more easily understood by a client than the more abstract and unfamiliar three-dimensional oblique drawing.

In reality an ornate Victorian column is modeled by light. Shadow describes the column's depth and detail of ornamentation, radius of curvature, and texture. A drawing of that column can describe the same characteristics if shadows are depicted.

The intent of this chapter is to establish basic shadow-construction techniques. The first portion defines a vocabulary and outlines fundamental rules. The second portion discusses specific shadow-construction techniques for multiview, paraline, and perspective drawings.

A shadow vocabulary is needed before attempting shadow construction. A few of the basic terms are discussed below.

Parallel Light Rays

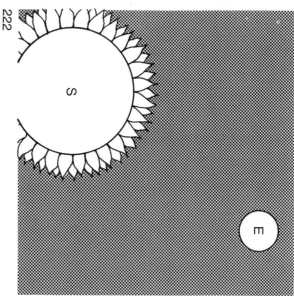

222

The earth's radius of orbit around the sun is approximately 93,000,000 million miles—nearly 150,000,000 kilometers (222). At this distance any two imaginary light rays reaching the earth are considered to be parallel. In drawing shadows the sun's light rays are drawn as parallel lines.

Sun Angles

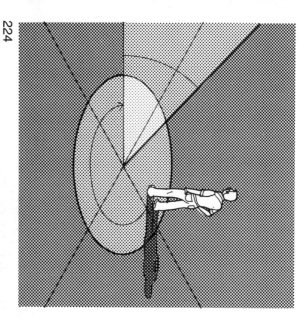

224

Two basic angles are required to describe the specific direction of the sun's rays (224).

Bearing or Azimuth Angle

Bearing or azimuth angles describe the plan direction of the sun's rays (223). Conventions for expressing bearing angles were described earlier (page 64).

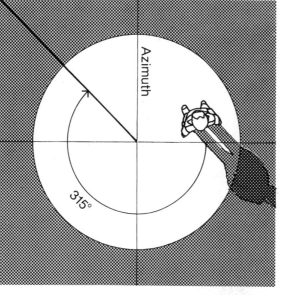

223

Altitude Angle

Altitude angles describe the true vertical angle formed by the intersection of a light ray and the horizontal plane (225).

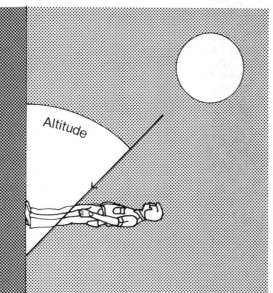

225

Shade

A shaded area occurs on the dark backside of a sunlit object (226). It receives no direct light. The edge that divides the shaded surface from the lighted surface determines the boundary of the shadow that is cast by the object.

Shadow

A shadow is a naturally projected image of an object's shaded area (226). Shadow areas also receive no direct light; light rays are blocked by an object, and the result is a dark shadow cast on a lighted surface.

Casting Edge

The casting edge separates the surface in sunlight from the surface in shade (227).

Shadow Line

Shadow lines separate surfaces in sunlight from areas in shadow (227).

Rays

Actual Rays (A)

Actual rays project directly from the sun. They refer more generally to the actual rays from any light source (228-230).

Bearing Rays (B)

Bearing rays are horizontal rays that point in the bearing or plan direction of actual sun rays (228-230). They are the horizontal component of actual rays.

Cut Rays (C)

Cut rays are inclined rays that point in the bearing direction of actual sun rays (228-230). They can be constructed at any altitude, provided that they aim in the bearing direction of the actual ray. Cut rays are useful for constructing shadows on inclined surfaces.

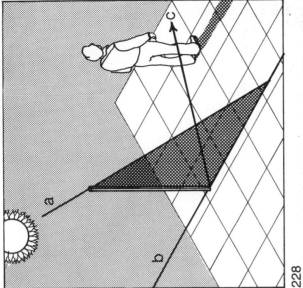

228

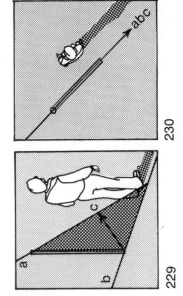

230

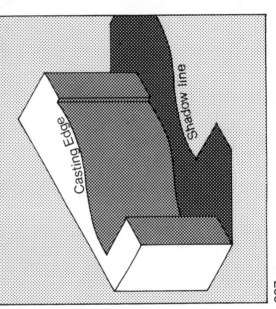

229

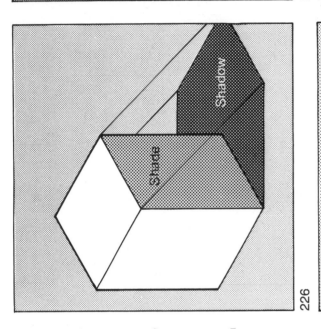

226

227

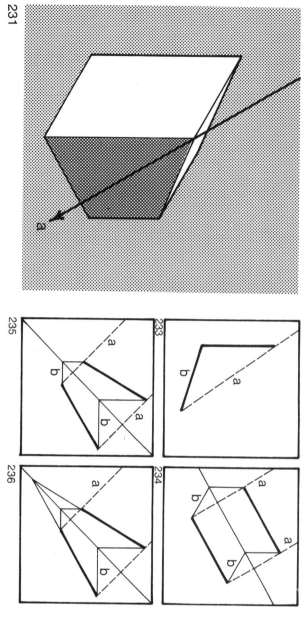

232

231

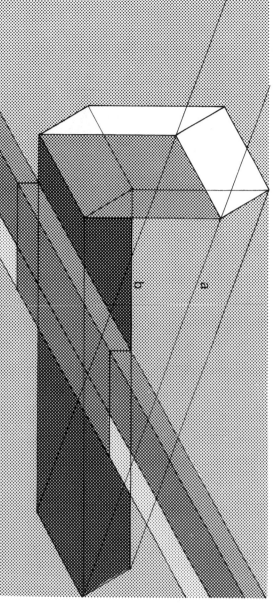

235

233

236

234

Shadow of a Point

The shadow of a point on an object must fall somewhere along the actual ray through the point (231). To find where the point's actual ray strikes another surface involves the construction of bearing and cut rays along existing surfaces or the imaginary extension of existing surfaces until the point's actual ray is intersected (232).

Shadow of a Line

To find the shadow of a line, locate the shadow of its end points. The shadows of lines or edges or horizontal surfaces can be constructed by following these simple rules.

1. The shadow of a vertical line on a horizontal surface lies along the bearing ray through the base of the line (233). The intersection of the bearing ray and an actual ray through the top of the line marks the end point of this shadow.

2. When a line and a surface are parallel, the shadow of the line on the surface is parallel to the line (234).

3. When a line and a surface are not parallel, the line's shadow on the surface is not parallel to the line (235). If the line is projected to intersect the surface, the line and its shadow meet at a common point on the surface (236).

All shadow construction, regardless of its complexity, must answer the basic question about every point that casts a shadow: where does the actual ray through a point strike another surface? Shadow construction involves answering this question over and over.

The following basic constructions are often used to solve shadow castings.

Shadow Box

The shadow of a line or an edge on a vertical wall can be found by constructing a shadow box (237). The true diagonal to a shadow box is always an actual light ray. The diagonals across its upper and lower faces are bearing rays. Construct the shadow box so that one of its upper edges contains the line or edge casting the shadow. The diagonal on the back face of the shadow box is the shadow of the line or edge on the vertical wall.

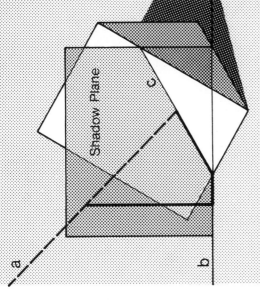

237

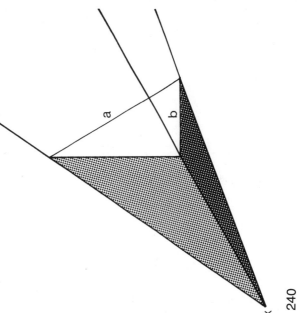

239

Shadow Plane

Shadow planes are imaginary vertical surfaces that slice through buildings and their surroundings in the bearing direction of sunlight (239). All actual, bearing, and cut rays that can be constructed to find the shadow of a point are by definition, confined to the surface of the shadow plane containing that point.

To find the shadow of a point, transfer the point along real or imaginary contours contained within the shadow plane until the actual ray through the point is intersected.

Shadow Wedge

If a line intersects a surface, the shadow of the line on the surface begins where they meet (238, 240).

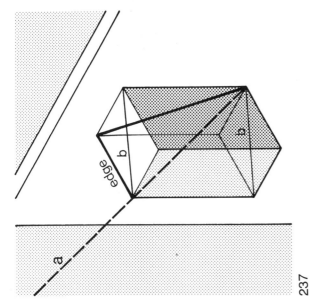

238

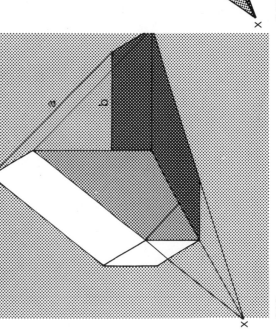

240

The following analogies may help to understand how shadow construction works. A total shadow configuration is often thought of as a composite of the shadows of its individual parts.

Inky-putty-infill Analogy

Imagine that areas not in sunlight are filled with inky putty (241). Remove the putty—the remaining inky surfaces are in shade and shadow (243).

Stick Analogy

Imagine that vertical edges are actually sticks or poles (242). Cast the shadows for sticks and connect their end points together.

Melting-plastic-triangle Analogy

Fix plastic triangles to vertical edges (244). Let their bottom edges melt to fit the terrain (245). The profiles of their melted bottoms are the shadows for vertical edges. Connect the tips of the triangles together to form the completed shadow. The drawings (page 181) illustrate magic melting triangles at work. The bottoms of the two larger triangles have melted to fit the embankment.

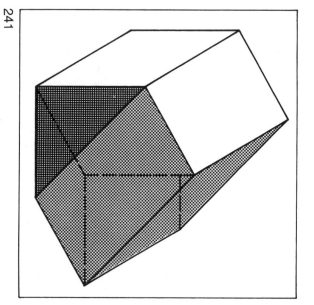

241

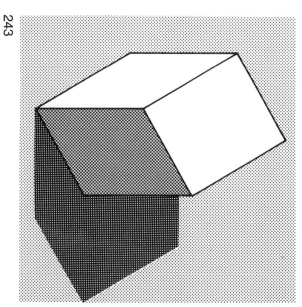

243

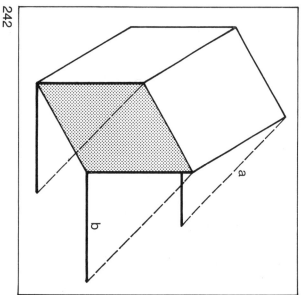

242

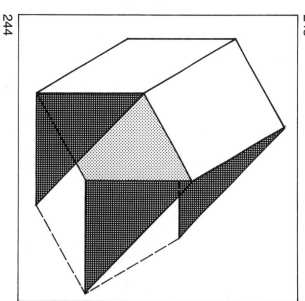

244

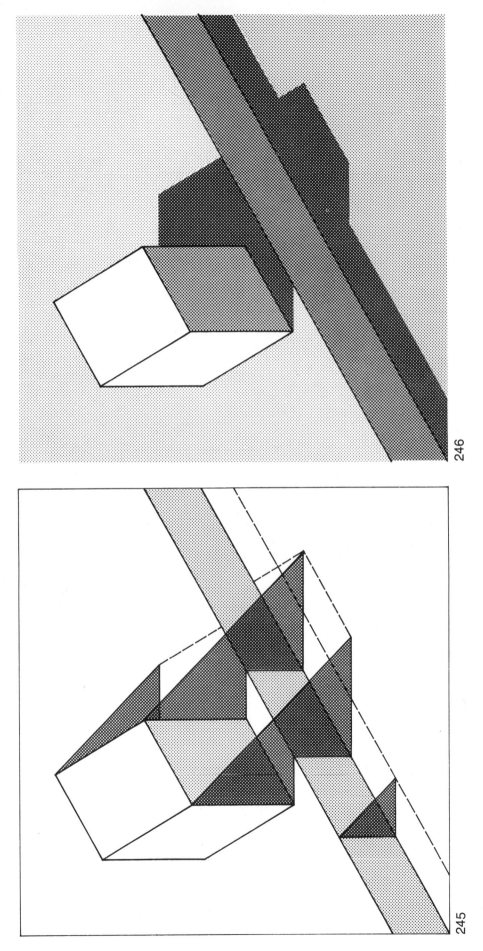

245

246

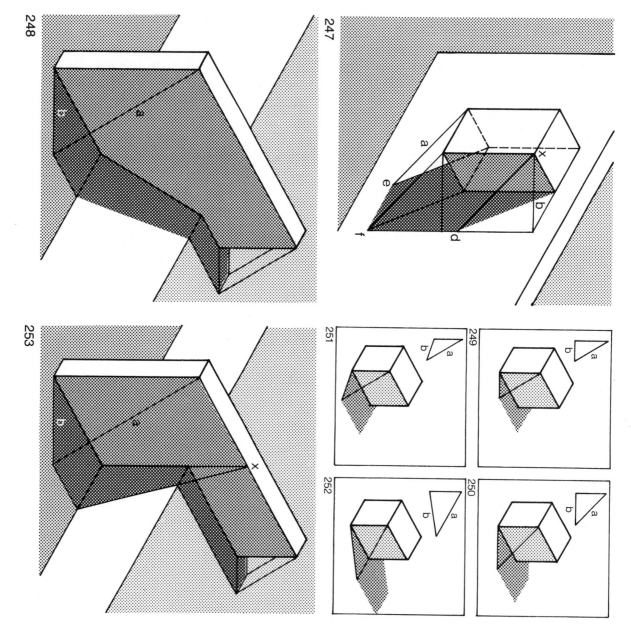

247

248

253

249

250

251

252

Constructing shadows in paraline provides a quick and understandable look at the behavior of actual, bearing, and cut rays. Remember that parallel lines remain parallel in paraline drawings. This rule applies to parallel actual and bearing rays as well.

Simple Shadows

The four small drawings (249-252) illustrate a simple method of casting shadows in a paraline drawing. The small triangle in the upper left-hand corner of each of the examples describes the actual and bearing direction of sunlight. The triangle's hypotenuse describes the direction of the sun's actual ray, and its base describes the direction of its bearing rays. All paraline shadow casting can be solved by using basic shadow constructions: the shadow of a point, the shadow of a line, shadow box, shadow plane, and shadow wedge. The following examples help to illustrate the behavior of shadows on different geometric configurations.

Block on a Wall

Construct a shadow box to find point d. Points e and f lie along parallels to line xd (247).

Wall on Stepped Ground

Cast the shadow of the wall on the upper and lower planes and connect the difference across the incline (248). The point labeled x is located at the apex of a shadow wedge (253).

Shadow Strategy

A solution to a shadow problem often requires looking at the whole problem and developing a strategy for construction. A single problem may involve separate shadow constructions.

Inside Walls

To find the shadows on interior vertical surfaces such as hollowed structures (254), lightly construct the edges defining the inside walls. Cast the shadows for these walls as if they were located outside. Construct a shadow box to find the shadow line darting across the far inside wall of each structure.

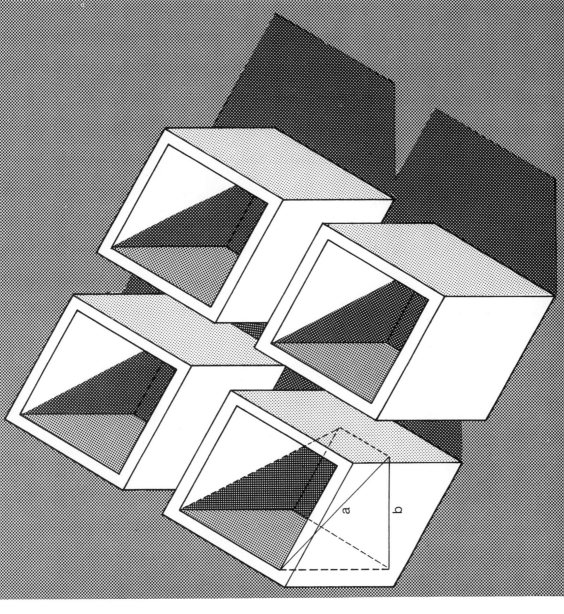

254

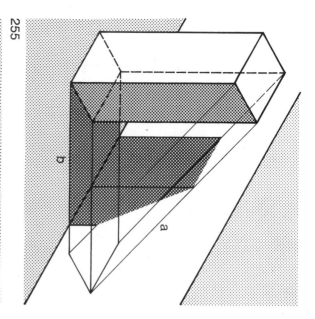

255

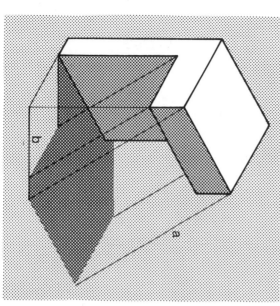

256

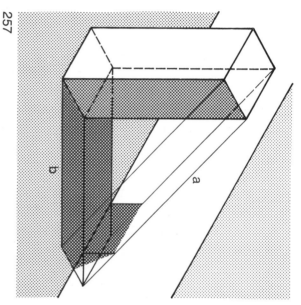

257

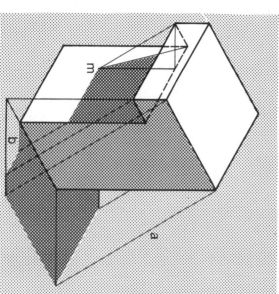

258

Block on Wall

The strategy for this problem (255, 257) involves first ignoring a part of the drawing and then remembering it and adjusting the shadow so that it is correct.

First ignore the wall and cast the shadow of the block on the ground plane. Remember to note where the block's bearing rays meet the wall and draw vertical lines through their intersections. The points where these vertical lines meet the block's actual rays mark the corners of the block's shadow on the wall.

Overhang

The strategy for this problem (256, 258) is to imagine that the drawing is more than it actually is. Imagine that the entire overhang structure is actually a solid block and cast the shadow for the solid block. Carve out the block to obtain the original configuration of the overhang. Subtract the excess portions of the shadow. Construct a shadow box to find the shadow for point m (258).

Block on Wedge

The problem here (259, 261) is to find where the block's actual rays strike the inclined surface. To do this, use shadow planes that slice the wedge like a loaf of bread in the bearing direction of light. Align these vertical slices in the planes of the block's actual rays. Actual rays strike the surface of the inclined block where they meet cut rays. The shadow of the block on the inclined surface becomes a connect-the-dots exercise.

Block on Block

This is an ignore-remember strategy and an imaginary-ground-plane problem (260, 262). Ignore the reclining block and cast the shadow of the tall block on the ground plane. Remembering the reclining plane, imagine that the ground plane for the tall block is at the height of the top surface of the reclining block. Cast the shadow for the tall block on the imaginary ground plane. Retain the shadows that fall on the real and visible surfaces. Part of the tall block's shadow falls on the ground plane and part on the horizontal surface of the reclining block. To complete the shadow, connect these shadows together across the vertical surface of the reclining block.

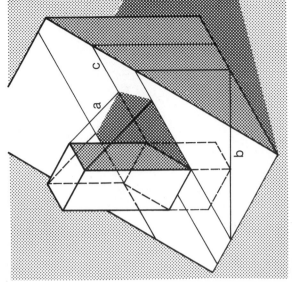

259

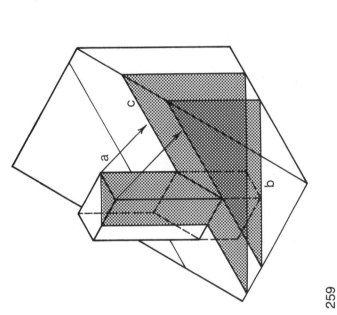

261

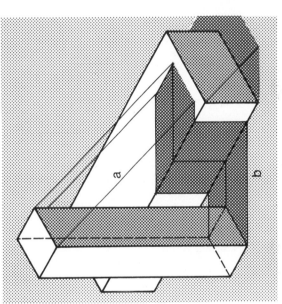

260

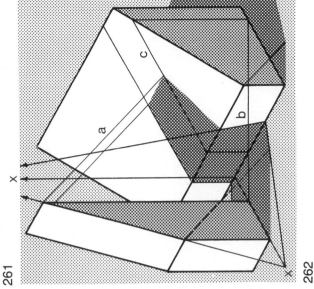

262

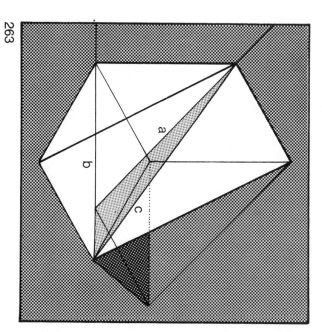

263

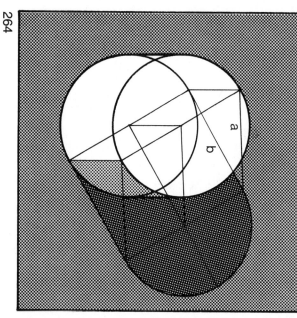

264

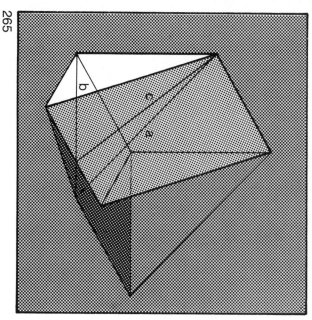

265

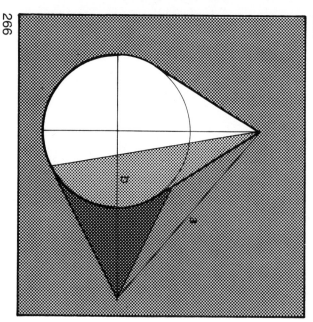

266

Wedge

Slice the wedge with a shadow plane. Using this shadow plane, compare the angle of the actual ray to the angle of the wedge's outline. If the angle of the wedge's incline is steeper than the angle of the sun's actual ray to the angle of the sunlight (263). If the angle of the wedge's incline, the wedge's inclined surface is in the angle of the wedge's incline, the wedge's inclined surface is in shade (265).

Cylinder

The shadow of a cylinder on a horizontal ground plane is the slipped profile of its casting edge (264).

Cone

Find the shadow of the cone tip on the ground plane (266). Find the shadow of the whole cone on the ground plane. Construct tangents from the base of the cone to the shadow of its tip. To define the shade side of the cone, construct lines from tangents at the base to the tip of the cone. More than half the cone's surface should be in sunlight.

Stairs

Compared to buildings, stairs are fairly small objects, but these small objects made up of a multitude of simple shadows. The time required to cast shadows on a simple stairway often exceeds the time required to cast the shadow for the entire building. Stairway shadows require time and patience for accurate construction. Here are a couple of tips for casting shadows on stairways.

1. Find the shadows of railings at the base and top of the stairs and then work toward the middle (267, 268). When similar shadow patterns emerge at the top and bottom, fill in the same pattern on the middle stairs.

2. Tread and riser planes can sometimes be extended to find shadow wedges (268).

268

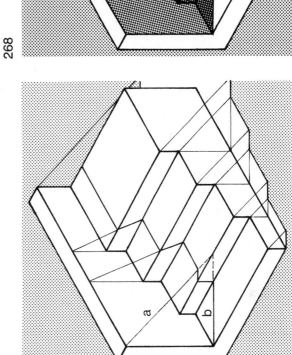

269

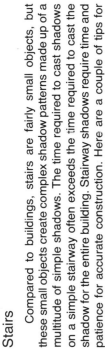

267

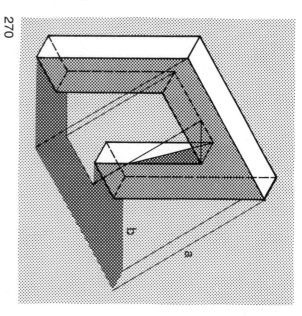

270

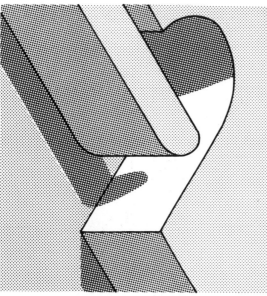

271

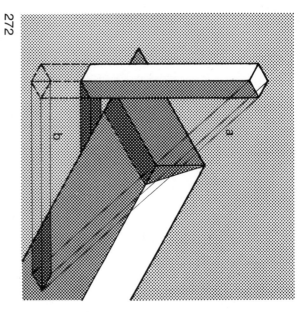

272

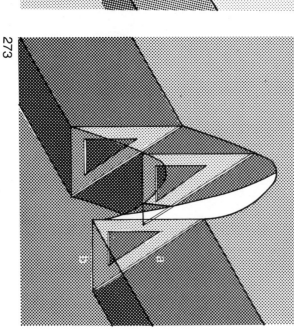

273

Hole in Wall

Cast the shadow for the whole plane and remove the hole (270). Of special interest is the thickness of the rectangular opening; part of its surface is in shadow. To find this shadow, construct a bearing ray on the underside of the opening. Draw an actual ray through the point where the bearing ray intersects the horizontal sunnyside edge of the opening. The intersection of the actual ray and the front vertical thickness edge marks the point at which this inside shadow line begins.

Ravines

Extend the base of the rectangular column down to the level of the ravine's floor (272). Cast the shadow of the column on the floor of the ravine.

Irregular Shapes

Break irregular forms down into points and find the shadows of the points. Use the plastic-triangle analogy to find intersections with vertical or inclined surfaces (273).

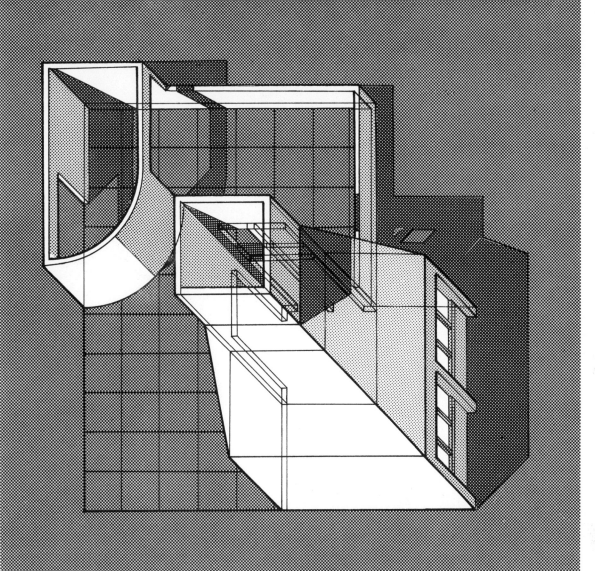

274

Complex Objects

Here is how to find the shadow of a complex object (274).
1. Break the object into simple shapes.
2. Find the shadows cast by each simple shape.
3. Draw the overall shadow configuration as a composite of the simple shadows.

Helpful Hints

When the intersection of actual and bearing or cut rays is not immediately evident or seemingly impossible, try constructing imaginary lines and planes as extensions of given lines and planes or simplify the drawing by taking away some of the surfaces. Replace them as the drawing is understood.

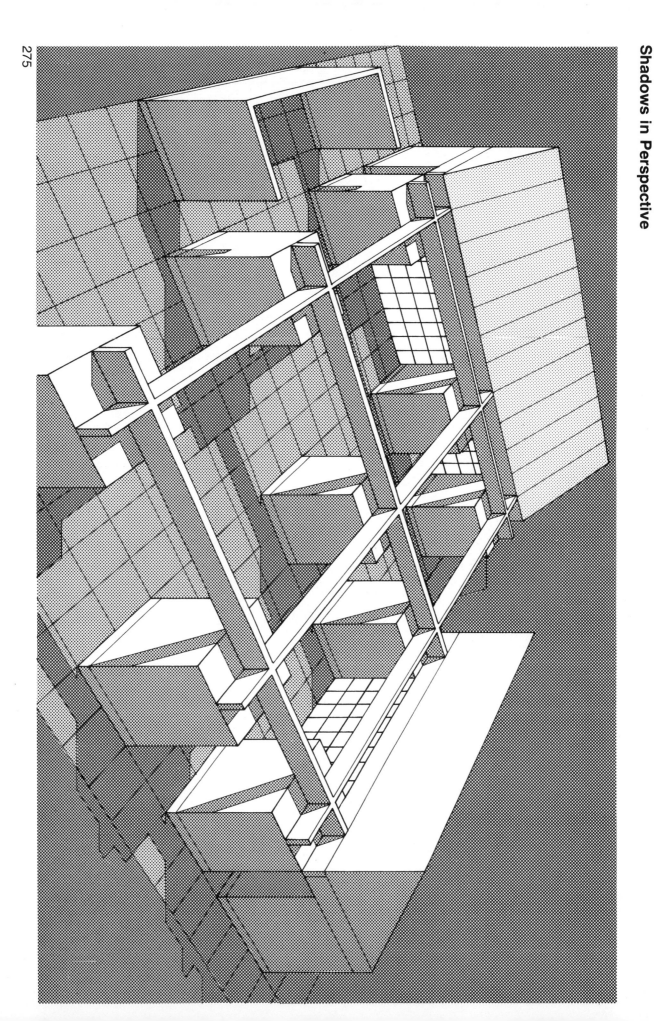

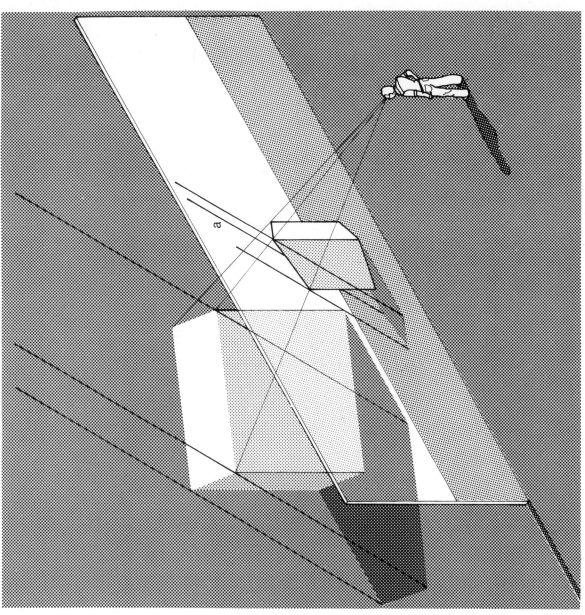

276

The techniques for casting shadows in perspective are identical to those for casting shadows in paraline. The difference is that the shadows must be constructed in perspective (275). This means that perspective construction techniques must be applied to actual, bearing, and cut rays, which sometimes have vanishing points. All the previously discussed ways of looking at shadow construction can be applied to drawing shadows in perspective: the inky-putty infill, magic plastic triangle, and stick analogies and the basic shadows of lines, shadow boxes, shadow wedges, and shadow planes.

The behavior of actual and bearing rays in perspective depends upon their relation to the picture plane. Two basic relationships are possible: actual and bearing rays can be oriented either parallel or oblique to the picture plane.

When actual and bearing rays are parallel to the picture plane, actual light rays are drawn parallel to each other in the perspective, and bearing lines are drawn parallel to the horizon line (276).

A different shadowcasting arrangement results when light rays are oriented oblique to the picture plane. In this situation actual and bearing rays appear to vanish in perspective.

The quickest and easiest method for casting shadows in perspective occurs when the light rays are parallel to the picture plane; this approach is discussed first.

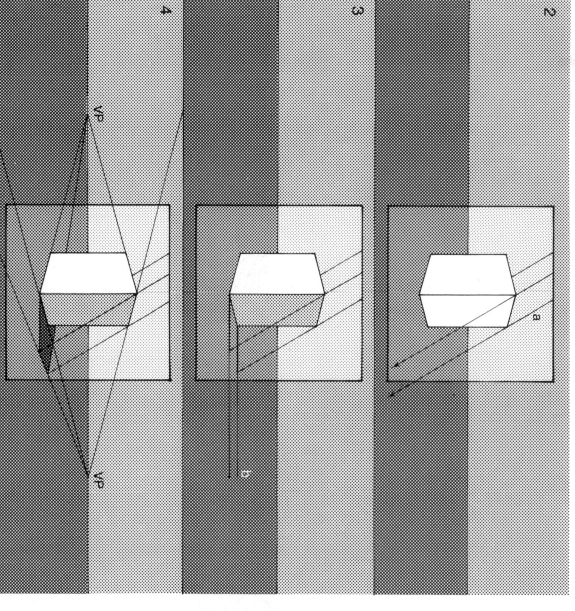

Light Rays Parallel to the Picture Plane

The sun's light rays can be arranged to orient either parallel or oblique to the picture plane. Each arrangement results in a distinctive set of rules for constructing actual and bearing rays in perspective. Here are the basic rules for constructing perspective shadows when light rays are parallel to the picture plane (277).

1. Avoid using one-point perspectives to illustrate shadows when the light rays are parallel to the picture plane. With few exceptions shadows in a one-point perspective tend to represent a building's form ambiguously.

2. Construct actual rays as true parallels in perspective.

3. Construct bearing rays in perspective as horizontal lines that are parallel to the horizon line.

4. Connect all the points where actual and bearing rays meet and look for shadow edges that share the building's vanishing points.

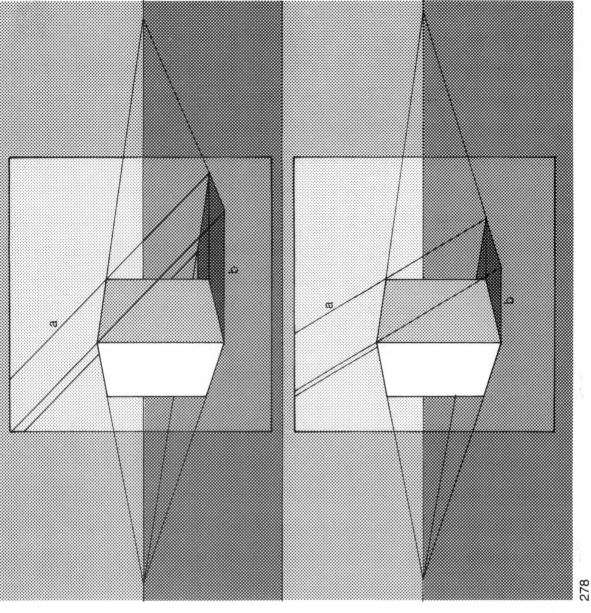

278

Shadows formed by light rays that are parallel to the picture plane fall from left to right or from right to left across the perspective visual field. They never appear to recede into the background or to advance toward the foreground of the perspective.

Varying the angle of the sun's actual rays results in longer or shorter shadowcastings (278). The angle that these actual rays forms with the horizontal plane expresses the true vertical altitude of the sun's rays. Since the sun is casting shadows parallel to the picture plane, the true bearing or plan direction of sunlight is the same as the orientation of the picture plane.

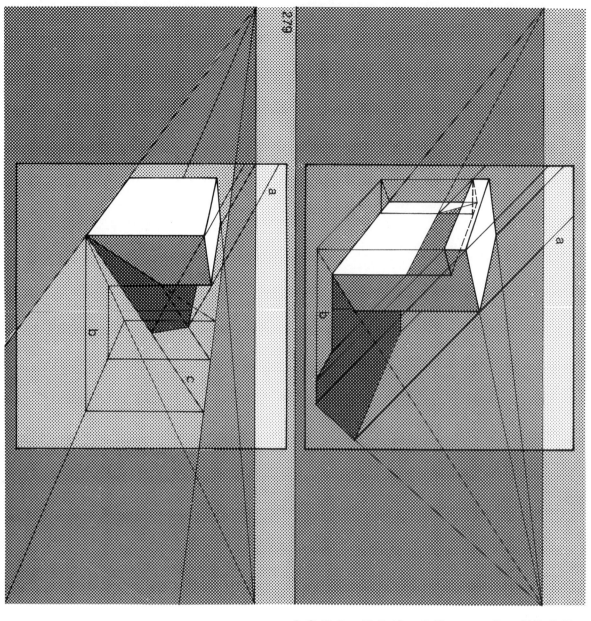

280

279

Here are two objects, an overhang construction (279) and a block on an incline (280), whose shadows were cast with light rays oriented parallel to the picture plane. The following set of rules for constructing actual, bearing, and cut rays should be followed for each shadowcasting.

1. Actual rays are constructed as true parallels in perspective.

2. Bearing rays are constructed parallel to the horizon line.

3. Cut rays are drawn as true parallels in perspective.

An object's horizontal edge and its shadow cast on a horizontal plane are in reality parallel; in perspective construction the edge and its shadow share a common vanishing point.

If the specific rules for casting shadows with light rays parallel to the picture plane are followed, any of the methods and techniques used to solve paraline shadow problems can be applied to perspective shadow problems.

The sloped embankment with the block was sliced like a loaf of bread (280). The profiles of these slices containing actual, bearing, and cut rays are used to locate the position where a pair of actual rays through two corners of the block would strike the embankment. Both slices are made parallel to the picture plane.

Light Rays Oblique to the Picture Plane

Actual, bearing, and cut rays do not vanish in perspective when they are oriented parallel to the picture plane. All these rays must vanish in perspective when they form oblique angles to the picture plane.

The following rules and observations govern the behavior of actual, bearing, and cut rays when they are oriented at oblique angles to the picture plane.

1. All bearing rays appear to vanish to a common vanishing point (vpB) on the perspective horizon line.

2. Actual rays always converge to a common vanishing point (vpA) that must be located somewhere along a vertical line passing through vpB perpendicular to the horizon line.

3. Cut rays must vanish somewhere along the same vertical line through vpB.

When vpA is positioned below vpB in the perspective setup, the sun is imagined to be shining over the shoulder of the viewer (SP) and shadows appear to extend back into perspective (281).

When vpA is positioned above vpB, the sun is located in front of the viewer (SP) and the shadows of objects are cast toward the foreground of the perspective (281).

The position of the sun moves higher into the sky and perspective shadows become shorter as vpA is located further away from vpB on the vertical extension line.

When the specific rules for casting shadows with light rays oblique to the picture plane are followed, any of the methods and techniques used for solving paraline shadow problems can be applied to perspective shadow problems.

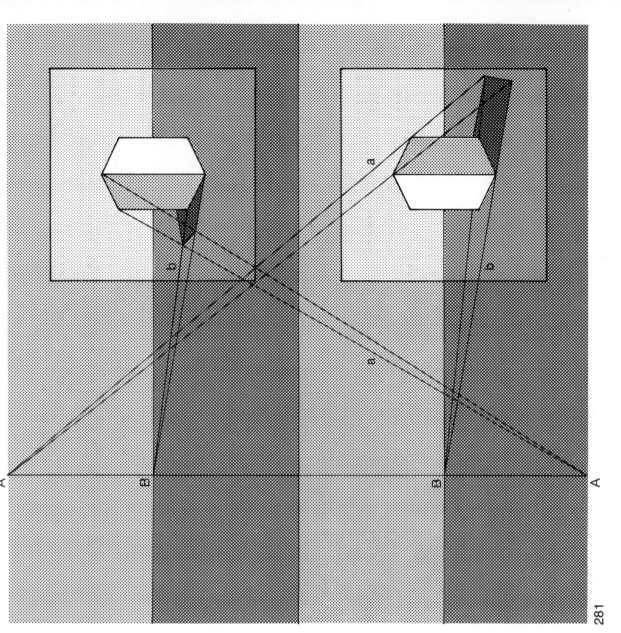

281

282

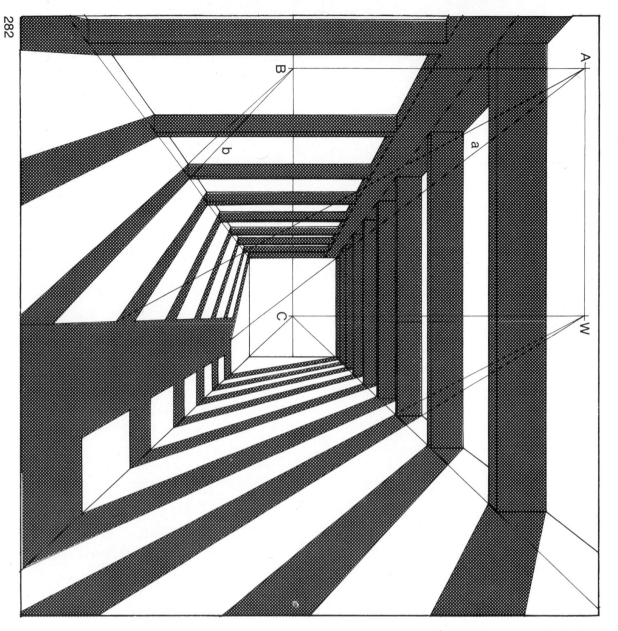

Special perspective shadow constructions are needed to lo-cate the vanishing points for the shadows of points and lines on vertical surfaces. These constructions are based on the shadow-box technique (page 179).

One-point Shadow Box

When an edge is oriented perpendicular to a vertical wall plane that vanishes toward C, the vanishing point (vpW) for the direction of the shadow of the edge on the wall plane lies at the intersection of a vertical ray through C and a horizontal ray through vpA (282).

Two-point Shadow Box

The vanishing point for the shadow of a line on a vertical surface lies at the intersection of line vpA-vpR and a vertical line through vpL (283).

The best way to understand the reasoning behind these constructions is to turn the perspective drawings on their sides.

For example, turn the perspective drawing (282) on its side. Imagine that line vpW-C is the horizon line. Vertical planes become horizontal planes, and vpW becomes the vanishing point for horizontal bearing rays. VpA, maintaining its fixed position in perspective, is located along a vertical line through vpW.

The same reasoning can be applied to a two-point perspective (283). Here, however, turning the drawing on its side results in a perspective whose vertical edges vanish toward vpR. The vertical through vpA must therefore also vanish toward vpR. Its intersection with the new horizon line (vpL–vpW) is vpW, the bearing-angle vanishing point.

283

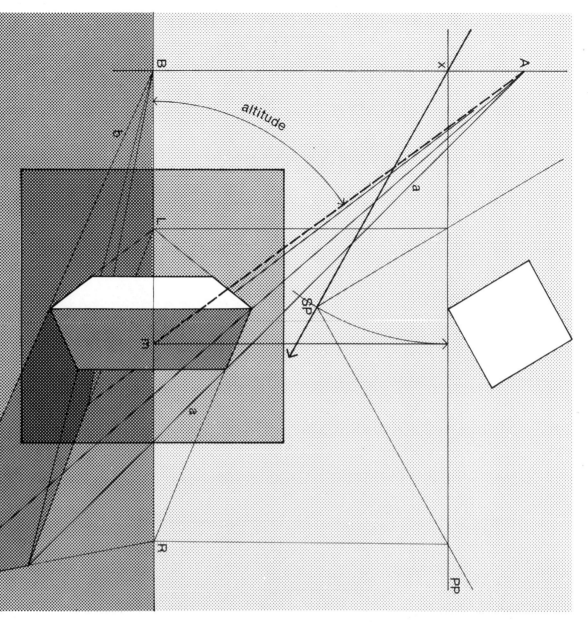

True Angles of Sun Rays

To measure the true bearing and altitude of the sun's rays in a perspective drawing, use the common-method setup (284, 285). The true orientation of the sun's actual and bearing rays can be measured in perspective as follows.

1. Mark where a line through SP in the bearing direction of sunlight intersects the picture plane and call this point x.

2. Tranfer this point of intersection down to the horizon line to locate vpB.

3. Swing an arc through SP about point x. Mark where the arc intersects the picture plane. Draw a vertical line from this point of intersection down to the horizon line to locate point m.

4. Construct a light vertical line through vpB. Extend a line from point m on the horizon line to this vertical line. Make the angle of this line through point m equal to the true altitude of the sun's rays. The intersection of the line from point m and the vertical line through vpB marks the location of vpA in perspective.

The true altitude of the sun's rays can be measured above or below the horizon line. If the sun is shining over the shoulder of the viewer (SP), measure the angle of the sun's altitude below the horizon line (285).

If the sun is located in front of the viewer (SP), measure the true altitude above the horizon line (284).

Use vpB and vpA to construct the object's perspective shadows.

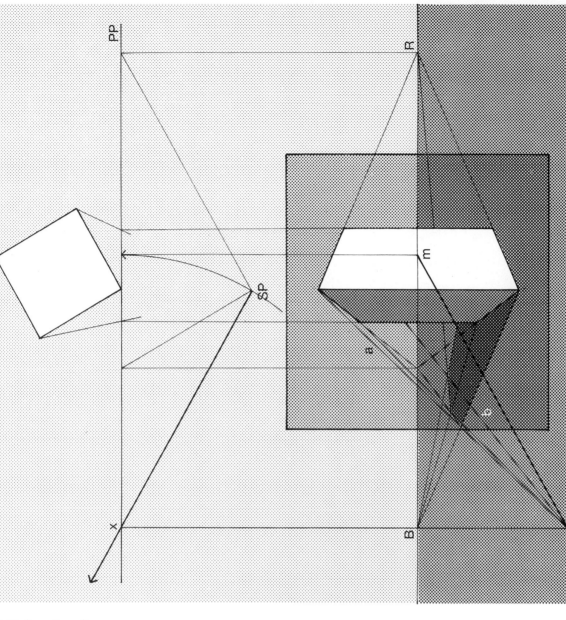

285

286

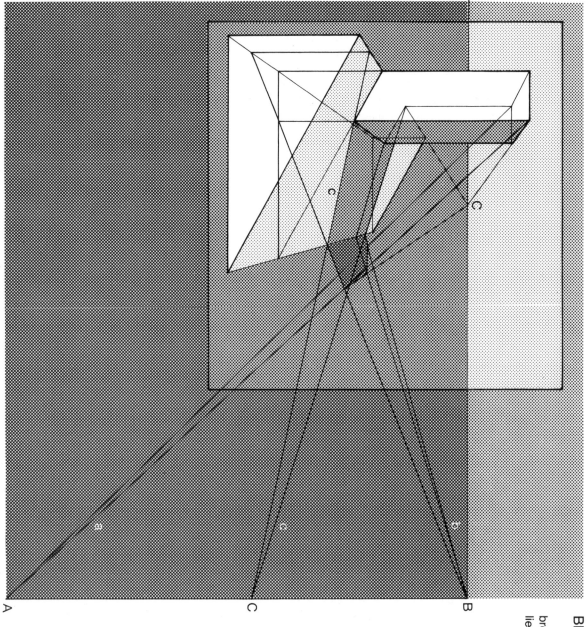

Block on Inclined Surface

Use vertical shadow planes to cut the wedge like a loaf of bread (286). The vanishing points for actual, bearing, and cut rays lie along a common vertical line through vpB.

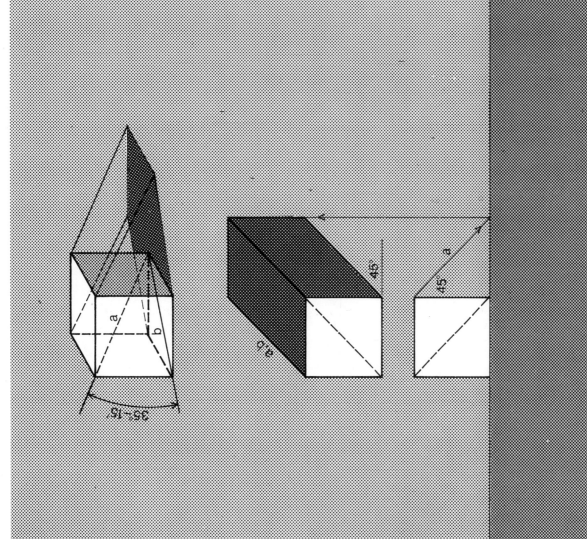

287

Common-method Shadows

There are two ways to construct shadows in plan and elevation drawings: the common method and the magic method. Each has its advantages and disadvantages. The common method requires two related views of the same building or object in order to construct shadows, while the magic method requires only one drafted and scaled plan or elevation. The common method is best for constructing accurate shadows of complex objects such as spiral staircases, origami sculptures, and corinthian columns. The magic method also casts accurate shadows but works best for simpler configurations.

Common-method Shadows

Common-method shadow constructions require a drafted and scaled plan and elevation view of the building to be cast in shadow. The setup is simple. Locate the plan directly above the elevation. The rule for drawing actual rays in plan and elevation is also very easy: simply construct actual rays at 45° angles in both the plan and elevation views (287).

In the plan view the direction of these 45° angles is not important. Shadows can be cast to fall toward the upper left, upper right, lower left, or lower right of the depicted object.

When casting lines are drawn at 45° angles in plan and elevation, the true altitude of the sun's rays is 35°-15', the altitude for the diagonal of a cube (287).

The shadows of lines, planes, and volumes on horizontal and vertical surfaces can be constructed by first finding the shadows of their points (288-290).

1. Pick a point on the object.
2. Lightly draw 45° actual rays through the point.
3. Begin at the point and move along the actual ray through the point in both the plan and elevation views, searching for the point's first intersection with the edge of a surface in either the plan or the elevation drawing.

4. Transfer this first intersection with the edge of a surface into the adjacent view. The intersection of this transferred line with the actual ray in the adjacent view marks the shadow of the point.

5. Do this for all points on the object. Connect the shadows of points together to form the completed shadow of the object. To check for accuracy and to draw shadows more quickly, use the basic shadow patterns (page 203).

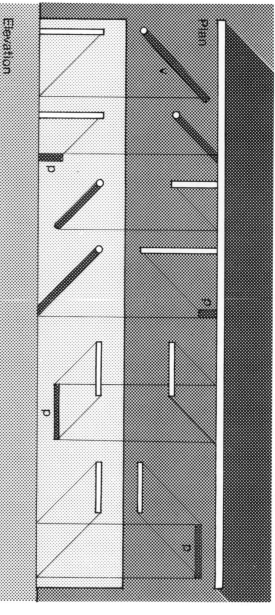

Plan

Elevation

288

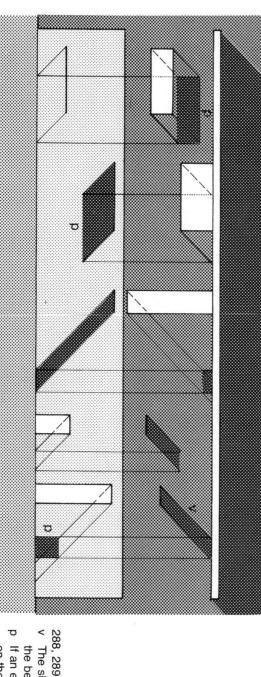

289

288, 289

v   The shadow of a vertical edge on a horizontal surface falls in the bearing direction of sunlight.

p   If an edge and a surface are parallel, the shadow of the edge on the surface is parallel to the edge.

Shadows in Plan and Elevation

290

In common-method shadow configurations a few basic shadow patterns for points, lines, and planes occur over and over.

1. The shadow of a point always falls along the actual ray through the plan view of the point.

2. The shadow of a vertical line falls along the actual ray through its point view in plan.

3. When a line is parallel to a plane, the line casts a shadow that is parallel to itself on the plane.

4. Vertical shadow planes containing actual, bearing, and cut rays appear as lines in plan.

290
v The shadow of a vertical edge on a horizontal surface falls in the bearing direction of sunlight.
p If an edge and a surface are parallel, the shadow of the edge on the surface is parallel to the edge.

291

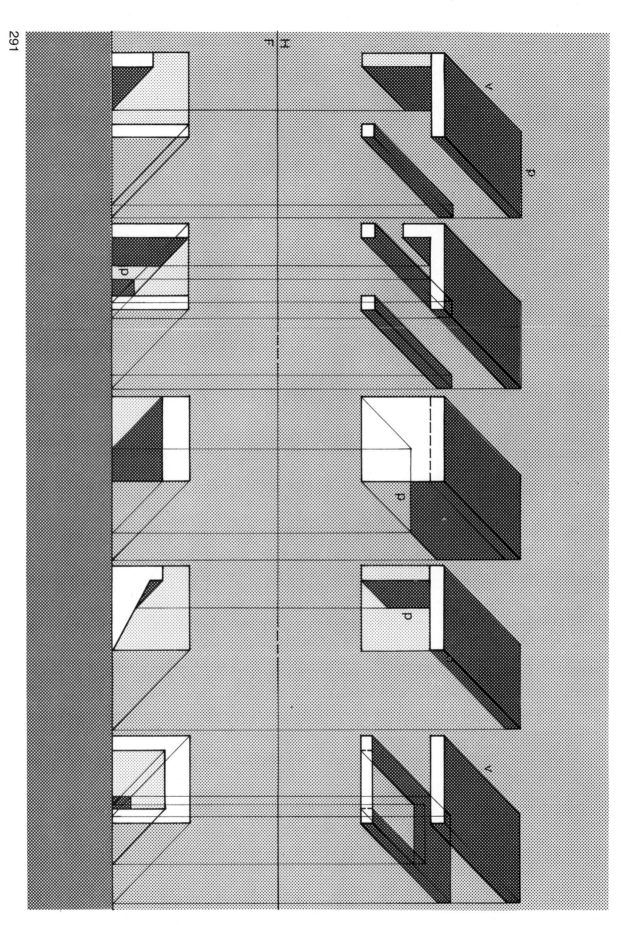

Apply the conservation-of-edges rule to check finished shadow constructions: every object edge that casts a shadow is responsible for a shadow edge.

In almost all cases object edges that cast shadows lie at the intersection of a surface in sunlight and a surface in shade.

The single exception to this rule involves curved surfaces such as a cylinder (292). In the case of the cylinder the break between sunlight and shade occurs along the continuously curved surface of the cylinder at points where actual rays are tangent to its curvature.

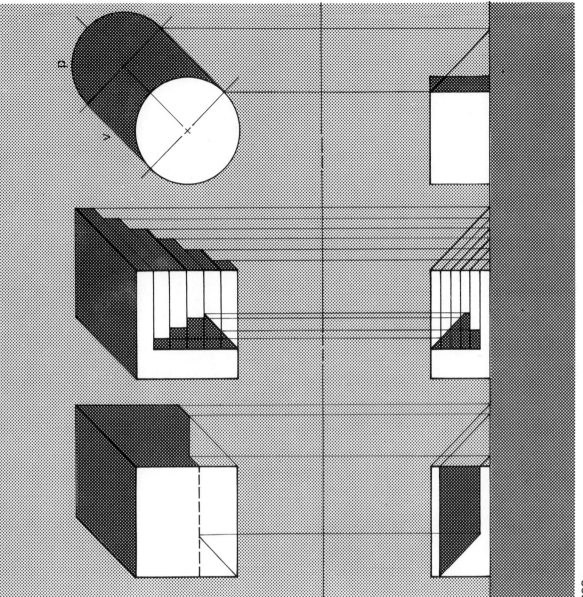

291, 292

v The shadow of a vertical edge on a horizontal surface falls in the bearing direction of sunlight.

p If an edge and a surface are parallel, the shadow of the edge on the surface is parallel to the edge.

292

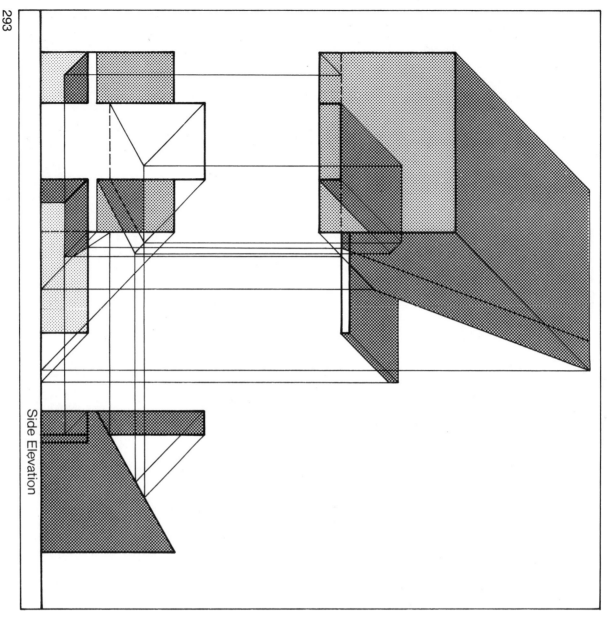

Side Elevation

Extra Views

It is sometimes necessary to construct additional elevations. Here a side-elevation view of the house is needed in order to find where actual rays through the corner points of the chimney intersect the roof plane (293). In this side-elevation view the roof plane appears as an edge.

In the common method actual rays can be thought of as diagonals of a cube. They are therefore drawn at 45° angles in the side elevations.

The point of intersection between the actual rays and the edge view of the roof in the side elevation is transferred horizontally to the adjacent elevation, where it can intersect the actual ray in that view to locate the shadow of the chimney on the roof. The plane of the roof is extended to aid in constructing the chimney's shadow.

Varying the Sun's Angle of Altitude

To vary the sun's angle for common-method perspectives, construct plan and elevation views of a light box with its diagonal at the true bearing and azimuth of the desired sun angle. Construct an auxiliary elevation view to draw the sun's angle at its proper azimuth. Use the plan and elevation orientations of the actual light ray as the diagonals for casting shadows.

Magic-method Shadows

Once mastered, the magic method of casting shadows in plans and elevations is more efficient than the common method for most design applications.

The magic method requires only the scaled plan or elevation view that is to be cast in shadow to complete the shadow configuration.

Depth measurements that are normally measured off the scaled companion plan or elevation view are estimated in your head, calculated on a piece of scrap paper, or drawn at a different scale than the given plan or elevation.

The magic method works well for casting shadows in architectural floor plans and elevations. It is especially useful for site plans. Site plans are often drawn at different scales than standard architectural elevations, and the magic method eliminates the need to draw elevations at the site-plan scale to project heights.

The magic method is set up in a slightly different way than the common method. In the magic method the conventional angle for the altitude of sunlight is 45° rather than the roughly 36° angle used in the common method. Two sides of a 45° right triangle are equal in length. This permits constructing shadows whose lengths are equal to the heights of object edges (294).

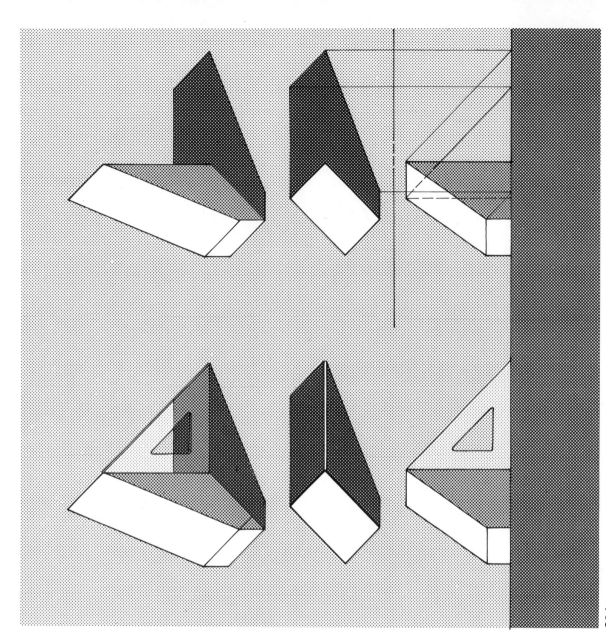

294

295

Varying the Sun's Angle of Altitude

Changing the altitude and bearing of the sun's rays varies the length and direction of shadows. The length of shadows sometimes tends to obscure the legibility of a drawing. This can be corrected by changing the typical 45° altitude. Adjusting the sun's altitude up or down from 45° causes the shadows in plan to become longer or shorter.

To change the sun's altitude, select a shadow-length (SL): vertical-object-edge (VE) ratio other than 1:1. For ease of construction make this ratio fairly simple such as 1:2 or 1:1.5.

Cast the shadows of all vertical object edges in plan view by multiplying the height of the vertical edges by the simple SL:VE ratio. Measure the multiplied length along lines drawn from the vertical edges in the bearing direction of sunlight.

Three rows of circles and squares with different shadow-length: vertical-edge ratios are shown (295). The top row has an SL:VE ratio of 1:2; the middle row, 1:1; and the lower row, 1:5.

Varying the Bearing of the Sun's Rays

The clarity of a drawing can sometimes be improved by changing the angle of the sun's bearing ray. For example, in a plan-view drawing depicting an office tower and an adjacent land-scaped park the shadow of the office building might obscure the detail of the park by blanketing it in shadow. By simply changing the bearing direction of the actual rays the shadow of the office tower can be made to fall elsewhere in the drawing.

Changing the bearing direction of the sun's rays is similar to swinging magic triangles about hinges that are cemented to the vertical edges of objects. The true vertical angle of the triangle, analogous to the sun's altitude, does not change: only the bearing direction of actual rays is affected (296).

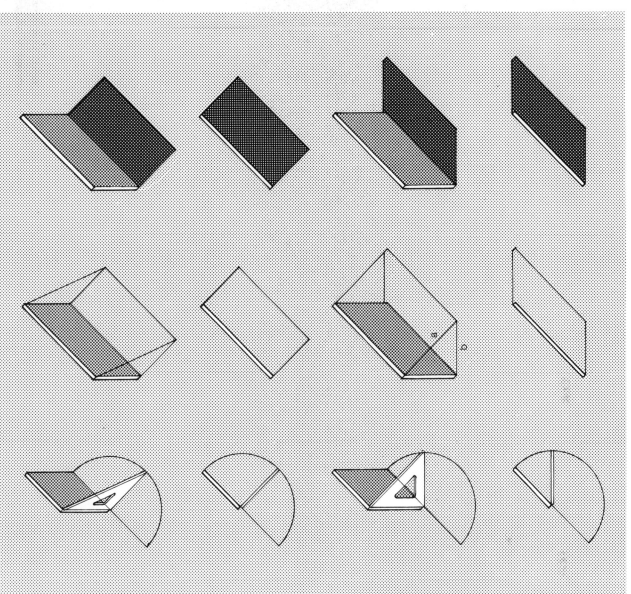

296

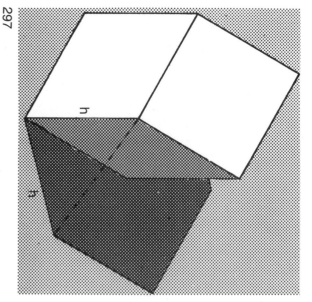

297

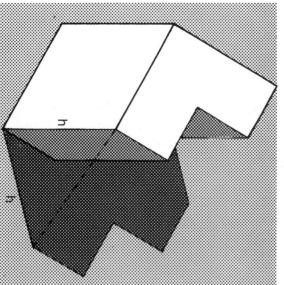

298

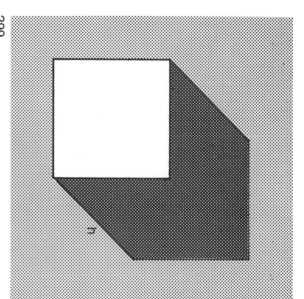

299

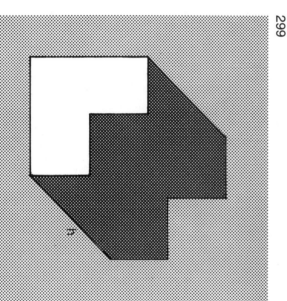

300

Basic Rule

Shadows add a three-dimensional feeling to two-dimensional drawings. They provide clues to the relative heights of objects in plan and the relative depths of objects in elevation.

The magic method is most often applied to shadow constructions in plan view.

In practice a designer knows the approximate heights of the vertical edges of a building. There is little need to construct a building's elevation to find the exact height with the magic method. Only one simple rule needs to be applied in order to cast shadows in plan.

The basic rule for the magic method is that vertical edges cast shadows that are equal in length to their height or, more simply, height of vertical equals length of shadow.

The shadow of the cube (297, 299) is constructed by measuring the height of the cube along the 45°-angle shadow line cast by the edge of the cube.

Once the shadows for each vertical edge are found, the end points are connected to form the completed shadow of the cube.

The cube's shadow conveys more information about its three-dimensional configuration than a simple plan view can provide. For instance, the shadow communicates that the cube is solid and rests on the ground plane. Without the shadow the cube might be interpreted as a square plane hovering somewhere above the ground plane.

Basic Patterns

Watch for the following relationships between lines and planes.

When a line is parallel to a plane, the line casts a shadow that is parallel to itself on the plane. Horizontal edges of the notched cube cast shadows on the ground plane that are parallel to themselves (298, 300).

When two planes are parallel to each other, the shadow of one on the other is identical in shape and size to the shape and size of the plane casting the shadow.

The circular top of the cylinder is parallel to the ground plane (301, 303). The shadow of the cylinder's top is a circle identical to the shape and size of the cylinder's top.

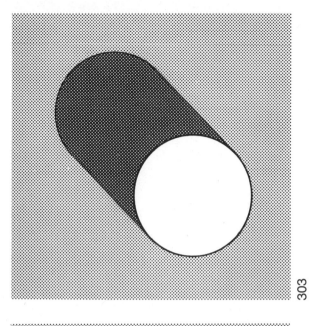

301

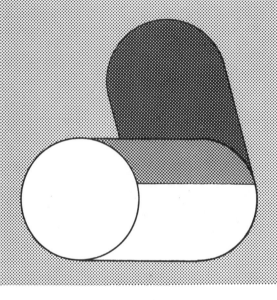

302

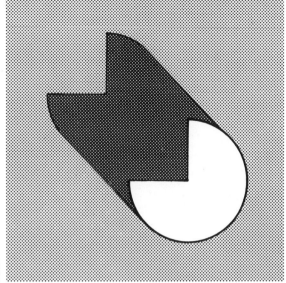

303

304

305

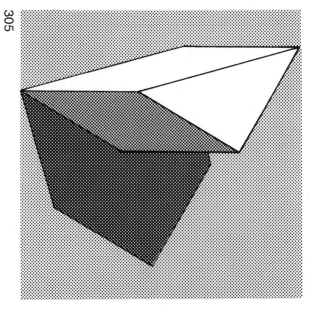

306

307

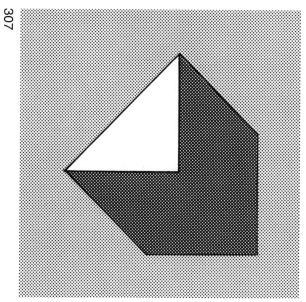

308

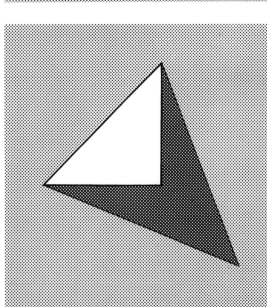

The same triangular shape appears in both plan views (307, 308), yet the shadow of each shape is different. The shape of the first shadow is cast by three vertical edges. The second shadow is cast by one vertical edge. Two of the three corners in the plan view of the lower triangle are level with the ground plane and cannot cast shadows.

Shadows in Plan and Elevation

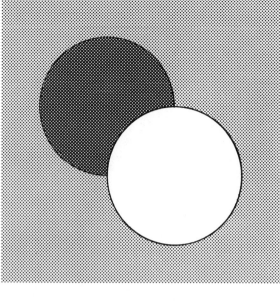

311

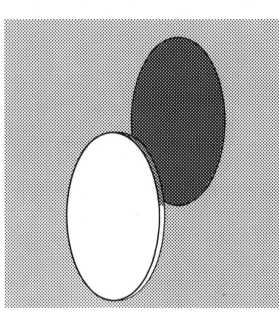

309

312

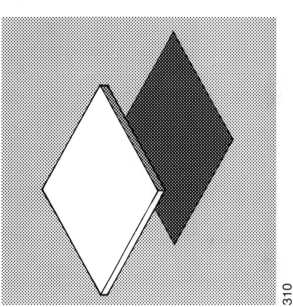

310

Hovering Planes

When a hovering plane is parallel to the surface on which its shadow appears, the shadow of the plane on the surface is identical to the shape and size of the plane (309-312).

Slipping Planes

As a rule slip the shadows of hovering planes in the bearing direction of sunlight to a distance that equals the height of the plane. The shadow is complete if the casting plane is a two-dimensional plane hovering above the ground. If it is solid underneath, complete the shadows for the vertical sides.

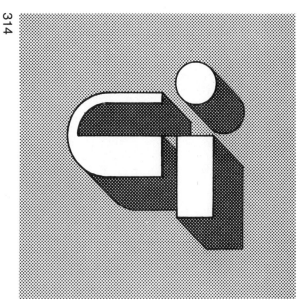

313

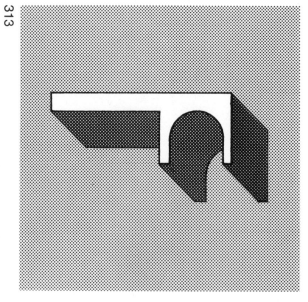

314

315

316

Inky-cardboard Analogy

The inky-cardboard analogy might help to explain how slipping a plane finds a shadow. Imagine that the back of a piece of white cardboard cut to the shape of the object casting the shadow is smeared with black ink. Press the cardboard to the paper and slide it along the surface at a 45° diagonal for a distance equal to the height of the object's top surface above the paper. The resulting inky trail bears an amazing resemblance to the object's shadow (313-316).

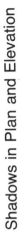

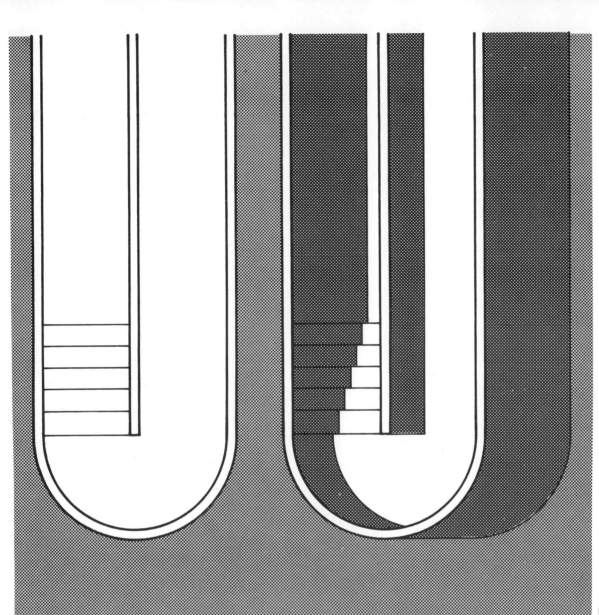

Here shadows fall from top to bottom along vertically oriented bearing rays instead of along the usual diagonal bearing rays (317). This does not affect the basic rule for finding shadow lengths. The height of an edge above the ground plane receiving its shadow is still equal to the length of the edge's shadow.

317

318

Plan

Elevation

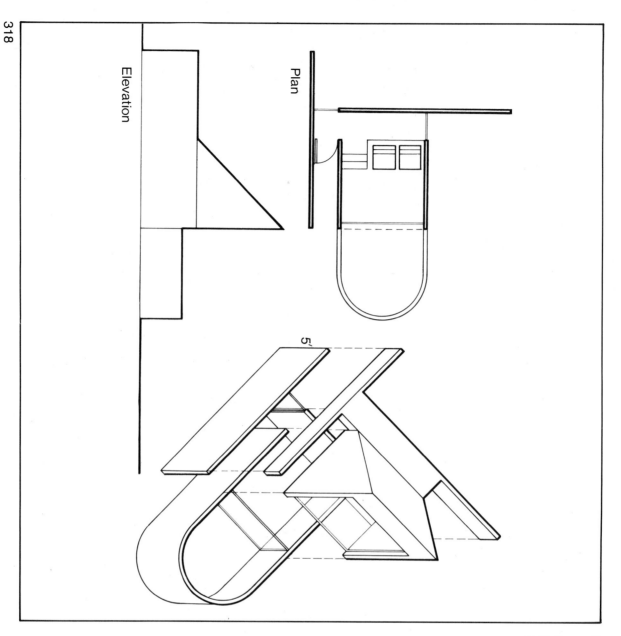

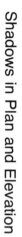

5'

Floor-plan Shadows

Floor plans are horizontal sections. The height of the section cut determines the length of wall shadows. Section cuts in plan are usually made 4' or 5' above the floor level of the floor plan (318).

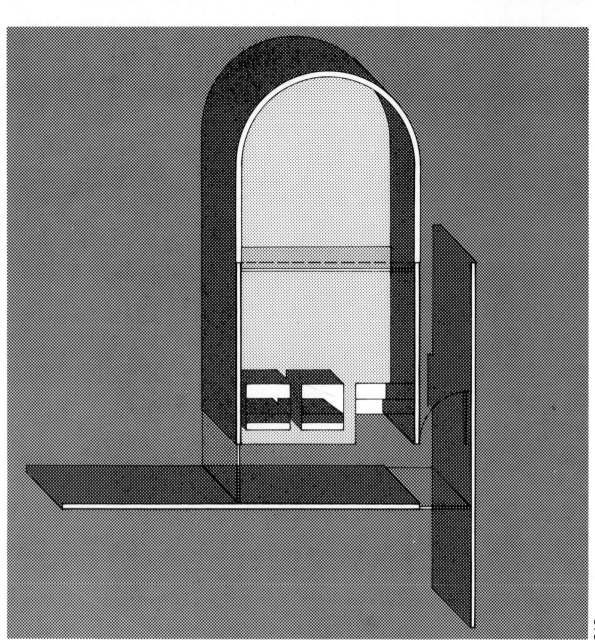

319

Shadows drawn on architectural floor plans help create a feeling of depth and a sense of the spatial characteristics of the design (319). If furniture is included in the floor plan, simplify its shadow construction by blocking it out and keeping it monolithic in character. Avoid too much detail.

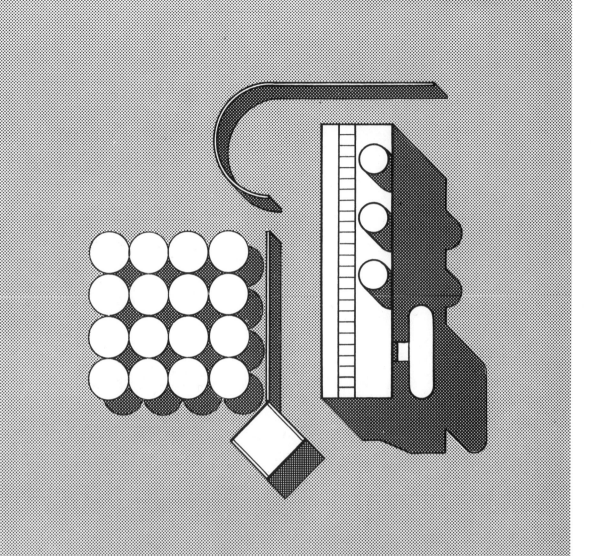

Site-plan Shadows

Trees are an important site-plan element (320). Avoid the time-consuming task of constructing the shadows of spheres in plan. Instead use the abstract spherical-tree convention.

1. Draw circular shadows for circular trees.
2. Slip the tree's shadow along a diagonal until the shadow's perimeter lines up with the center of the tree.

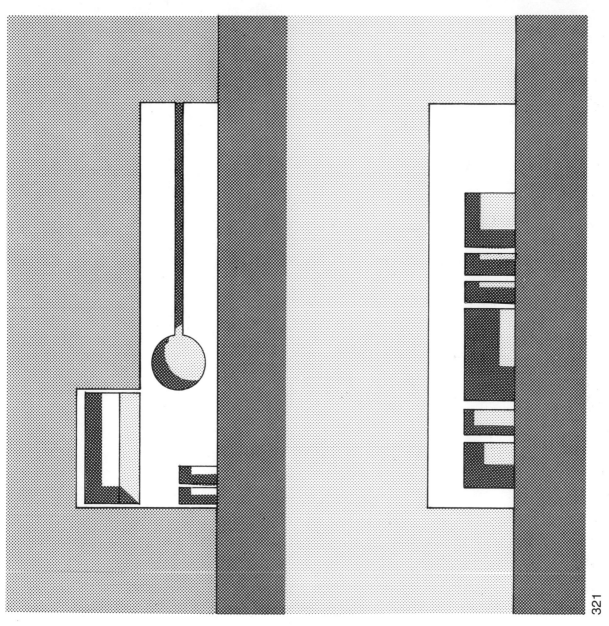

321

Elevation Shadows

Shadows in elevation are constructed with the same techniques used in plan drawing. Shadows in elevation help to provide a sense of depth. The relative depths of the openings (321) are visually apparent: the wider the shadow, the deeper the opening.

Inclined Surfaces

To find the shadow of a vertical edge on an inclined surface, construct a partial auxiliary elevation (322). Draw the fold line parallel to the bearing direction of sunlight. Use an actual ray of sunlight to determine where the shadow of a point intersects the inclined surface. For conventionally cast shadows draw the actual ray of sunlight at a 45° angle to the fold plane.

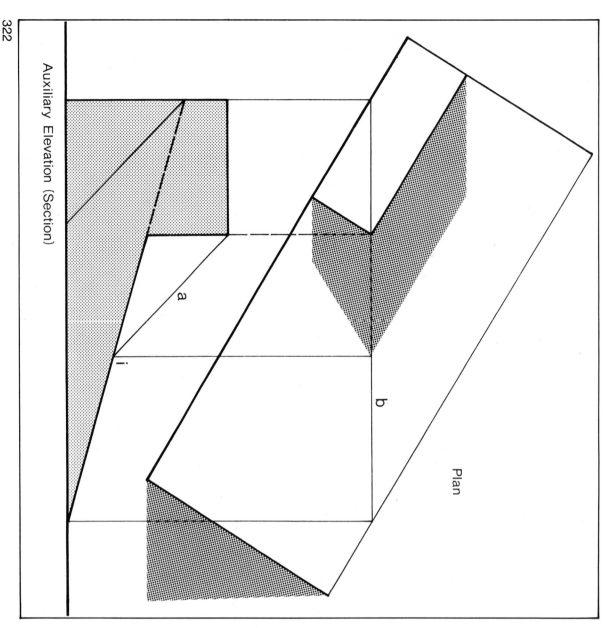

322

Plan

Auxiliary Elevation (Section)

322

a   True angle of actual ray
b   Bearing direction of sunlight
i   Intersection with incline

Multiple Horizontal Surfaces

Cast the shadow for a vertical edge onto each horizontal surface in its path. Measure the length of the edge's shadow so that it equals its height above each surface.

The shadow of the rectangular block (323) falls on two surfaces: the surface of the square block, indicated by dashed lines, and the surface of the ground plane. Its height above the surface of the square block is less than its height above the ground plane, and the shadow is shorter on the block than on the ground plane.

The shadow of the rectangular block cast in the plane of the square block's surface (324) falls short of the square block, and no part of the rectangular block's shadow falls on the surface of the square block.

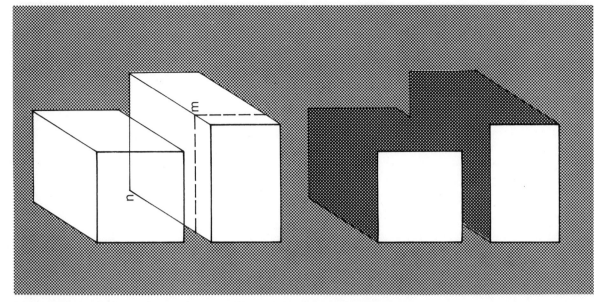

324

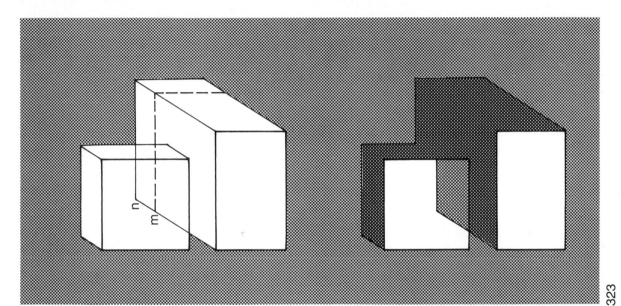

323

323, 324
m Shadow of block on block
n Shadow of block on ground

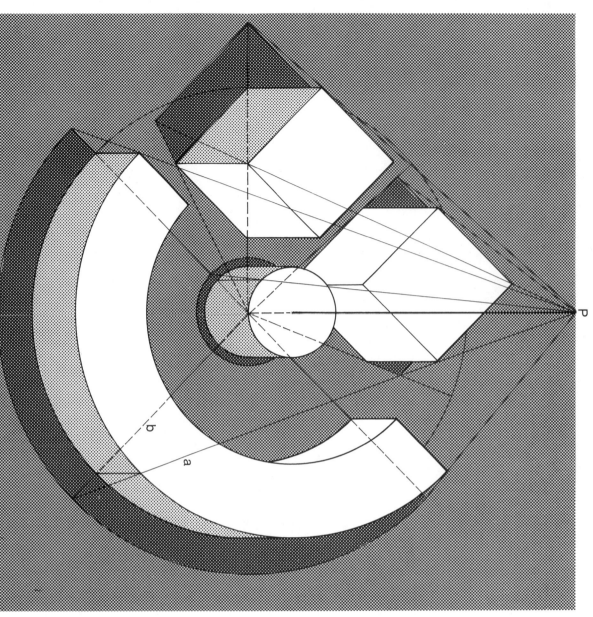

Unlike the sun, light radiating from man-made sources such as floodlamps, streetlights, and chandeliers is not far enough away from the objects that it illuminates to be treated as parallel light rays. To draw the shadows of objects illuminated by point sources of light, follow these simple guidelines:

1. Actual rays must originate at the point source of the light (P).

2. Bearing and cut rays must radiate from a vertical line through the point source of light.

3. Use bearing rays to find where actual rays strike horizontal surfaces.

4. Use cut rays to find where actual rays strike inclined surfaces.

These guidelines apply to all types of design drawings: paralines (325), perspectives (326), and multiviews.

The completed network of construction lines for casting the shadows of objects illuminated by point sources of light resembles a plastic-triangle evergreen tree. The point source of light is located at the top of the tree, and the vertical shaft through the point source of light is the trunk.

In reality the edges of shadows caused by point sources of light are not sharply defined. They tend to be fuzzy, because the light does not radiate from a single sharp focus but rather from a point that is as large as its mechanical source of illumination. An example is an incandescent light bulb: the source of light is as large as the diameter of the bulb.

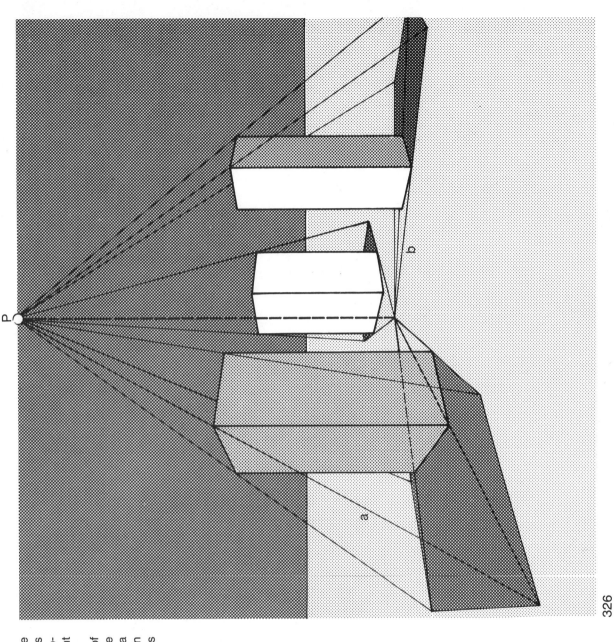

326

Index